The Emergency Teacher

The Emergency Teacher

The Inspirational Story
of a New Teacher in an
Inner-City School

Christina Asquith

Foreword by Mark Bowden
Introduction by Dr. Harry K. Wong

Skyhorse Publishing

Copyright © 2007 by Christina Asquith
Foreword copyright © 2007 by Mark Bowden
Introduction copyright © 2007 by Dr. Harry K. Wong

All Rights Reserved. No part of this book may be reproduced in any manner without the express written consent of the publisher, except in the case of brief excerpts in critical reviews or articles. All inquiries should be addressed to Skyhorse Publishing, 555 Eighth Avenue, Suite 903, New York, NY 10018.

www.skyhorsepublishing.com

10 9 8 7 6 5 4 3 2 1

Library of Congress Cataloging-in-Publication Data

Asquith, Christina.
  The emergency teacher : the inspirational story of a new teacher in an inner city school / Christina Asquith ; foreword by Mark Bowden ; introduction by Harry K. Wong.
      p. cm.
  ISBN-13: 978-1-60239-193-2 (alk. paper)
  ISBN-10: 1-60239-193-9 (alk. paper)
  1. First year teachers—Pennsylvania—Philadelphia. 2. Classroom management—Pennsylvania—Philadelphia. 3. Middle school teachers—Pennsylvania—Philadelphia. 4. Middle schools—Pennsylvania—Philadelphia. 5. Urban schools—Pennsylvania—Philadelphia. I. Title.

LB2844.1.N4.A77 2007
371.1—dc22
                                        2007028967

Printed in the United States of America

Contents

To my Mom and Dad

and

To Mark

Foreword

by Mark Bowden

It was eight years ago when Christina Asquith, my young colleague at *The Philadelphia Inquirer,* told me she was taking a leave from reporting and writing to teach a sixth-grade class at a troubled middle school in North Philadelphia.

It was a bold move. Christina was an extraordinarily talented and ambitious journalist, and in the two-year internship program she was completing at the paper, she was already launched in what had become a very competitive field. But Christina was passionately interested in education, which meant that she had both the itch to teach and a desire to write about it. She wasn't sure which would ultimately win out. If she decided to stay with teaching, this would be a good way to start, she told me, and if she decided not to teach, but instead to report and write about education, the firsthand experience would greatly inform her writing.

She got more than she bargained for.

Philadelphia's school system was so desperate for teachers in 1999 that they were willing—and this is only slightly stretching the truth—to take anyone. They had a program for "emergency" certification. Typically, teachers spend their college years preparing for a classroom and then log many hours working and observing alongside veteran instructors before taking over a class of their own. Christina had none of this. She even signed up too late for the one-week instruction course. The school district recruiter was unfazed.

"Can I really teach without any experience?" she asked.

"Believe me, we need you more than you need us," he said.

Christina was set before a class of sixth graders at Julia de Burgos Bilingual Middle Magnet School, then in a massive gray stone building with all the charm of a nineteenth-century prison, on the corner of Eighth Street and Lehigh Avenue. Christina had thirty-three rambunctious early teens (most of them mature well beyond any sixth-graders she had ever known), all of them fluent in Spanish but less so in English, from some of the most troubled neighborhoods in the city. There was minimal to no support from school administrators. The whole experience, from the existence of an "emergency" program to lure the naive and idealistic to the reality of Julia de Burgos, was like a bad joke. This heartbreakingly earnest, slender, blond, pretty, twenty-five-year-old woman from the suburbs of New Jersey was being offered up cynically. The job was hard to fill because no one wanted it. She had no lesson plans, no guidance, and, as it turned out, no books (she would eventually discover boxes of old, outdated, and undistributed books on her own). It was like someone was playing a trick on her. The bigger trick, of course, which Christina was quick to see for herself, was on the kids.

"I hate the fact that untrained teachers are being assigned here," said one veteran teacher at the school who remembers Christina and noted that the program that lured Christina is still in place today. More than ten novice teachers were handed classes this year alone. Only an experienced teacher at this school could fully comprehend the folly of the emergency certification program.

It's more than a folly; it's a disgrace. That and the general condition of public education in parts of Philadelphia and other big American cities is as clear a statement as society can make that children in certain neighborhoods—most of them Hispanic and black—simply don't matter. Christina's starting salary that year was $30,000—less than half of what her internship paid at the newspaper and $8,000 below the starting salary of her suburban counterparts, who were teaching at schools that were not hiring people off the streets to teach and who had, among other things, actual textbooks. In a society concerned about the escalating violence and lawlessness of inner-city neighborhoods, or a just society that paid salaries commensurate with the level of a job's difficulty, any teacher willing to tackle Julia de Burgos would be making top dollar.

Many of the untrained recruits take a quick look and flee. Christina watched as her fellow recruits dropped out, dumping their classes in midsemester on the teachers who stayed. She also saw something even worse: teachers who had given up long ago, but who stayed in place, going through the motions, waiting out the years to qualify for a pension. There were varying degrees of abdication, from those who simply threw their most difficult students out of class, leaving packs of unsupervised teens to roam the halls, to one male teacher who simply ignored his students altogether, spending class periods reading the newspaper at his desk. "Failure is not an option," the school principal had intoned impressively in a staff meeting at the start of the year, which sounded firm and inspirational, and turned out to be literally true, as teachers were encouraged to simply falsify grades on exams and report cards in order to meet assigned goals.

Christina was tougher than that. She battled her way through the full year, never more grateful for her fluent command of Spanish, buying books and supplies for the children out of her own thin wallet—her parents helped with the rent—and finding a small network of skilled teachers inside the school who inspired and counseled her. Along the way she fell in love with her students.

I visited her class midway through that year. I had sent three of my children to public schools in Philadelphia, but nothing prepared me for Julia de Burgos. The only thing that struck me as normal about the school was her class. It was warm and boisterous and fun. There were kids in the back of the room who were off in their own worlds, and there were brassy kids clearly unconvinced that being in school was worth their while, but Christina had the full attention of a core group of smart, focused, genuinely curious children eager to learn. As I left that day, Christina asked me what I thought, and I didn't have a terribly coherent response. I was shocked, but I didn't want to jump to any conclusions—I didn't know if the herds of wild children in the halls were a temporary problem or the status quo—and I didn't want to discourage her by being too critical. I told her that, at the very least, she had a great story to write. I was moved by her courage and accomplishment.

I also encouraged her decision to keep notes and to think about shaping the experience into a book, which, much to my surprise, she did. Here is the remarkable result. I was lucky enough to be one of this book's first readers, and I love it for reasons apart from its startling revelations about a deeply troubled school system. It would be a good enough book if that was all it did, but it does much more. It captures Christina's heart, the sheer tenacity and decency she showed in refusing to abandon her idealism. In it are portraits of teachers both heroic and appalling, and of administrators right out of some black comedy about bureaucracy. Most captivating, though, are the loving stories of her students whose sweetness, helplessness, and neediness is heartbreaking. Her battle to be the teacher they deserved is inspiring. It is a fascinating story of stubborn ingenuity and courage, and as warm and revealing a portrait of a troubled urban school as you will ever read.

Christina left after that year, after months of painful deliberation. I know how hard the decision was for her. She had taught herself how to control a class and to teach in the worst of circumstances, and she knew the island of sanity and learning she had created for her students would very likely disappear once she was gone. She went on to earn a masters degree in education at the London School of Economics, and then covered the war in Iraq as a stringer for the *Christian Science Monitor* and other newspapers, writing about education issues in that war-torn place.

Since she left, Julia de Burgos has moved into an impressive new building at Fourth and Lehigh, but still suffers the same problems. Classes remain very challenging and overcrowded; there are fewer classroom supplies than there were seven years ago; teachers are still quitting (both those who walk away and those who stay in place); and wild children still roam the halls, preying upon the kids who are trying to learn, and occasionally their teachers—in one recent and heavily publicized case, a substitute filling in for an "emergency" teacher who quit was assaulted so severely that he landed in the hospital.

I hope *The Emergency Teacher* is a wake-up call. The only real remedy for challenging urban schools is not to recruit brave volunteers like Christina, but to offer salaries that equal or exceed those paid in the suburbs. Why would anyone who is not a saint take a harder job that pays significantly less? Schools like Julia de Burgos don't need novices, even ingenuous and dedicated ones like Christina; they need the most resourceful, experienced, and dedicated teachers money can buy.

Introduction

By Dr. Harry K. Wong

The statistics are staggering and hard to imagine in any other industry: Almost a third of all new teachers leave the classroom after three years, and close to 50 percent leave after five years. Each resignation can cost the school district upward of $50,000. The turnover is a primary cause of the chaos in underachieving school systems like Detroit where less than 25 percent of high school students graduate on time—if ever.

How can a team of teachers and school staff prepare, plan, and sustain a functioning, effective school program with such instability?

"The exit of teachers from the profession and the movement of teachers to better schools are costly phenomena, both for the students who lose the value of being taught by an experienced teacher, and for the schools and districts, which must recruit and train their replacements," says renowned University of Pennsylvania education professor Richard Ingersoll.

"There is a growing consensus among researchers and educators that the single most important factor in determining student performance is the quality of his or her teachers," he says.

In *The Emergency Teacher* we have a captivating case study of a new teacher's experience illustrating why so many are driven from the profession. This makes the book an excellent new-teacher training tool. Fast-paced and well-documented, *The Emergency Teacher* gives names, faces, and emotion to those alarming statistics. This true story relates the experience of young Philadelphia journalist Christina Asquith after she quits her newspaper job to become an emergency certified teacher. She is sent into the toughest school in the city, Julia de Burgos Bilingual Middle Magnet School, and assigned to be the sixth grade teacher for English, social studies, and reading.

Christina was just like so many of the new teachers I meet and train each year. Full of energy and determined, she did not go into teaching to make money. She dreamed of giving low-income children a chance in life through education. She writes of her motivation to quit her newspaper job and teach:

> Most of my friends were setting off for well-paying jobs with Internet start-ups or glamorous new magazines. I wanted to "make a difference in a child's life," as the Philadelphia Department of Education recruitment posters promised. I felt like the failing inner-city schools were an injustice that I should stand against, not only with words but also with real action.

Her idealism and high expectations are so common among new teachers. In the book I've written with my wife, Rosemary, *The First Days of School,* I call this stage "Fantasy." All teachers go through it. Christina watched movies like *Lean on Me* and *Stand and Deliver* and fantasized about rescuing a group of students through sheer will, ingenuity, and pluck. Her enthusiasm ought to be applauded, but enthusiasm is no substitute for knowledge and experience. So often, though, these positive expectations collide with the sober realities of the job, and teachers move from the fantasy stage into what I call "Survival."

Within weeks, Christina realized that she was wholly unprepared to actually teach, and she received no support from her administration and few supplies. The honeymoon period between her and her students wore off, and her disorganization made the students anxious and rebellious. Here, she describes the desperation both she and Ms. Rohan, her team teacher, were feeling by October:

> We had nothing to teach with and six hours of classroom time to fill. We were two untrained, inexperienced teachers about to invent their own sixth grade from scratch, without even textbooks. We could barely keep our heads above water; how did we build a lifeboat?

Induction Versus Mentoring Programs

The Emergency Teacher does a powerful job of documenting a problem widespread in public school systems: the lack of trained teachers and its effect on student learning. Christina illustrates one of the major reasons why new teach-

ers don't succeed in making their dreams come true: They lack support from
the school administration.

All school districts should offer a structured induction program to welcome, introduce, and give ongoing training to new teachers, but few do. Many
new teachers, like Christina, are tossed classroom keys and told to "sink or
swim." As we know, too many sink. The fear, vulnerability, insecurity, and isolation that Christina experienced are typical. Proper teacher training and insti-
tutionalized, ongoing support could save new teachers from a disastrous year,
and retain them for another year.

The administrators at Julia De Burgos Bilingual Middle School in
Philadelphia seemed to treat the new teachers as an afterthought. Either they
were too busy running around trying to organize the school, or they had been
worn down by all the new teachers coming and going, so they treated Christina
with cynicism.

When Christina did ask about training, she was given only a mentor. Giving new teachers a mentor is a common mistake that afflicts underperforming
schools. A mentor is not induction; these two terms are not synonymous. Induction is a structured process used by districts to train, support, and retain new
teachers. It is a highly organized and comprehensive staff development process
involving many people and components, and typically continues as a sustained
process for two to five years. Mentoring is important, but it is only one compo-
nent of the induction process.

In this book, Christina describes how she was ignored by the other teachers on her first day and how her mentor show little interest in helping her become a better teacher, but want Christina just to sign her time sheet so she
could receive payment! In far too many instances, a mentor is simply a veteran
teacher who has been haphazardly selected by the principal and assigned to a
new teacher, resulting in a "blind date," as Jon Saphier (2001) calls it in his
book *Beyond Mentoring.* Sharon Feiman-Nemser, in her 1996 *ERIC Digest* article "Teacher Mentoring: A Critical Review" writes that after twenty years of
experimenting with mentoring as a process for helping new teachers, few comprehensive studies exist to validate its effectiveness.

People crave connection. New teachers want more than a job. They want
hope. They want to contribute to a group. They want to make a difference. Induction programs provide that connection because they are structured around
a learning community where new and veteran teachers treat each other with

respect and all contributions are valued. Christina successfully made friends with the other teachers who supported her professional development, but there was little leadership from the administration, which ought to have had the most invested in keeping her.

Christina also had a poor relationship with her school's principal. Rarely will a college education class prepare a teacher for the emotional stress this can add to a teacher's many other hurdles. We watch her grapple with the idiosyncrasies of her superiors, and see how she took solace in the friendship and support of a group of teachers who socialized together each Friday afternoon. Christina's poignant description of her isolation will resonate with and offer comfort to other new teachers, but isolation is a new teacher's worst enemy. It is emotionally taxing and prevents teachers from sharing successful strategies that benefit the students. I always tell teachers: "Steal! Steal lesson plans, classroom management tricks, successful teaching strategies, and whatever else you can." Christina wisely did that, and we are happy to go with her as she builds up her classroom.

All administrators should take heed of Christina's experience and look to it to understand how they can offer more support to their new teachers. In my 2003 book *New Teacher Induction: How to Train, Support, and Retain New Teachers*, my coauthor Annette Breaux and I discuss step-by-step how school districts can set up a support program, a recommendation based on extensive research including thirty successful induction programs from other schools. Had Christina's school had an induction program like the ones we describe, her experience would have been very different. If you are an administrator, ask yourself: "How do we support and retain our new teachers?" If you are a new teacher or are considering teaching, I encourage you to ask your school administrators: "Do you have an ongoing induction program, and what do you do to support new teachers?"

If they don't have a good answer, try to look elsewhere. A good induction program can include a pre-school-year workshop, a welcome center, a bus tour of the neighborhood, study groups, mentors and coaches, portfolios and videos, demonstration classrooms, administrative support, and learning circles. It should last for at least three years.

New teachers come into the profession having invested years of their lives and tens of thousands of dollars with the vision of making a difference in the lives of young people. It is a crime when they are just thrown into a classroom with no training or support.

Managing a Classroom

The second important lesson to be learned from *The Emergency Teacher* is the importance of classroom management as opposed to discipline. Whether emergency certified teachers or graduates from the college of education, too few teachers grasp the critical difference. Therein lies the key to their success.

In the beginning of her school year, Christina was typical of the millions of devoted and committed teachers who fret about their next day's lessons. Each evening, she asked herself, "What am I going to teach tomorrow?" So, she planned what she would cover or what activity she would do in class the next day. She thought this was teaching because most teachers cover or do activities first, then they discipline when things go wrong—and when things did go wrong, Christina spent the next evening again fretting and wondering what she could do to get the students to pay attention to their lessons, and thereby have fewer behavior problems in the classroom. She asked that perennial but incorrect question: "What can I do to motivate my students?"—thinking that motivated students will be more attentive and better behaved. The next day, however, the cycle repeated itself, and Christina continued to cover and discipline.

The problem, Christina later realized, was that she was not spending any time managing her classrooms. She was reacting to problems as they arose. So many teachers fall into this trap. If classroom management procedures were taught, almost all class discipline problems would disappear, and more time in the classroom could be spent on learning. *The problem lies with teachers not knowing the difference between classroom management and classroom discipline.*

When you go shopping, you expect the store to be well managed. If it is not, you're likely to say, "Does anyone around here know what they are doing? I could run this place better." Shopping in a well-run store means you expect the place to have a pleasant ambiance conducive to shopping. The temperature is perfect, the aisles are clean, the merchandise is well organized, and the personnel are inviting.

An effective shopkeeper does not manage the store by posting a sign outside the front door with the store's policy telling you how you are to behave inside the store, then running around the store taking away privileges from customers who do not behave and giving perks to those who follow the rules. No restaurant, office, cruise ship, or church is managed in this manner; yet this is how some teachers "manage" their classrooms—with consequences and rewards.

In the late fall, Christina read *The First Days of School* and began to understand the importance of managing a classroom, using the many techniques in the book to instill order. Until that point, Christina had been waiting until a problem arose and then condemning the infraction. For example, each time certain students wanted to throw away paper, they stood up, took a dramatic basketball shot, and bowed as the rest of the class cheered. Christina either admonished the student or pretended she didn't see the infraction. However, after reading *The First Days of School,* she learned that the better solution was to have a procedure in place for throwing away garbage—and to teach that procedure and practice it. This strategy can apply to all areas of the classroom. Christina describes how her class turned around once she started implementing procedures and classroom management strategies:

> For a week I continued to devote all my energies to classroom management. Each morning we reviewed the class procedures and did exercises on them. We practiced lining up to leave for lunch. We practiced throwing away garbage. We ran drills on pencil sharpening and what to do if you had a question. One morning I devoted an hour to practicing passing back papers. My class didn't turn around all of a sudden and completely, as in that movie *Dangerous Minds* when Michelle Pfeiffer teaches her students a karate kick and then suddenly they're her angels. Nor was there one big meaningful moment when my students and I finally "got it," as in *Lean on Me.* The spitballs returned the following day, in fact. But once I was consistent with teaching the procedures, the Rodolfos and the Ronnys left the dark side and joined my team.

Such a dramatic turnaround in Christina's class illustrates that with the right teaching strategies, and good support and training from the school administration, all teachers can succeed in any classroom.

Conclusion

Christina entered teaching not for the money, but for the dream—the dream of making a difference in the life of a child.

Even though you don't know the outcome of her story, we've given you enough hints to know that Christina experienced many feelings of frustration and despair. These emotions were not for herself, but for her students. She had failed them miserably—she felt. But Christina turned that experience into a book for other teachers to benefit from, and there is so much to learn from her experience.

To the many teachers who relate to Christina's journey, I have this advice:

Stay steadfast in your dreams. Give each student your all, for you may never know if you've succeeded with that child. It may be years, even decades, later that one of your students will think back to you and recognize what you meant in his or her life. Eyes will wistfully close and silent thank-yous will be etched in the mind as that former student transforms into the better person you so diligently wanted all of your students to be.

You have the capacity to touch the life of every child who sits in your classroom waiting for the bell to ring. Never lose that dream. It's the reality all children deserve.

1
Julia de Burgos:
A Short History

It is a free school system, it knows no distinction of rich and poor . . .
it throws open its doors and spreads the table of its bounty for all the children of the
state. Education, then, beyond all other devices of human origin, is the equalizer
of the conditions of men, the great balance wheel of the social machinery.

—Horace Mann, Secretary of Education, Massachusetts, 1837–1848

On a blustery November afternoon in 1905, in a working-class Philadel-phia neighborhood, dignitaries rode trains into Broad Street Station to witness the opening of one of the first public high schools in the nation. U.S. President Woodrow Wilson, then head of Princeton University, led a procession of bigwigs including Pennsylvania Governor Samuel Whitaker Pen-nypacker and the CEOs of railroad companies, transatlantic steamship con-cerns, and carpet mills—business luminaries of the great Iron Age—to the corner of Eighth and Lehigh avenues.

Inside the auditorium of the new school, called the Northeast, distin-guished guests took the podium in top hats and canes and declared the school a symbol of democracy, freedom, and equal opportunity, all distinctively Ameri-can virtues. The major newspaper of the day splayed the event across the front page: A FREE HIGH SCHOOL FOR WORKING CLASS BOYS? This high school was headline news.

"We want men of capacity who are able to turn their hands to anything. This capacity is one characteristic of real Americanism," Woodrow Wilson said at the opening ceremony. "Benjamin Franklin was such a man as this, who would invent such practical things as an improved pump on the one hand and establish the Philadelphia Philosophical Society on the other. The distinct note of Americanism is fitness for anything—adaptability to the age, to its thought, its action and its utterance."

Designed by famed architect Lloyd Titus, the brand-new Northeast stood a full city block in length, a towering school of limestone and silver granite, with a black iron gate ringing the grounds and a battlemented center turret flanked by projecting gable ends that reached one hundred feet from the ground into the sky. The three-story structure had transom panels and gargoyles leaping from the cornices. Two stone lions guarded the front four steps leading up to the entranceway. The $400,000 construction cost was unprecedented at a time when most grammar schools were housed in churches, homes, and abandoned farmhouses. The school's focus was vocational training. It had a large manual training department, with a forge room in the basement and a wood-turning room on the third floor. The principal, Dr. Andrew J. Morrison, made it known that each boy would have his own forge and anvil. Powering electricity through the building were two Corliss engines the design of which the boys were to study. The building dominated Lehigh Avenue like a medieval castle built in the imposing style of a traditional English boarding school.

The idea of taxpayer-funded public schooling for the masses was largely unheard of. At the time, education—and the idea that all children ought to attend school—was a progressive, controversial concept, though its popularity was spreading. Among the earliest education proponents were Massachusetts Secretary of Education Horace Mann and former U.S. President Thomas Jefferson. They argued that democracy would never succeed—and equal opportunity would never be realized—without free schools for all. However, throughout the 1800s their arguments fell on deaf ears. Even parents disagreed. They wanted children at home doing manual labor. In the 1800s, primary schooling, if it happened at all, had traditionally fallen to churches and parents. Informally organized groups of parents contributed to a teacher's compensation, either by paying what amounted to a pittance or offering a gift, say, of food, like a bushel of wheat. Older and younger children were taught together. Most boys left to work on the farm or in factories by thirteen years of age. Only upper-class children benefited from trained tutors or religious leaders, and these students were then funneled into Ivy League universities.

The industrial revolution would change that attitude. The Pennsylvania Assembly was one of the first states to create a Free-School Law, in 1834 and 1836, which became the basis of a statewide system of tax-supported grammar schools for young children. Throughout the 1800s, other states followed, and eventually government-funded grammar schools became common.

High schools, however, were still rare in 1905. Some of the first high schools were Boston English Classical School, started in 1821, and Philadelphia's Central High School, which opened to a distinguished pool of male students in 1838.

Nineteenth-century boys would need preparation to do more high-tech industrial jobs, and high schools made for perfect training centers. Philadelphia, a city that had been a "center of politics, religion, intellect, arts, and letters," according to historians Nathaniel Burt and Wallace E. Davies, was transforming itself into the "Workshop of the World," or so said the city's chamber of commerce. Philadelphia had become an industrial giant, dominant in steam locomotives, textiles, the railroad, and all things iron, steel, and coal. Transatlantic steamers charged down the Delaware River from Liverpool and Antwerp, only two miles from the Northeast school.

Northeast Philadelphia was packed with so much industry that local neighborhoods took their nicknames accordingly: There was Brewery Town, a German section of Northeast Philadelphia packed with factories like the Schaefer Brewing Company, along with Gasoline Alley, a burgeoning transportation industry hub near Broad and Lehigh that began with carriages and wagons and moved on to Packards, Cadillacs, Fords, and Studebakers. Northeast Philadelphia was home to the largest textile industry in the world. Philadelphia produced more textiles than any other American city, employing 35 percent of the city's workforce, with 7,100 separate companies, most of which were clustered within a few miles surrounding the Northeast Manual Training Center. Carpet manufacture was were another homegrown Philadelphia industry.

Also headquartered within a mile of the soon-to-be neighborhood high school, Northeast Manual Training Center, were prominent companies such as Baldwin Works, which built one of the first American-made locomotives in the 1830s, and by 1884 had thirty-eight buildings and nineteen thousand employees; the Quaker Lace Company, with eighty looms spinning tablecloths and lace curtains; John Bromley and Sons, the oldest and largest carpet manufacturer in the country; and the Stetson Hat Company, which produced three million hats by the 1920s. With more than twenty buildings (including its own hospital), thirty acres of floor space, and thirty-five hundred employees, Stetson was the size of a small town.

Immigrants, who doubled Philadelphia's population from 500,000 in 1870 to 1,000,000 in 1920, lacked mechanical skills in a day when demand for such labor was surging. As the Philadelphia economy surged forward, the interests of educational proponents entwined with those of capitalists, and that made high school an appealing idea.

From its first year, the Northeast Manual Training Center would enjoy decades of success as one of the nation's most prestigious public high schools. Graduates like Herbert Max Abramson and Edgar E. Bailey grinned from yearbook photos, wearing ties and meticulously slicked-back hair. They listed their aspirations to be "A Harvard Man," and to "Own a Railroad." The school would host a number of dignitaries, including two U.S. presidents, Albert Einstein, Babe Ruth, Herbert Hoover, Amelia Earhart, and movie actress and World War II pinup Ann Sheridan. It would win scores of awards. Even as the concept of public high schools caught on in the 1930s and 1940s and enrollment became commonplace in America for both boys and girls, Northeast was still one of the most well-regarded high schools in the nation.

* * *

Social change drastically affected Northeast and many urban high schools like it. The Northeast school was now required to serve all boys, rather than handpick the most talented. In the past, boys with limited ability went straight into the job market. Now they were going into the schools. Students ranged dramatically in ability and motivation. At the time, many thought this widening access to education was a horrible idea that would dilute the pool of the most talented. To handle the growing rolls, IQ tests were given, and boys were divided into low-IQ sections, called 9-A, and honors-type classes, in which they were pushed forward. Truancy accounted for 75 percent of the school's troubles, and was attributed to the fact that boys who lacked interest in education, or were needed to work, were being forced into the schools, along with the sons and daughters of blacks who had migrated North from Alabama and the Carolinas.

By 1950, it was readily apparent that Philadelphia's heyday had come and was going. The Northeast alumni, a giant and tightly knit group of city businessmen with strong affection for their alma mater, felt their school, like most urban schools, was in decline. They began to meet, at first furtively, then publicly. Ironically, in 1951 the Northeast received the Francis Bellamy Award for school of the year. It would be the last year that the school received any national awards.

In the fall of 1956, a rumor ran through the hallways of the Northeast: the school was moving. Northeast student Don Hackney, class of 1957, remembers a sinking feeling in his stomach as news bounced off the lockers. Principal Charles A. Young called all the boys to the auditorium.

"Word was flying around that they were moving the school," recalled Hackney almost forty years later. "We went to the auditorium, and the principal addressed us. We were respectful gentleman—the Men of the Northeast—so we wouldn't have created any really volatile situation. We listened to the principal, but we were very upset. How could they do this? We didn't want to move. They were going to take our trophies and all the things we'd worked so hard to win and put them in a new place?"

It was true. The school's powerful alumni had been meeting since 1952 to plan the school's move. They had lobbied city officials and the board of education members, many of whom were Northeast alumni themselves. They gave two reasons for the move.

First, they complained that the school at Eighth and Lehigh was old and deteriorating, and that a new building was needed. Second, they deemed the building overcrowded, with enrollment bursting and projected to increase. Students needed the space offered only in the suburbs, they said. They found a plot of land ten miles north. They used their powerful connections to make their voices heard.

In truth, records show the school's population was actually declining. What they didn't mention in the public record was that the neighborhood was changing rapidly, and in the eyes of the Northeast alumni, for the worse. Old yearbooks show a steady increase in African American enrollment starting in the late 1940s. By the 1950s nearly half of the student body was black. They replaced students from white families who were moving to the suburbs.

Records show the plan for a new building was hatched officially on March 11, 1953, when Frederick C. Fiechter, president of the Northeast Alumni

Association, submitted a proposal to the school board. In May 1953, the new site was purchased for $500,000. One year later, the school board authorized $6 million for the new forty-three-acre Northeast school. At the time, $6 million was considered an extravagant amount of money for a new building. Construction began at Cottman and Algon.

The alumni had cited the school's deteriorating condition in arguing for a new building. However, after the alumni secured the new building, the city voted to keep the old Northeast School open anyway. The school left behind would not close; it would be renamed Thomas Edison High School, and it would serve the mostly black neighborhood. It was a fifty-year-old structure in desperate need of repair, but almost all the money would go to the new school.

William H. Loesche, chair of the school board's business committee, was a lone voice at a 1954 school board meeting when he called the new building a "luxury." "We should possibly be spending this money on replacing and repairing some of our older buildings in the city," Loesche noted in the *Bulletin*. The article went on to say: "But other members overrode his objections."

The physical moving of a school is, in fact, not that unusual. Northeast traces its history back to a Girard Street location, in the 1880s, when it was an annex to Central High School, a school that had also moved several times as late as 1938. However, when a school moves, it usually brings its students with it. Under school district policy, students from the Eighth and Lehigh neighborhood were too far away to be allowed to attend the new Northeast building. The new school was sectioned off for its new neighbors—white residents who had fled the inner city for the suburbs.

One exception was made. Grandchildren of Northeast alumni still living near Eighth and Lehigh would be allowed to move to the new location. This clause allowed almost all white students still attending the Eighth and Lehigh school to transfer.

Once again, the Northeast would be at the forefront of an educational trend. In 1954, the Supreme Court's *Brown vs. Board of Education* decision had officially forbidden school segregation. However, in Northeast's case, no one was technically forbidding black students from attending. The alumni just created all the right geographic circumstances for it to be practically impossible. Hence, they would be the leaders of de facto segregation, a movement that spread quickly throughout the city high schools and is, at the turn of the twenty-first century, the reason schools are more segregated than ever before.

At the time of Northeast's move, its student population was 50 percent Caucasian and 50 percent African American. By 1958, in the span of about two years, the old Northeast—Edison High School—became almost entirely African American. The new Northeast was 100 percent Caucasian. It would stay that way for the next thirty years.

The board also approved the transfer of the "name, traditions, and specialized courses of the school" to the new location. The best teachers left, too. According to a December 1956 *Sunday Bulletin* article, the school took the principal, five department heads, and the athletic director.

This "created some resentment in the community and among some of the veteran members of the faculty, the greatest number of which will stay at Eighth and Lehigh," according to a minor mention made in a November 1956 *Bulletin* piece. If there was an outcry within the community, it was either not strong enough to even receive much press, or was ignored.

The new school principal tried, however unconvincingly, to smooth over the frustrations of the students left behind. "There was some justice to the resentment of the loss of their school name and traditions, but the boys have now come to see that there is also a privilege in helping build traditions for a new school, and, in a sense, being a pioneer class," Dr. Robert Wayne Clark, Edison's new principal, said at the time. Shortly thereafter, he transferred out himself.

A placard with the school's new name went up. On the first day, in September 1957, senior Ron Ford, who is black, walked down the once familiar halls. The trophy case was gone. So were the stained-glass windows and the plaque dedicated to the three hundred Northeast graduates who'd given their lives to World War II. He peeked his head into his old classrooms. His favorite math teacher, the one who was tough but fair, had left for the new Northeast. His coach, the main reason Ford had aspired to Northeast, had left, too, and he'd taken the team's red-and-white uniforms with him. That year they lost the basketball championship to Overbrook High and its rising star Wilt "the Stilt" Chamberlain.

"I was distraught," said Ford. "If you could wear the red and black of the Northeast, you were looked up to. It was a source of pride and wanting to belong, and that was taken away and given to someone else. The goose bumps you got from the football and basketball games were not there. We had packed houses every game. Girls from Kensington came. All that changed. They took that away. The building may be the same, but it's not just a building that made the Northeast."

Meanwhile, ten miles north, little had been spared in the construction of the new Northeast school. Of the $6 million budgeted for a new school, $1 million had been spent on athletics, including three grandstands seating 6,700; fields for football, baseball, hockey, and soccer; four tennis courts; a quarter-mile track; and three parking areas. Several uproars made it into the local press, but none of them had anything to do with the inequality between the schools. One was over the fact that girls were being granted access to the great Northeast! Another had to do with changing a line in the school song from "the walls made of granite" to "the strong and sturdy walls." And the alumni were in a state over sports teams changing names from the Archives to the Vikings.

The new Northeast opened to students in February 1957 and dedication day, a few months later, brought a huge celebration and decades of alumni with it. There were open-house tours, a laying of the cornerstone, an alumni dinner, and speakers, including the board of education president. There was an alumni banquet. President Dwight Eisenhower was invited, but declined at the last minute. A plaque in his name was dedicated to the Northeast that said, "For nearly 70 years this school has played an essential part in the training of young citizens. The completion of the modern building indicates your determination that the school shall increase its splendid contribution to your community and nation in the years ahead, April 27th 1957."

Back in Philadelphia, businesses that once demanded that schools train boys had disappeared. In the half-century after 1925, the city lost two-thirds of its industrial jobs and virtually all its great firms. Of the twenty-five large companies operating in Philadelphia in 1925, only one remains a major player.

The textile industry's flight to the suburbs dealt the hardest blow to the North Philadelphia neighborhoods surrounding Eighth and Lehigh. In 1928, 350 of the city's 850 textile firms operated in North Philadelphia, employing almost 35,000 workers. Of these businesses, 265 remained by 1940 and only seventy by the 1960s. Hardwick and Magee, across the street from Northeast, didn't survive much past the 1950s. The Stetson Hat Company, famous for its millions of Western hats, closed its doors in the 1960s, as did the Quaker Lace Company down Lehigh Avenue on Fourth street, set back by the invention of knitting machines capable of making lace. Across North Philadelphia, hundreds of formerly proud giant factories were continually downsized until they were nothing but rotting hulks of brick, mangled wire, and chemicals.

***

It was the early 1960s, and the future was dim for students at Edison High. The school board announced that a new citywide program intended for "slow learners" would be installed at Edison. The board warned principals not to use the program as a dumping ground for students with discipline problems, but that seemed inevitable. The historic U.S. Supreme Court *Brown vs. Board of Education* decision to end segregation in 1954 had created the opposite effect: Edison's student body was almost 100 percent black. The Supreme Court decision only hastened white flight across the city. In the 1950s, the student population of Philadelphia's Simon Gratz High School was divided evenly between whites and blacks. Ten years later it was 100 percent black. In Philadelphia, 1961 marked the last year in which there were equal numbers of whites and blacks in the city schools. After that, the population would become two-thirds black and continue to segregate. By 1971, the number of the city's Puerto Rican students, concentrated in North Philadelphia, had grown to 3 percent of the school population. Edison was the school primarily serving them.

As civil rights protests arose in the 1960s and 1970s, minority parents began to echo the same complaints about Edison's deteriorating condition that their white predecessors had made prior to the 1957 move. That move had faced little protest by black parents then, but times were changing, and white flight was now held up by neighborhood activists as blatant racism. Resentment over the state of the old school building—which was dilapidated and infested with rats—boiled over.

In October 1968, a student walkout to protest the conditions spread violence throughout the city. The students at Edison High School were active participants. An article in the *Bulletin* read, in part:

> 200 Negro students refused to return to classes after a false fire alarm. They marched to Kensington High School for Girls, shouting for the girls to join them. The group, followed by 40 police, then marched to Dobbins High School, which was still 50 percent white. Three white boys were outside waiting for the bus,

and the blacks shouted, "We want whitey," but the police surrounded the white students until the bus arrived to escort them away. The principal held the Dobbins students inside the school until 4:00 PM as the police tried to disperse the Edison students. When a riot broke out, a white boy, 17 year old Elliot Abrams, was stabbed.

The Vietnam War dealt another blow to the school. Hundreds of Edison boys volunteered or were drafted. By war's end, the principal tallied the deaths and was astonished to see that sixty-six Edison students had given their lives in the war. When Northeast students died in World War II, an enormous plaque was mounted in the auditorium listing their names. Edison's fallen heroes didn't receive any recognition. Their "ultimate sacrifice" would go largely unnoticed by anyone outside of Edison.

By the 1970s, parents had organized and were campaigning for a new building. The seventy-year-old high school was by far the city's oldest. Pieces of plaster fell from the ceilings. Paint peeled. Heating systems broke down. When sections of the school became too dangerous to occupy, the city had the custodian board them up. Soon, nearly half of the school was sealed off and boarded up. Graffiti marked the transoms and white moldings. Bars went up across the windows.

In 1972, after a long neighborhood campaign, activists came within just a few votes of winning city funding for a new school building. They'd secured a site one mile north, at Second and Luzerne. It was across the street from a graveyard, in a neighborhood that happened to be largely white. The local residents vociferously opposed moving Edison into their backyard. At the eleventh hour, Philadelphia Mayor Frank Rizzo, the notoriously racist, bat-wielding former police commissioner, blocked the plan. Years of work were defeated.

Test scores at other high schools—Overbrook, Simon Gratz, and Ben Franklin—were falling, but Edison fell the furthest. When students took the California Achievement Tests in 1976, a whopping 80 percent of Edison students scored in the bottom percentile nationwide, indicating that they were "functionally illiterate," according to *The Philadelphia Inquirer*.

In 1979, seniors from Edison and neighboring schools tried again. They boycotted classes. They marched on the board of education, complaining they were getting a "rotten education." They said instruction was inadequate, and that they wouldn't return to class until the situation had improved. Their pleas were largely ignored.

By the 1980s, Edison was widely regarded as the city's worst school. A September 1982 article in the *Inquirer* summed it up: "The way most people think of Edison, if they think of it at all, is as just another ghetto school with a legacy of racial problems and gang infestation."

***

The North Philadelphia neighborhood surrounding the school had continued to evolve and change. A wave of Puerto Rican immigration swept through North Philadelphia in the early 1980s, and the new arrivals eventually became organized and politically vocal. The neighborhood elected a Latino city councilor, Angel Ortiz. Philadelphia also had its first black mayor, Wilson Goode. The city's population was still declining, and blacks were now in the majority. Those community groups involved in the nearly thirty-year battle for a new school building to replace the deteriorating one finally had representation in government. The dream was gaining strength.

In 1988, a sprawling new school building opened at Second and Luzerne, the same site it had requested fifteen years earlier (the majority of the white neighbors who'd once opposed the plan had since moved to the suburbs). The new school, with grassy lawns, a pond, and a parking lot, cost upward of $50 million. At the time, it was the city's most expensive school. It was to be bilingual, an educational idea that had become trendy in recent years.

The teachers and principal took the new trophies and whatever stained-glass windows and historical plaques still remained. In the old building, the blinds were drawn and chains snapped shut. The parking lot emptied but for junked neighborhood cars. The school building at Eighth and Lehigh was condemned and closed.

A year later, neighbors watched a bright blue and yellow banner go up across the front entrance. A cleaning crew came in. The city sealed off the most dangerous sections of the building, closed the auditorium completely, and slapped on a fresh layer of paint. The news spread rapidly: The neighborhood schools were overcrowded and an additional middle school was needed. The school at Eighth and Lehigh was having a "grand reopening." To meet the specific needs of the community, it would be Philadelphia's first bilingual middle school. It would be called the Julia de Burgos Bilingual Middle Magnet School.

At the time, administrators sang the praises of bilingual education. The city said the school would offer bilingual programs in which Spanish-speaking students learned English, and English-speaking students learned Spanish. Students could apply from all over Philadelphia.

It sounded perfect on paper. But even at a wealthy, well-run school the goals of bilingual education were challenging to meet and required years of teacher training. In a North Philadelphia school already beset by discipline issues and financial constraints, bilingual education was little more than rhetoric. The *Philadelphia Inquirer*'s 1989 story about the school described a chaotic and ill-prepared opening year: "[Principal José E. Lebron] didn't know he'd be the principal of the district's first bilingual middle school until July. He had to recruit a staff and oversee setting up a curriculum before school opened in September. And then there was the building. Home to two different schools over more than eighty years, the old Edison High was in need of more than a little repair."

"I walked in one day and said 'No way are we going to open in September,'" Lebron was quoted as saying to the *Inquirer*.

By 1989, the school had only a handful of Spanish-speaking teachers. Implementing a bilingual curriculum was unrealistic. Into the early 1990s, research emerged showing that students learned new languages at a faster pace in elementary school, anyway. Principal Lebron transferred to Edison High School and took with him much of the energy of the new project.

Newly immigrated students joined Spanish-speaking cliques of friends and progressed through years of school without learning any English. Cries continued against the school's condition. In 1989 it was eighty-three years old and falling apart. This was the last building to which mothers wanted to send their ten-year-olds. The city couldn't deny it. They agreed the building was too old and coughed up $2.3 million for rehabilitation. There were plans to construct another middle school, they promised. They wouldn't use the structure as an educational institution for long, they promised. It would only be "temporary."

The school at Eighth and Lehigh would remain open for the next fourteen years. In its final years, I arrived.

2
They'll Take Anyone

A weather-beaten, gray stone edifice stood on the corner of Eighth and Lehigh in North Philadelphia. The roof had four turrets with menacing gargoyles arched forward. Surrounding the building was a moat of concrete ringed by a black iron gate. Somehow, vandals had sprayed graffiti on the slanted roofs. This could not be a school.

I yanked open the only door that wasn't chained shut and saw a little placard with the words MAIN OFFICE down the hall. Inside, a woman behind the counter shuffled through papers. She glanced up over the glasses perched on her nose.

"Hi, my name is Christina Asquith," I said. "I'd like to teach here."

Most schools had their staff in place by July, but the city of Philadelphia still lacked fifteen hundred teachers—more than 10 percent of the teaching staff. The district was desperate to hire anyone, or they'd have thousands of kids without a teacher that September. I was a twenty-five-year-old journalist and had recently finished a two-year internship with *The Philadelphia Inquirer*. I ought to have been looking for a job in journalism, but the other day I had come across an advertisement at the bus stop: "Change a Life. Be a Teacher." The ad showed a sweet young boy with a yearning look on his face.

Although I'd worked for newspapers since college, I was frustrated with the industry as of late. I wanted to make a difference, particularly by covering urban school systems, but from the distant perch of the newsroom I felt out of touch with the real problems inside the classroom. Teaching was always something I had a passion for, but I didn't want to go back to school for years to get an education degree. As I'd quickly learn, I didn't have to.

Julia de Burgos was one of a handful of so-called Spanish-English bilingual schools in Philadelphia that I would most likely be placed at because I was

13

fluent in Spanish. The woman behind the counter was Mrs. Jimenez, the assistant principal. She was friendly and offered to give me a tour.

"The school used to be called the Northeast Manual Training Center, but they renamed it twice, and now it's called Julia de Burgos Bilingual Middle Magnet School, after the Puerto Rican poet," she said. She told me she had taught here for a decade, but that the school was almost one hundred years old.

The school felt like a museum filled with history. A dimly lit staircase led up to an antique stained-glass window that filled the archway with the colored light of a church. The school hallways formed a square, with a courtyard in the middle and three sets of staircases leading from the basement to the third floor. Several years had passed since I'd stood in the long, shiny hallways of a school, and I was flooded with memories of my own private school in Northern New Jersey.

Mrs. Jimenez was unfazed when I told her I had never taught before. "Mmmm, yes. Well, we really need teachers," she replied. Even though the school needed some serious renovation, the pretty murals of Puerto Rico and handmade signs displaying school pride gave the place a sense of spirit.

This would be tough, but if I were going to do this, I didn't want a school that anyone would teach at. I wanted to teach kids that no one else would take. When Mrs. Jimenez offered to write a letter requesting I be assigned here, I happily agreed. She looked slightly surprised.

***

"Can I really teach without any experience?" I asked Eppy, the recruiter for the Philadelphia School District. Most districts require new teachers to have graduated with a bachelor's degree in education from a four-year college. Additionally, aspiring teachers had to log at least forty hours in the classroom training alongside a real teacher.

Eppy waved my concerns away. "Believe me, we need you more than you need us," he said.

I had no direct experience in a classroom, but had always dreamed of being a teacher. I took several education classes my first year at Boston University, but I eventually switched to journalism because the classroom seemed too confining at such a young age. I wanted to go out and learn about the world first, and journalism was a vehicle to travel, meet new people, and explore different subjects. Immediately after college I moved to Chile for one year to write for a newspaper. Upon my return I was accepted into the *Inquirer*'s two-year internship program where I gravitated to education and wrote of stories about testing, school life, and teachers' programs. For two years I volunteered in the Big Brother/Big Sister program of Philadelphia and for the Salvation Army Boys and Girls Club. I thought I would be better in high school, teaching maybe English, science, or history. I was imagining the famous teacher movies: *Stand and Deliver*, *Dangerous Minds*, and *Lean on Me*.

"The real need is in the middle schools," he was saying. "I was a middle school teacher." Eppy was overly friendly, like a salesman. He never stopped grinning and looking relaxed, even as he constantly interrupted our meeting to take phone calls that always seemed to involve an emergency.

We spent about two hours together on that first day, and by the end Eppy convinced me to take middle school. He warned me to hurry with my application forms, though, because it was already July.

"It's not the eleventh hour, Christina. It's quarter to twelve."

I had a million things to get: a criminal-record check, a doctor's physical, and a form from the FBI saying I had no reported history of child abuse in Pennsylvania. And I needed to enroll in a certification program at a university. After years writing about education, interviewing principals, reading about the troubles of urban schools, and pleading to see a real classroom in action, I was excited that I'd finally be able to uncover how schools really work.

At twenty-five, I was full of determination to change the world and make a difference. A year as an inner-city teacher would be a chance to help children in need. Why were inner-city schools failing? Maybe I'd find the solutions, perhaps even write about it afterward. But I'd worry about that part later. I hadn't been in middle school in more than a decade. I didn't even know any twelve-year-olds. The school district wasn't really going to let me do this . . . were they?

While I waited for Eppy to process my application I devoted all of July to training myself to be a teacher. I read *The First Days of School*, by Harry and

Rosemary Wong. Rather than comforting me, it opened my eyes to how much I didn't know. What was a lesson plan? How did I decorate a classroom? How did I discipline a child? How would I get parents involved?

I pored over teaching books that explained concepts like name charts, pencil-sharpening procedures, and positive reinforcement. I learned all kinds of new details about preteens that I had long forgotten, such as the most important thing a child wants on the first day is security. Transition frightens them, and teachers should explain every small detail, such as how to pronounce the teacher's name and classroom locations and schedules.

I scribbled down tips for myself: "Don't mark X on the answers that are wrong, just mark C on the answers that are correct." "Never, ever raise your voice." "Teach a new vocabulary word each day, and call it, 'Word of the Day.'" The most important thing was to "plan and plan extra."

My boyfriend, Pete, helped. He was tall, handsome, outdoorsy, and the only person who supported my dream to teach. He was in his first year of residency at a local hospital, but before medical school, Pete had taught for a year in New York City. He was encouraging and gave me solid advice, such as "never kick a student out of class to be disciplined. That sends the message that you aren't the authority. Handle all your own discipline." Together, we reviewed his old lesson plans.

"Just remember that you're in charge. The most important thing is discipline," he said. "You gotta sit them down first, then teach."

He told me not to smile until Thanksgiving, either. "There are two different types of teachers—the ruler-cracker and loving pushover. Who are you going to be?" He explained that, in his school, the female teacher across the hall from him was soft and fuzzy, and won over the kids with warmth. Her class was always chaotic, but the students covered her desk with gifts at Christmas. They listened because they loved her.

Pete was the opposite, a real "hard-ass" teacher who demanded quiet and didn't let the kids get away with anything. When a fight broke out in the hallway one morning, he'd jumped in and put a red-faced boy in a headlock, pushing the kid's chin into the floor. The rest of the students saw this and knew not to mess with him. He never let the slightest infraction slide. That may sound harsh, he said, but these kids craved borders. My strictness would pay off, and I'd be glad, he promised. For example, he recalled a day in the spring when he conducted a physics experiment. He was able to leave half his class unattended while he and several other students went to another floor to study velocity. His students behaved. Other teachers saw this and marveled at his control. He bragged for ten minutes about it. When he reminisced about teaching, he grew nostalgic.

"This will be the best thing you've ever done," he said, giving me a hug.

Then he gave me a piece of advice.

"Never enter a showdown you can't win," he said.

"A showdown?" I asked.

He nodded. That night he demonstrated a judo move in which I was to grab his wrist, wrap it around in a circular orbit, and grip him in a headlock. This could nail someone in three seconds, regardless of weight. I tried it a few times, but it didn't really work when I did it.

"Just in case," Pete said.

My family was much less supportive.

"Are you crazy?" said Jon, my brother, a twenty-seven-year-old stockbroker who lived in a mini-mansion in the New York suburbs. "Don't you know what happened to Jonathan Levin? Is that what you want to happen to you?" he asked.

Jonathan Levin was the wealthy son of then Time Warner chair Gerald Levin. He had eschewed his family fortune and fame to become a beloved English teacher in an underprivileged school in the Bronx. In 1997, two of his students arrived high on drugs at his Upper West Side Manhattan apartment, robbed him, and shot him to death.

"That's not going to happen," I said uncertainly.

"Why do you have to do that? Do what your friends are doing," he said.

Most of my friends were setting off for well-paying jobs with Internet start-ups or glamorous new magazines or in bureaus of the *Wall Street Journal* or *The New York Times*. Why didn't I want to do that, too? I didn't know. I wanted to "make a difference in a child's life," as the Philadelphia Department of Education recruitment posters promised. I felt like the failing inner-city schools were an injustice that I should stand against, not only with words, but with real action, especially these days, as the economy boomed and people in their twenties were becoming Internet millionaires overnight. In the newspaper the other day, I read that some rich Wall Street guy rang up a $200,000 tab at a restaurant and left the waiter a $40,000 tip. Yet, in the same city there were children who lacked textbooks. Something was wrong with this. Once inside the schools, I would understand the problems and then find solutions. I could take those solutions to politicians and make a change in schools across the nation.

"Go into advertising, real estate, finance," Jon was saying. "You're crazy. It's the ghetto. It's dangerous."

I didn't say anything. I couldn't articulate my beliefs, and I couldn't stand up to my brother. He filled the silence.

"Oh, man, wait until Dad hears this one," he laughed. "Dude, I'm going to earn your annual salary in one day."

As the summer drew to a close, the Philadelphia schools still needed to recruit hundreds of warm bodies. It offered $1,500 sign-up bonuses. A few hundred more signed on, and a couple hundred additional bodies joined in September and October. Like me, they would be too late for the one-week induction seminar, so they received no training at all. I didn't want to imagine the kind of unqualified, uninterested teacher who would take the job at the last minute just for the sign-up bonus.

By the time school started, more than eleven hundred random people—one in ten teachers—had wandered off the street and been handed classroom keys. They were directed to the most troubled schools, and when September started they stood in front of their classrooms. They had no educational experience, no guidance, no instruction, and scant support. Like me, many had no clue how to teach.

It may seem unbelievable that someone could simply walk off the street and into a classroom, but in Philadelphia and many urban districts, this was exactly what was happening.

The thriving economy of the late 1990s drew potential teachers and college graduates into other, higher-paying jobs. This occurred just as birth patterns gave rise to a massive increase in student enrollment. At the same time, an aging workforce meant that scores of teachers were retiring. This perfect storm in the education employment world led to one of the periods of greatest demand for new teachers in thirty years. An estimated seven million new teachers would have to be hired between 1997 and 2007, according to the U.S. Department of Education.

In 1999, Philadelphia was the fifth largest public school district in the nation, with 210,247 students, twelve thousand teachers, more than two hundred schools, and a $1.6 billion annual budget. Like most big urban areas, the school system had turned abysmal in the 1970s—correlating with the disappearance of big industry and white flight to the suburbs—and hasn't turned around since. These days, 78 percent of eleventh-graders couldn't even complete basic-level work in any major subject, according to scores on the SAT-9, the city's standardized test.

City officials had been trying for decades—without success—to turn the system around. The latest trend strove to make schools run like businesses, an approach that was gaining in popularity in urban districts across the country. In the spring of my year teaching, the school board fired its school superintendent and replaced him with a "chief executive officer," using a business title to indicate their intention to bring corporate-style accountability to a public system. Plans were afoot to turn dozens of schools over to for-profit companies. Voucher programs, in which children use public money to attend private schools, were also being pushed by the governor's office. So were merit pay, teacher accountability measures, and teacher recruitment.

Missing from this list were proposals to improve teacher recruitment and training. The city was desperately trying to recruit hundreds of warm bodies, and yet leaving us to prepare for the job without guidance.

To meet demand, schools hired "emergency certified" or "alternative certified people." These were candidates who didn't have a university degree from a college of education; neither did they have a major in the field in which they planned to teach, such as chemistry, math, or English. They also didn't have to take any state or school district teacher exams. In the case of Philadelphia, all teachers typically had to take the Praxis exam, designed by the Educational Testing Service. It's a battery of tests to assess prospective teachers' basic knowledge of math, reading, and writing. Emergency certified teachers would not have to take that test until after three years on the job.

By 2000, forty-five states and Washington D.C. allowed for emergency certified teachers, and their ranks were growing. In Texas, one in four new teachers was emergency certified. In Detroit—the city with the greatest numbers—one in three teachers was uncertified. In poor rural and inner-city schools, their numbers are even greater.

Many people opposed the idea of emergency certification, pointing out that the equivalent in medicine would be to solve a hospital's doctor shortage by doing away with medical school and board examinations. Yet others said that looser standards allowed people to change careers and go into teaching without having to go back to school for three years. In these instances, schools benefited from diversifying their teaching ranks with successful professionals, such as scientists, mathematicians, entrepreneurs, and writers. One popular national program, Troops to Teachers, gave former military commanders emergency certifications to become teachers and eventually school leaders. Teach for America was another popular national program that recruited college graduates, placed them in underprivileged school districts, assisted them in getting their emergency certifications, and ran training courses. It also acted as a support for new teachers in their first year.

These programs gave between one to six weeks of summer training, but new teachers like me, who applied directly to the school district, often received less. I would receive only a few days. Supposedly that was enough to take on a classroom of the city's toughest-to-teach children.

In 2003, a Philadelphia think tank found otherwise. When Philadelphia's emergency certified teachers finally did take the basic licensure tests—the Praxis exam—the think tank uncovered: "Less than half of the emergency certified teachers passed the basic mathematics test." Only two-thirds passed the reading. Only 60 percent passed the writing.

"Their inexperience makes classroom management a problem," stated the report titled "Once and for All" by the "Learning from Philadelphia's School Reform Project." In math, science, and bilingual classrooms—the areas that were the hardest to find teachers for—half of all new teachers were uncertified. This meant a child in Philadelphia's public schools had less than a 50 percent chance of getting a math teacher who could do basic math.

The report concluded: "The data makes clear that students in Philadelphia have not been able to count on getting a teacher who has mastered basic academic skills."

***

"I was just about to call you," Eppy said. "You're scheduled to come in on Thursday, September 9. Bring all your things, and then hopefully we'll process you to start by the following Monday."

That was a week after school starts! "I thought I was ready to go," I said.

I'd been sitting on a completed application for at least a month now. Meanwhile, thirty-three kids would show up to an empty classroom—all because of a delay in processing? I had also heard from another new teacher that the school district was running a one-week induction program for new recruits, which I had missed because Eppy hadn't told me about it.

Eppy encouraged me to *calmate*, Spanish for "relax". "You're a Type A personality, Christina. You need to relax or you'll never make it through the first year teaching."

On September 2 Julia de Burgos held a welcome-back day for all the teachers, and I decided to turn up despite my lack of a formal assignment. I felt uncomfortable, but Mrs. Jimenez looked pleased to see me. She probably knew I hadn't been hired yet, but we both acted as though I had so I wouldn't miss anything. Everyone hugged and talked about summer vacation and about children. The library had elegant architecture, with sixteen-foot-high ceilings, original wood trim, and grand windows and wooden tables. I saw teachers had hung student projects on the walls. Mrs. Jimenez told me the teachers were divided into six Small Learning Communities, like teams, and mine would be the TV/Communications Team, also called the Bilingual Team. I found a seat at their table.

There were seven other teachers, all from Puerto Rico, the Dominican Republic, and Venezuela, all in their thirties and forties. They wore lots of gold jewelry and had long, painted fingernails. They spoke in Spanish to one another. They spoke English to me.

We played some get-to-know-one-another exercises, in which we interviewed the teacher next to us, and then we each had to stand up and say one nice thing about the person we spoke to.

"Christina learned Spanish in high school and then lived in Chile for a year after college," said Marjorie Soto, the English to Speakers of Other Languages teacher next to me. Everyone smiled.

A woman entered and everyone fell silent. For a few minutes she stacked and restacked the papers on the podium, as though relishing her ability to command silence. A few wisps of short, grayish brown hair clung to her forehead, and her conservative business suit hung unevenly off her round frame. She had thin grayish lips and wore large, thick eyeglasses. Silently, she passed around her resume and a mission statement that said, "All ye who enter here prepare to succeed. Failure is not an Option."

Her resume said she was a career school administrator but for a brief stint of teaching in the 1970s. This was her first job as principal. The teachers began to gossip about her in Spanish: Assigned at the last minute, she was the school's third principal in four years. She was a *gringa*, in a school whose students were 85 percent Hispanic and 15 percent African American. And she did not speak Spanish. Judging by the stiff body language of the teachers at my table, the principal was not going to be popular.

"It's hard to believe, but only two weeks ago the superintendent of schools called me himself. I was on the beach on vacation with my family at the time. He asked if I would be willing to be principal here."

She laughed a little to herself. "Two weeks is hardly enough time to prepare an entire school for a new year. I've been working hard each day from 5 AM until 6 PM. I am committed to moving this school up."

She walked from behind the card catalog in a sweeping manner, as though on stage in a grand theater. Her words sharpened.

"We have nowhere to go but up," she began. "Julia de Burgos is one of the worst middle schools in all of Philadelphia. It has the lowest test scores of any other middle school. Student attendance is 70 percent. Teacher attendance is not much higher."

Another teacher shook his head, as if to say her numbers were not correct, but the new principal was looking to the back of the library, as if speaking to an amphitheater of people. She continued to tick off offenses.

"The number of violent incidents here each year is inexcusable. The state is investigating the school for problems with its special education students. Starting this year, no teacher will be allowed to suspend special education students," she said. "We'll find a way to deal with them."

This sounded ominous. Was she hinting at grade inflation? That would be a major story for the *Inquirer*, but of course I didn't work there anymore. No one there even realized I had become a schoolteacher. Most people looked at me strangely when I told them. A few weeks earlier, I was chatting with a police officer in Rittenhouse Square, and I mentioned my new job. He was happy for me until I revealed the location at Eighth and Lehigh Avenues in North Philly.

"Whaddaya, nuts? That place is a toilet," he said. "We get called in there every day."

Glancing around the library, I tried to imagine hardened city cops arresting the kids. The principal rambled on, and teachers stared stone-faced or rolled their eyes toward the high ceiling. I wondered how often they'd heard this "there's-a-new-sheriff-in-town" speech.

"Failure will not be an option. I will work until they spread my ashes in the Poconos to turn this school around," she promised.

The principal gave a thirty-minute speech about her life growing up and what motivated her as a principal. She said she had moved among twelve foster homes, and although she was gifted, she also had undiagnosed dyslexia, which many teachers interpreted as stupidity. It was a moving speech.

"I know what it feels like to be alone," she said. "I don't want any child at this school to ever feel alone. Find a way to have magic in every child."

We received the school-year calendar, and the veteran teachers huddled together, laughing, pulling out red pens, and circling each holiday with flourish. There were two days off for Thanksgiving, a week for Christmas, Martin Luther King Day, Presidents' Day, spring recess, Good Friday, Memorial Day—by June 15 it was all over. That totaled five weeks of vacation out of a ten-month work year. I couldn't believe it. That seemed like a really generous benefits package.

The Venezuelan teacher happily flipped through the calendar. "Another holiday here," she said, drawing a big red circle around each day she'd have off work. She looked up to see me staring at her.

"Believe me, you're going to be doing this," she chuckled.

No, I'm not, I thought. I looked away.

The Venezuelan teacher nudged the teacher next to her. They rolled their eyes and shared a knowing look.

Later, one of them volunteered to be my mentor, which the Philadelphia School District provides for all new teachers. I was grateful and thanked her. Then she told me we'd spend exactly six sessions of forty-five minutes each together, and each time I'd have to sign a piece of paper so she'd get paid.

"Oh, okay," I said.

I was the only new teacher on our team.

***

Despite Eppy's foot-dragging, my persistence paid off, and I landed a processing date before school started. Processing took four hours, during which I received a speech from the union, an explanation of all benefits, an official teacher ID card with photo, and—most important—my pick of school.

When they called us up, more than one-third of the group didn't have proper documentation (such as an original copy of our college diploma), and were sent home.

I imagined the thirty-three kids who would now have to start school without a teacher—and only because some teachers had brought photocopies of their college diplomas. The only reason I knew to bring the original (which my parents had sent by FedEx) was because I called Eppy so frequently that he finally happened to mention it.

Then the big moment: They handed us a computer printout of all the open positions and began calling our names. "Pick the school you want," we were told . . . and nothing more. How completely random. We didn't even interview with the principal? Teachers all around me were mumbling, "I have no idea ..." And the union workers circled us, saying things like "Don't go there!" and "That school is outta control."

I scanned the sheet and recognized a lot of the schools' names. These schools routinely made the evening news for shootings, arson, and violence against teachers. The veterans steered clear of these schools and left them for the new, untrained teachers, who were given last pick. I quickly found Julia de Burgos and saw two openings for sixth grade. That was what I wanted. Forty-five minutes passed and they still hadn't called me. What if someone else requested that position?

A librarian sat next to me. "I was going to pick Olney High School, but the union lady said it was one of those bad schools, you know?"

I wanted to tell her that I planned on picking a so-called bad school, because I was going to turn around a classroom, and then take what I'd learned and change education policy so schools everywhere could be improved. But something held me back. Perhaps a realization that, one day, I might not feel so holier than thou.

Finally, my name was called. No one else wanted Julia de Burgos. I got it!

When I got to school, I raced down the hallway with my good news. I couldn't wait to tell my team their vacancy was filled.

About sixty teachers sat in the library and there were some leftover doughnuts and orange juice during a break between meetings. I saw Marjorie Soto, the ESOL teacher who had introduced me the other day. She used to work in finance in Manhattan and still had a hardened-chic look, with her short, spiky hair, and a rainbow-colored ring on her finger. I rushed over to tell them my good news.

As I sat down, Marjorie Soto looked up, bemused.

"Oh, you're back?" she smirked. The conversation stopped.

"You're here?" asked another.

"We thought you transferred somewhere else," said a third.

"What? I called to say I was being processed this morning," I said weakly.

Marjorie Soto turned to her friends: "No, that's the rumor you all started. You said, 'Oh, I bet she bailed. She doesn't belong here.'" They laughed together and went back to their conversation.

She doesn't belong here? I slipped my teacher card into my bag. Why not? Maybe I asked a lot of really dumb questions, but it was for the right reasons.

Afterward, the head of the Bilingual Team, Mrs. G., approached me. She asked if I wanted to be the sixth-grade bilingual teacher. I would teach English, social studies, and reading to my class in the morning. Then, after lunch, I would send my class next door to the team teacher, who also had a class of sixth-graders. She taught science and math. She would send me her students.

The team teacher would teach in Spanish, and I would teach in English, but use my Spanish when necessary.

"I can tell you're not aggressive," Mrs. G. said. "I'm posting someone outside your door for the first day."

"Can I see my room?" I asked, but Mrs. G. said she was busy. Mr. Marr, the seventh-grade social studies teacher, who was on a different team, must have felt sorry for me, because he offered to take me when no one else would. We headed up the stairs.

On the way up to the second floor, we bumped into Danyelle, a young teacher starting her second year. She was taping a poster to her door.

"I thought you were leaving?" Mr. Marr asked her.

"Nah. I couldn't get into another school, so, oh well," she trailed off, and returned to her room.

At the end of the hallway, toward the back of the school, he showed me Room 216, your standard classroom in that it had a big teacher's desk at the front near the blackboard, and dozens of small desks attached to chairs. The dim space creaked even when we stood still. It was spacious, with three blackboards and only a few cracks in the ceiling panels, although it had uneven wooden floors. There were twenty-three desks. Mr. Marr was already lugging in from next door what eventually added up to ten more desks.

"You'll need these," he said.

The teacher's desk was wooden, like an antique from Laura Ingalls' one-room schoolhouse. I stood behind it, and then knocked on it for no reason. "What happened to the teacher who taught here last year?"

"He left. He refused to ask for help. He thought he was Jaime Escalante or something," he said, referring to the famous teacher from the movie *Stand and Deliver*. "The teacher before him left, too. A lot of teachers hate coming to work here," he said in a soft voice. "The kids know the teachers who hate them, and they hate them back."

Mr. Marr left me alone. The few signs around Room 216 looked like splotches of bright paint splattered on a gray board. As I lay down my bag of supplies, the breadth of what I'd undertaken was like a massive storm cloud that suddenly broke open and drenched me. Tears welled in my eyes. What had I done? This was crazy. I don't know how to teach! I fought off panic and reached into my bag for some supplies.

Four giant READ! signs went up over the doorway. My nameplate belonged on the inside of the door window, facing outward. The back wall would be perfect for my world map. By the door, where I'd line up students, I planned on making a "college board" with information about different universities. For myself, I posted one wrinkled page behind the desk. It was a list of advice my mom, whose dream had been to finish high school, had given me years ago: "Go for It." "See Things as They Really Are." "Hang onto Your Dreams."

My parents were immigrants from England. My dad came from an upper-class British family. My granddad ran a refinery during World War II and had received the Order of the British Empire from the queen. He later sent my dad to boarding school and eventually on to Harvard University. My mom, on the other hand, had dirt-poor, working-class roots. Her father was a electrician, and she had five siblings. When my mom was fifteen, she came home from school one day to discover she wouldn't be going back. She had to find a secretary's position in an office. She was devastated, and even now, thirty-five years later, the memory brings tears to her eyes. The message to me was simple: Missing out on an education was the world's worst injustice. Everyone deserves a good education and a chance in life.

A few years later, my mom left home for London, where she met my dad at a dance. Their marriage was unusual in that it crossed class lines in a very class-obsessed society, and perhaps for that reason they were thrilled to leave England so my father could enter Harvard University Business School in 1964.

They sailed across the Atlantic Ocean and past the Statue of Liberty, arriving as immigrants with a strong belief that if you worked hard you could get ahead in America. My mom worked as a secretary while my dad finished business school and went to work on Wall Street. They bought a four-bedroom house in the New Jersey suburbs, where my brother and sister and I were raised. My parents love their adopted country and believe in the classlessness of America. They taught me to look beyond income and race. They believe in the power of education as a vehicle of social mobility and a great equalizer.

"Hang onto your Dreams." That cliché jumped off my mother's quote page with relevance and meaning. For hours I doted on my classroom. The last rays of sunlight strained through dirty windows when I finally picked up my bag to leave. It was my twenty-sixth birthday, and Pete had something planned to celebrate. I flicked off the lights and stepped into the hallway, surprised at how late it had gotten. The assistant principal's office door was shut tight, and the dimming sky cast a few shadowy fingers down the hall. Next door were the blackened windows of Room 217. Shouldn't my team teacher be preparing her room, too? Alone in this spooky castle, I crept down the stairs, and then ran down the hallway to the fire-escape door. A heavy chain hung from one side, but had no padlock. Panting, I flung the door open, realizing the next time I came back here the building would be filled with kids.

The liquid-black stretch of asphalt where I parked my car looked miles away. I kept one foot propped in the door, huddled my shoulder bag to my chest, and purposely averted my eyes from the outside stairwell. A few years back, I'd been told, a man dragged a thirteen-year-old girl across this parking lot, into that stairwell, hit her over the head with a gun, and raped her. Teachers warned me to stay away from the rear of the school, where heroin dealers stalked the corners. I felt scared, but there was little choice at this point. I had decided to come to North Philly, and I couldn't be afraid of the parking lot. I had to be brave. I hurried toward my lone car, my legs lurching forward, still thinking about the first day of school, worrying about one simple question:

What was I going to teach?

3

The First Days of School

The first day of school, even the first few minutes of class, can make or break a teacher. What you do can determine your success, or failure, for the entire school year.

—From *The First Days of School*, by Harry and Rosemary Wong

It was 7:30 AM on the first day of school. A yellow bus pulled up to the curb of Julia de Burgos Bilingual Middle Magnet School. I idled in the car, fervently rereading papers a last time and watching fellow teachers carry crates and poster boards into the school. In the school alcoves, dead autumn leaves blew into circles with discarded plastic bags from the corner store. Pairs of ratty sneakers dangled from a telephone wire. Kids were swarming in front of the shiny blue front doors in groups that doubled, then tripled, in size. I couldn't believe an entire classroom for which I had no preparation awaited me, full of students expecting me to teach them.

The night before, I'd driven myself crazy sharpening pencils, scratching out name tags, and writing a welcome message to parents and students translated into Spanish. I finally collapsed in tears. Pete comforted me into a fitful sleep. "You'll be great, don't worry." Now I had to get out of the car. Time to open the door or drive away.

My bulging shoulder bag knocked into students as I made my way through the crowd. I pushed inside, passing two security guards setting up their table. In the main office, teachers rushed around and pointed at papers. "Good morning," I said to no one in particular, and no one answered. Quietly, I removed my class list from the top mailbox, disappointed the secretary hadn't labeled it with my name yet. Seeing my class list for the first time was jarring: Juan

Jimenez, Ernesto Gutierrez, Vanessa Pena . . . who were these strangers? The scent of brewing coffee wafted out from the guidance counselor's office. I looked for a familiar face—Mrs. Jimenez, anyone. I searched up and down the halls, but I recognized no one. The stairs to the second floor were empty, too.

The door handle of my classroom rattled as I pulled on it, and the yellowed windows shook in their frames. I stepped in cautiously, as a child might climb into the cobwebbed attic of his home for the first time. Room 216 was not cozy, but wide and sparse with a musty, abandoned smell. Inside my classroom, I was crushed to see most of my signs had peeled off and drifted to the floor. Later, teachers would introduce me to a blue, gummy substance that held up against the humidity, but for now I had to shut the signs away in the closet. Five rows of little desks, erasers filled with chalk dust, bulletin boards for student work, the teacher's filing cabinet—everything was here. I crossed the room and gazed out onto the roof where a wet sneaker lay like a dead rat. I flipped on the bluish overhead lights and half expected a student to jump out at me. Except for the uneven floorboards and dangling wires, Room 216 looked almost pretty—better than I had remembered.

I dropped everything onto my wobbly desk and faced the thirty-three empty chairs. For a moment, my idealism and excitement faltered. Everything in the room seemed to sigh wearily: another new teacher. I'd read up on the vicious circle of poverty that trapped kids like these, and wondered if the same went for new teachers. Given the few resources and meager training, were we, too, just climbing on a merry-go-round, in for a wild ride but always pinioned on the same circle? I couldn't bear the thought, so I pushed it out of my mind. There was so much to do. I began copying names from my class list onto index cards and taping them to desks. The clock read 8:00 AM; I picked up my class list and left for the auditorium.

Rather than meet in the classroom, as I had done on my first day as a sixth-grader, students met in the auditorium, and teachers went to collect them. The hallways were filled with kids, running in different directions and asking for certain rooms. No one seemed to know where to go, not even the teachers. They say that students need security on the first day. More than anything, they want routine, and to know "Am I safe?" Yet our school didn't seem safe at all. It felt completely disorganized and unprepared for the eight hundred students who had just poured out of the buses. It felt like we were a cast of actors rehearsing for a Broadway play, when suddenly the curtain opened to a packed audience. No one had their scripts or stage directions, and a quarter of the actors hadn't even shown up.

The auditorium sloped downward in rows of wooden seats to a stage enclosed by velvet curtains. Dozens of kids scattered among those chairs turned to eye me as I hurried down the aisle and sat down. Many kids had parents sitting beside them. Onstage was the principal, holding a clipboard, along with two other teachers. They were looking at me. I jumped up and joined them.

For weeks I'd been preparing for this moment. I'd done everything from sharpen pencils to reread new-teacher guidebooks. I'd read all the materials the school district gave me on the Big Issues. Race—how would I be culturally sensitive to students' Hispanic and African American origins? Self-esteem—how would I be encouraging and never make them feel bad? Bilingual education—how would I teach everything in both languages, so the Spanish speakers wouldn't feel left out? Even though they were sixth-graders, I prepped a speech inspiring them to attend college, and not local colleges but Ivy League ones, where—in my mind—admission directors would be sympathetic to underprivileged minority kids and offer them scholarships. Later, I would discover that it was statistically unlikely that more than half of the students would even graduate from high school, let alone make it to higher education. In his book, *The First Days of School*, Dr. Wong says many new teachers have grandiose ambitions, and he calls this "the Fantasy Stage." (It is replaced, apparently, by "the Survival Stage." Great.) These dreamy goals reflected my own biases and unrealistic expectations, and showed how I carried the snobberies from my world into theirs—a move I would pay for later on. Another self-imposed goal was that every one of my students would learn to read at grade level by June—a Herculean feat, I would later realize. But back then I simply didn't know better.

"Ms. Asquith?" The principal looked at me expectantly. My hand trembled as I lifted up my student list.

"Good morning. Buenos días," I shouted. "Alvarado, Chanta. Antonetti, Ivetteliz. Byers, Sharmaine. Castillo, Iris." I choked on that second name and on this one too: "Colon, Yahaira." My group pooled by the wall. The girls carried black-and-white composition notebooks. The boys stood empty-handed.

I thought back to my own first day in sixth grade—my mom put me in a gray dress with white tights and penny loafers (it was 1984). My blond hair was tucked behind my ears, which bore tiny pearl earrings. I was flat-chested, makeup-free, and barely combed my hair unless my mom made me. The boys all wore ties and jackets.

Here at Julia de Burgos, the girls had jet-black hair, shiny and slicked straight back into high buns, or parted, swept across their foreheads, and pinned behind the right ear. They wore dark fitted jeans that tapered down to Timberland boots. Gold or silver hoops dangled from their earlobes and matched several overlapping chains and necklaces. Some girls had glitter painted across their eyelids. They looked polished, confident, and tough. I barely got a look at the boys, but they wore baggy, low-riding pants and had buzz cuts. A few had the beginnings of a moustache, but most were baby-cheeked and clear skinned. I thought sixth-graders were eleven. Some kids here were pushing thirteen.

"Get in line, please," I said. I straightened them out and started walking. The only line I'd led before this was a conga line; I never realized how hard it would be. Students veered all over the place. They were tight-lipped and shy, yet wandered off like curious ducklings. Some slid ahead of me, and some dragged their feet in the back. They touched everything—the fire extinguisher, the bulletin boards, doorknobs. Instead of stopping them immediately and making my first lesson how to walk in a line, I continued. After all, I was the English teacher, not the how-to-walk-straight teacher. To accommodate, I tried to walk backward to keep an eye on them. I stumbled. A few giggles. Outside Room 216, I stopped them and perfected the line before entering the class, as I had read I should.

"Look for your name on the desk," I said, as they snaked in quietly and sat down.

There were some teacher basics I had picked up: A good teacher has a "procedure" for every classroom activity. For example, lining up, using the bathroom, asking questions, and being dismissed. Students as young as eleven and twelve like procedures because they provide order, which helps them avoid doing the wrong thing and being laughed at by their friends. Kids laugh at each other for every little thing, from mispronouncing the teacher's name to sitting in the wrong desk. Students will do whatever it takes to avoid being laughed at. Another situation that strikes terror into the hearts of eleven-year-olds is not being able to find their classroom. A sixth-grader lost in the hallway is a sixth-grader vulnerable to running into a seventh- or eighth-grader and getting beaten up. These painful possibilities keep students awake the night before the first day of school, and procedures help them avoid these nightmares. I had come across the concept of procedures in my studies, but not recalling what it was like to be eleven years old, I had brushed it off for broader, weightier theories that interested a twenty-six-year-old. Later, when I reintroduced myself to procedures, it would serve as the turning point for my classroom. At the moment, though, this oversight was about to spark my unraveling.

With an uncertain hand, I put chalk to chalkboard and wrote, "Ms. Asquith." When I stood back and looked at it, the handwriting was light and slanted downward. Quickly, I erased it and tried again, pressing harder and writing each letter hugely. The last three letters still slanted downward.

As I turned around and saw everyone watching me, I felt like the emperor with no clothes. I was a big faker, down to the starched pinstriped blouse intended to make me look serious. My shoulder-length blond hair, which I preferred loose and curled, was blown straight and restricted into a no-nonsense ponytail. My lipstick of choice was matte brick, which I never wore, but had specifically selected over softer, shimmery shades to create the impression that I was mature and purposeful. The veterans had even told me to lie and say I'd had years of experience. But I couldn't fool anyone, and it felt wrong to start off the school year with a lie when my success would depend on creating a trusting and mutually rewarding relationship with these kids.

"Hey everyone, I'm Ms. Asquith. And I'm a new teacher, so, uh, I'm extra strict."

A silence hung over us as the classroom waited for me to say something. I stood behind my desk. Good teachers never sat at their desks, I'd read, so I merely clung to mine.

"Um, I, uh, grew up in New Jersey, and I went to college, and wrote for newspapers for six years. My parents are from England." With that, I walked back to the front of the room and pulled down the map and pointed at the small island across the Atlantic. "I also lived in Chile for a year. I'm not from Chile, that is. I just worked there for a year . . . as a journalist. . . ."

Over the loudspeaker, the assistant principal announced it was time for the Pledge of Allegiance. Several students didn't want to stand up. "C'mon," I insisted, even though I wondered if people from a commonwealth had to pledge allegiance to the United States. There was no flag. I drew one on the board. Only half the kids recited it, and some barely stood up. The solemn stillness returned.

"Hablo Español. Is there anyone who speaks only Spanish?" I said in Spanish. Several students raised their hands. I said in Spanish: "Our goal is to learn English this year. I expect you to speak English to me most of the time."

Then I repeated it in English. For a few minutes I proceeded in both languages. This took twice as long. It also made everything I said stilted and incoherent. The kids looked confused. Was this bilingual education? I made a mental note to look into exactly how bilingual education worked. I switched into English.

"Um, okay. Let's go around the room and say your name, age, and the street you live on," I suggested, hopefully.

The chubby boy with spiky hair in the first row looked up at me, pleading with not-me-first eyes. Desperation made me ruthless. "You. C'mon," I pushed.

I took a couple of deep breaths. So far, so good. No one was eating me alive. In fact, they seemed intimidated. My door opened softly, and my supervisor, Mrs. G., peeked her head in. She quickly counted my students and left. Mrs. G. didn't teach. She was head of the Bilingual Team in addition to being my direct supervisor, just under the principal. I pretended to be too involved to notice her, but I was pleased she saw my controlled classroom, after she had said I was "not aggressive enough."

"Time to take roll," I announced, admiring my use of such a classic teacher phrase. As I ran through every name, slowly and methodically, the students gazed off into the distance, bored. A few fidgeted. To my horror, only fifteen students from my list of twenty-seven were present. Five other students sitting in desks weren't on my list. My eyes met those of one nameless boy, and he looked down. That was strange. I didn't say anything. I made a mental note to ask the main office. A half-hour or so into instruction and no fights had broken out. I thought I must be doing very well. A swell of good feeling ran through me, and I eagerly shared this accomplishment with my students.

"Hey you guys, this is going to be a great year for us. I expect a lot from you, and I plan on working my hardest," I said. "You know, it's important to me that we are proud of each other, and that, uh, you all learn and everything."

I took some index cards off my desk. "Please follow the directions on the board and copy down what's up there." They dropped their heads obediently. They listened, and even raised their hands, though timidly. This was easy. They didn't seem to be the hardheaded thugs I had been warned about. I wasn't going to have to "break them down." I was going to be able to teach them. The morning swam along, until the door opened again at 9:30 AM. Mrs. G., again, and she wasn't alone.

"Good morning, Ms. Asquith. Good morning, T61," she chimed. A line of students shuffled behind her.

"We don't have another sixth-grade teacher for T62's class, so we will be combining the classes for now," she said.

My heart sank as another dozen or more students piled into the room, some carrying desks and clanking them against the walls. Had Mrs. G. only realized this morning that she was one teacher short? The little heads passed in front of me, like candies on a conveyor belt. I wanted to protest, but their little faces looked alarmed. Imagine arriving on the first day and being told you had no teacher! They looked ashamed as they found seats in the corners and climbed up onto the radiator. I covered my desperation with a happy face, a survival tactic I would come to master throughout my year.

"Of course," I said with a weak smile, "I'm so glad you are joining us."

Mrs. G. played along and then escaped out the door. I counted thirty-three students. What worried me was that there were fifteen more students on my list unaccounted for. What if they came in tomorrow? I began to sway and reel on my imaginary tightrope. The combined classes meant I had both groups in the afternoon, which meant I needed another two hours of material to teach. I had anticipated one lesson for T61 in the morning, and then repeating the lesson in the afternoon to the other group. Suddenly, I was left with three hours to fill. Groping around my desk drawer for more index cards, I was thinking so hard I was no longer seeing anything in front of me.

"Miss?" a student called out. I looked up. Thirty-three pairs of hands rested on desktops waiting for instruction. The bright colors of new T-shirts and jackets dotted the room.

"I need to go to the bathroom," he said.

"Um, okay."

In the fifteen seconds it took me to search for a piece of paper and write, "pass to bathroom," a conversation started in the back. I didn't want to do discipline on the first day, so I ignored it. "Where's the bathroom, Miss?" the boy asked, walking to the door.

"I don't know. Just ask when you get out there."

Facing the class, I employed another classic teacher phrase by telling them, "Clear your desks, please." No one really had anything on their desks. The door opened again. It was the bathroom boy. "It's locked. Miss."

"Well, try to find someone to open it."

He disappeared again.

"Okay, class, we're going to make personal information cards."

A student in the back raised his hand.

"Miss, can I sharpen my pencil?"

"Sure." As I passed out index cards, he snaked around several aisles before arriving at the pencil sharpener. A few students twittered and looked to see my reaction. I glanced away, pretending I hadn't noticed. Another student raised his hand.

"Miss, I don't have a pencil." I returned to my desk to search for one.

Another student raised her hand.

"Miss, my Band-Aid is loose."

"Um." Bringing Band-Aids had not been one of my Big Issues. I pretended to rifle through my desk, knowing there were none there. "Don't worry about it."

Encouraged by my attentiveness, several students began raising their hands.

"Miss, can we go by our other school from last year and say hi to our old teacher?"

I fumbled to answer everyone's questions and keep the class moving. Finally, I interrupted, "Look, everyone, please stop talking and write down your full name, address, and phone number on your index card."

But that unleashed a torrent of questions, and when I couldn't keep up, they shouted them out.

"Miss, I don't know my address."

"Miss, how you spell Lehigh Avenue?"

"Miss, we don't got a phone."

"Miss, how you spell Lehigh Avenue???"

From the back, a little girl, whose name tag read VALERIE, shouted, "Meessss, yo no entiendo." "I don't understand." I rushed around trying to accommodate everyone. Several students chatted with one another. I ran to the back to help Valerie. An hour, maybe two, slipped past. By the time we finished personal-identification index cards, the class, like an orchestra with each musician playing a different song, had spun off in thirty-three different directions. I was trying to conduct each one. Everyone was calling my name, and when I turned to quiet one group, another one flared up. Several more students asked to use the bathroom, and when I started saying no, two girls claimed to "have my P."

"No, no one else is using the bathroom," I said. I thought this made me strict. But then, one girl started to cry, and later she reported this to Mrs. G., who informed me as though I were a sixth-grader myself, that students had a right to the bathroom.

By 11:30 AM, I had to go to the bathroom, too. What were teachers supposed to do? At any given moment, at least one student from each corner of the room, and the middle, was calling my name. "Mmeeesss Asquith!"

A little boy, his eyes bulging madly, waved his hand. I rushed to his desk. His name card said, "Miguel, 11 years old." He had baby fat still bulging from his cheeks, like a chipmunk furrowing nuts. He had clasped his hand across his mouth, eyes wide with terror. Was Miguel about to become that "he-threw-up-on-the-first-day" kid?

"My tooth came out," he said.

I kneeled and saw a baby tooth cupped in his palm, like a little bird.

"Open your mouth," I said. I checked to make sure it wasn't some joke on me—no student was gonna get one past this teacher. But his tongue had blood on it. I smothered a little laugh and put my hand on his head.

"Does it hurt?" He shook his head.

"Good, then sit tight."

Later, I wondered if a lost tooth merited a visit to the nurse. I really had no idea. But I also had no idea where the nurse's office was, or how to give him a hall pass to get there, if he even needed one. So, lost-tooth Miguel wasn't moving. That seemed fine with him.

***

To my relief, the first week continued much like the first day, which I described to Pete as gentle pandemonium. I taught a list of eight topics given to me by Mrs. G., including class rules and the fire-drill and salute-the-flag procedures. Some days it took me hours simply to review one topic, other times I sped through a lesson in three minutes. For example, the dress code. I stood in front of the class and read aloud some of the rules: no bandannas, no gang colors, no low-cut tops or miniskirts, etcetera. Then I posted the rules on the blackboard, and moved on. I thought that was it; that was teaching.

Most lessons were like chaotic streams of consciousness, punctuated by my occasional lecture on "sitting still." Yet, overall, my impression was that the kids were sweet, obliging, and eager to endear themselves to me. So I received a few crank calls each night—Pete had told me not to list my phone number on that yellow Welcome! sheet—that was hardly a major inconvenience. My sister, Nikki, who was also a schoolteacher, warned me this could only be the honeymoon period, during which time kids act well-behaved, while gathering data on the new teacher, assessing how much they'll be able to get away with later on. (I wish I had listened.)

But at the time, I had such low expectations for my students, stemming from my own misconceptions about inner-city youth, that any small gesture of obedience was magnified in my mind. I recall my first week of teaching as a golden time. Sunny, cool September days, in which I drove back to my apartment around 4:30 PM, physically exhausted and bedraggled. The doormen understood I was a new teacher and that I had a really hard job. We would share a smile. They would greet me with an appreciative nod. Then, I either went for a run along the Schuylkill River or slipped to a pub around the block to correct homework over a much-needed beer, spreading papers across the dim bar. My dutiful pressing of animal stickers onto worksheets occasionally earned me a "you a teacher?" comment and a charity beer. I devoted the rest of the night to lesson planning at my computer. One big surprise was the time required to correct a day of class work and homework, and then prepare for the following day's lesson—in several subjects. It took at least three hours a night. But so far, my phone conversations with Pete and my sister were happy: Teaching was easier than anticipated. Ms. Vinitzsky, one of the helpful veteran teachers, told me it took five years to learn to teach. But I didn't think it would take me so long. The students liked me. I interpreted their docility as a sincere openness to working together to make ours the best class possible. I smiled at every cute thing they did. They were "really good."

***

"When your desks are clean, I will dismiss you," I said, kneeling to check the aisles. Our room had adapted to us. Balls of paper gathered around the wastebasket. Desks once aligned perfectly were slanted and shifting, like magnets, toward desks of nearby friends. Students had stuffed many of my handouts, primarily the welcome letter to parents, into the wire shelf under their seats.

At 2:47 PM, the principal spoke over the loudspeaker:

"Remember, failure is not an option! Thank you for all doing your best. Please have a safe weekend. Third floor may prepare for dismissal."

"Pedro's row may go first," I announced. Students poured out of the room, chirping "bye." Several girls crowded at my desk.

"Miss, we thought you didn't speak Spanish, and we was all gonna play tricks on you," cooed one girl with sleek black hair.

An 180-pound twelve-year-old stopped on his way out. The class called him Big Bird. He stretched out his meaty hand to shake mine.

"Tank you, Miss," he said, his binder tucked under his arm. Big Bird wanted to be a lawyer. He spoke to me as though he already was one. "Good job teaching this week," he offered.

I erased the board, and then wandered around the aisles for a few minutes, straightening desks, picking up pencils, and smiling to myself. I made a quick cell phone call to Pete, and we made plans to meet for dinner. "What a fantastic week!" I said. He congratulated me. "All right!" He laughed. "Wait until the spitballs start."

A form for Mrs. G. caught my eye, and I picked it up to take it to her. I left my room and turned the corner toward the lockers and Mrs. G.'s office. School had ended five minutes ago, but already the place had emptied. Mrs. G.'s door was shut, windows dark, as were several others. The only sign of life was a guy from the cleaning crew, pushing his cart down the hall, and a portable radio playing rap music.

Back in my room, I felt a pang of loneliness without my students. True, it was only the second week, but we were already like a real class. Each day when I dismissed them for lunch, they ran up to my desk with questions and begged to eat with me. I wasn't supposed to care about being popular, but all that attention made me feel like a rock star. They each had their own needs. Luis, an eleven-year-old with porcelain skin and owlish eyes, stopped me each day before lunch to shyly ask, "Miss, is there a band at the school? I kinda know how to play trumpet." Several students pushed past him with their own requests. I promised him I'd look into it.

Leaning back in my desk chair, my plan was to chip away at the piles of paperwork the main office needed. I was swamped with all the forms that accumulated between 8:20 AM and 2:57 PM each day: attendance sheets, emergency phone numbers, emergency lesson plans, special education forms, weekly lesson goals. The main office constantly had more paperwork for me to fill out, and I never had time to do it. I knew they needed it to organize the school, but I needed to organize my classroom. I imagined the confusion I was causing, multiplied by the dozens of new teachers, multiplied by the fact that this happened every year, and I began to understand why the system was so disorganized.

Quickly, my mind drifted to the lessons of the upcoming week. Actual teaching was even harder than I had anticipated. A quarter of the class spoke no English and a quarter no Spanish. How did I get everyone to understand the assignments? The other stumbling block: My class contained close to forty students, and it was a fluid bunch, with new arrivals and departures each day. My class list was never more than 50 percent correct, and any student I sent to the main office was bounced back with a "looking into this" note. I had spent the first week reviewing class rules, only to have half the class turn over and a dozen new kids who needed to learn from scratch. I had lost track. To whom had I taught what? I had four Juans, two Marias, two Vanessas, two Miguels, and a Yahaira, whose name I still couldn't pronounce correctly. I tried to sort them out with HI, MY NAME IS stickers for their shirts, but they tore them off at lunch. There was no sign of my team teacher yet, either.

I also had to teach a procedure for every little thing: how to walk into the classroom (slowly, directly to seats), put their books away (under desk, not on floor), sharpen their pencils (before class begins), throw things away (no basketball shots), speak to the teacher (soft voice), speak to each other (never). And that was only the beginning. After figuring out what to teach, I was confronted with the problem of how to teach. I'd tell them. Blank stare. They forgot. I'd tell them again. They said they forgot, again. How could I make information stick in their little heads so they didn't turn the room upside down with forty different approaches to things? This was frustrating, as I was anxious to start teaching reading and writing. Not that I had any books yet.

Instead of the administrative paperwork, my hands drifted over to a stack of cream-colored journals we had begun writing in that week. Pete recommended journal writing, and so I asked Mrs. G., and she sent fifty small notebooks to my room. They were the first items I had gotten from her.

The students had already decorated the covers with hearts and stars, their names in bubble letters and scribbles. Some had applied the names of famous wrestlers, like THE ROCK. The girls tended toward loopy, curly writing, punctuating each line with circles and squiggly lines. The boys mostly scrawled stick-like letters, and generally wrote fewer words. Most chose print instead of cursive, neatly following the blue lines. It appeared as though they had made an effort. Reflecting on their first week of school, most eked out just a paragraph.

> The first week of school we lear. The rules of school and the rules was. Dont eat gum dont scream in class, Respect Each other and when I came inside the room I was shide because I dirent now anybody in the room by Reinaldo."

How should I handle their mistakes? I tried to be positive and not criticize, so I marked, "WOW! You remembered a lot of rules." I crossed out his mistakes and rewrote the words correctly in big letters above. I smiled at the paper. On Monday, they would rewrite the entries.

Next, I opened Melinda's journal. She had spent the morning designing her name in several styles on the first few pages until I stood over her desk. Her entry explained everything.

> I wsc can see you gean. and see the weay at put on your leasek. and the ware that you wrac my hare an;d the are teat you wrao your hare.

I read it over and over but couldn't even decide if this was English or Spanish. She was twelve and had moved to Philadelphia from Puerto Rico when she was eight years old, which meant four years in the city's public schools. It also meant four teachers had passed her through, despite her illiteracy. Not me, I thought. My students would be held accountable. I struggled to think of something constructive to note. "I'm excited for all you will learn this year!" I wrote. Then I repeated it in Spanish, just in case.

The next journal belonged to Vanessa, the kind of girl, even at twelve, who got noticed. With long black hair and a dimpled smile, her beauty had already earned her unwanted attention throughout Julia de Burgos. Either the boys would harass her with catcalls or the girls would sneer and make catty comments. Most likely out of fear, Vanessa stuck to my side, asking to eat lunch in the classroom and insisting on sitting in the front row. We got along. She was also intelligent. Instead of journal writing, I'd given her an essay question for a competition I'd found in a teen magazine.

"Write a 150-word essay about what your mother means to you." The prize was a $5,000 scholarship toward college.

Dear editor,

I'm a typical 12-year old Hispanic girl, with typical interests like talking on the phone and watching movies. One day I hope to be a famous writer. My home is Philadelphia, which is called the city of Brotherly Love, but in my neighborhood police sirens seem more common than the birds chirping. Yet despite this negative influence, I have something positive—my mother. She is a 33 year old factory laborer, and the best role model for me. A single mother most of her life, she left school to earn a so-called living for herself. She has made bad decisions, like getting into a relationship with a verbally-abusive alcoholic who I call my father. But thanks to my mom, I have the happy life of a 12-year old, with a television, a phone and the confidence to succeed. My mom finds time to visit my school, and pushes me to study for A's. Although she has struggled most of her life, that struggle is not for herself. It is for me. My mom believes I can go to college, and looking at all she has accomplished, I am inspired to believe that too.

Vanessa

Underneath, I wrote: "Great job. I will send this in. Keep up the good work."

An hour had passed, and I had only corrected a handful of journals. The sun was setting. I had better hurry. The next journal was already bent up and torn a little. Most students wrote their names boldly across the front. But

Jovani didn't take up much space, on the journal or in the classroom. In the top corner, penciled in tiny letters, was "jovani."

The boys called Jovani "LD," which I thought was a nickname and almost used myself until I overheard the special education teacher, Mrs. Q., say it. LD meant learning disabled. Jovani barely noticed. Skinny with floppy arms, he didn't walk as much as trip across the room. He had a wandering eye, and a needy, guileless way. When students in the class waved their hands, Jovani practically jumped out of his seat to wave his, too. Once, I called on him.

"Yes, Jovani?"

He stared at me, startled. I waited. He waited. I called on someone else.

He looked about ten years old. In his journal, he had drawn a row house. Nothing fancy, just a rectangle, topped by a triangle, with six squares for windows, a rectangle for a door, a sun, and some squiggly lines, which appeared to be birds. On the roof, he wrote, "Jovani adn Ms Asauith." On the second page, he had answered only my second essay question. I suspected someone had helped him. "What are some of the problems in the world?"

"That people are mean to each other."

The rest of the journals fell somewhere between Jovani's and Vanessa's. These students didn't seem to belong in the same classroom. I didn't know how to assess any students because I had no clue what sixth-graders were expected to know. I shoved their journals in my canvas teacher bag and turned the flimsy lock on my door. Room 217 next door remained dark.

***

That weekend, panic set in. I still had nothing to teach. My class was still behaving okay, but the hallways were getting out of control. A whirlwind of student mobs had stampeded down the hallway on a recent day. I peeked my head out to see what was wrong and saw them leap into the air and smack their binders against the hallway wall. I didn't see any other teachers intervening, but weren't we the authority here? There were some hall monitors, called NTAs (non-teaching assistants), but students had begun to ignore them, and there didn't seem to be any consequences. I thought the principal was supposed to patrol the halls, but she was never around.

Looking for materials to teach, Pete and I hit the bookstore with a vengeance. Who knew when Mrs. G. would deliver textbooks to my class? She told me to teach school rules and procedures. And she kept reminding me that mine was a bilingual classroom, "Because, after all, we are a bilingual magnet school." I didn't know what the hell bilingual education looked like in practice. At a weekly teachers' meeting, the veterans all talked about September being Puerto Rican History Month, when we'd teach activities about the Taino Indians, the original natives of Puerto Rico. But I had no materials about how to do that, and everyone was out the door the minute the meeting ended. The veterans seemed annoyed with me, and everyone had their own set of emergencies. When I asked my mentor for help, she gave me a stack of various workbooks on the Taino Indians. Then she told me to sign her pay sheet. Later in the year, her other efforts to "mentor" me included stapling some colored cardboard in decorative patterns around my blackboard, and a quick lesson on how to fill in the grades for bilingual instruction listed on my students' report cards, even though I wasn't actually teaching it.

Left to my own devices, I turned to Pete.

Pete's idea was to draw up a week's worth of lesson plans. From my own pocket, I bought *The Elements of Style*, by Strunk and White, for English class; several workbooks; and *Chicken Soup for the Kid's Soul*, for reading class. We couldn't find anything for social studies.

At home I typed up my first worksheet. The Worksheet—that ancient teaching relic. Every pedagogue knew the Worksheet was a rote-learning teaching technique of the 1970s. In today's classrooms, teachers did activities and projects that had goals and objectives. I would get to that stage, I promised myself. The Worksheet was just a stopgap measure.

That night we went downtown for dinner and then to our favorite hangout, The Pen and Pencil Club, a late-night journalists' haunt. At that point, if anyone were to have asked me what I did for a living, I would have said, "I'm a journalist, teaching for a year." Yet, already, I felt strangely distant from my old profession. Dinner was strained. Pete was leaving for a few weeks for a medical rotation in western Pennsylvania. As usual, we talked about teaching and my students. We were tired. He felt I was stretching myself too thin trying to make assignments for each individual child. I said I thought I had no choice. He thought Mrs. G. and the veterans sounded like bitches, and I should steer clear of her and do my own thing. At the bar we drank Yuenglings and smoked a few cigarettes, and as we got drunk we chatted with the bartender and people at the jukebox.

"Chris," Pete said later, "you're being too easy on the students." In the swarm of advice of recent weeks, it was easy to focus on the pieces I liked and ignore the rest. This one I ignored. He had also mentioned something about how the really bad kids wait to show up during the third or fourth weeks. He had said I should be stricter because this was only the beginning. Only the good kids show up in the first weeks.

***

The MIA sixth-grade team teacher arrived in the third week. Ms. Rohan was in her early thirties, and after a decade drifting among odd jobs she had gone back to school to pursue a career in teaching. She was Irish Catholic. Bobby pins held back her fiery red hair, and she possessed an easy laugh. She was unmarried, and after a few weeks' teaching, to make ends meet, she began working as a waitress at Applebee's restaurant on the weekends. We met in the doorway between periods, and I wanted to hug her. There was only time to nod introductions, like doctors switching shifts in the emergency room. "Where have you been?" I asked. "Waiting to be processed," she said, giving me a fed-up look that sealed our friendship. Half my class drained out of Room 216 into Room 217 with the lime paint. Just in time. My list had climbed to thirty-eight students, and seas were stormy.

On paper, my class became T61, and I had them for four periods between 8:20 AM and lunch, which was about 11:30 AM. During this time, I was to teach them English, social studies, and English to Speakers of Other Languages (ESOL) reading. They also had one period with a different teacher, taking an elective such as gym, art, or creative writing. This was my planning period. Ms Rohan had a similar schedule with T62, except she was to teach science, math, and ESOL in Spanish language. After a twenty-minute lunch and another planning period, we switched classes and repeated the same lesson to the other group. On paper, this meant the students received English and Spanish instruction and still kept on task with subject matter.

But little went as indicated on paper, as I had already learned. I was T61 and Ms Rohan T62. The T stood for TV/Communications team, which was one of five theme-based teams the administration had divided students into years ago based on some million-dollar grant aimed at vocational training. Yet there was nothing TV/Communications-oriented about our team, or any of the other teams. The TVs hanging from our ceilings didn't even work. Another administrative categorization: Ms. Rohan and I were also on the Bilingual Team, which encompassed the second floor. The Bilingual Team took all the students who hadn't mastered English or any student whose parents had requested bilingual-program placement. This designation as "bilingual" earned our team an extra $1.7 million in federal grant money, referred to as the Portal grant.

Our so-called bilingual education program seemed very complicated, yet the reason none of it worked was simplicity itself: Ms. Rohan didn't speak Spanish. She must have been assigned to Julia de Burgos after the school district realized there were no more Spanish-speaking teachers, and it was almost October. There was a brief discussion about my teaching science and math in Spanish, but I balked. I didn't know how to teach science or math in English, let alone in Spanish, which required a vocabulary of words like cells, membranes, photosynthesis. Ms. Rohan didn't want to teach reading or English. So the bilingual program in practice never got off the ground for sixth-graders.

Ms. Rohan, however, was a caring teacher, and certified, meaning she had recently finished her master's degree and was armed with professional training. When I told her I had only a day of training, she said something along the lines of, "What the hell? Why did I spend $30,000 on a master's degree for a job you just walked off the street into?"

We both shrugged and made a deal: I would help her with the Spanish; she would help me with teaching. This evened us out, but it hardly mattered. We were the blind leading the blind, as neither of us had any books—in English or Spanish. We certainly didn't have English books for Spanish speakers, which was really what we needed.

Ms. Rohan was stunned when she learned we had no books. "What have you been teaching?"

"Um, I bought a grammar book at Barnes and Noble, and I'm using that," I said, feeling like I was admitting to child abuse. I grew defensive. "I've been asking for books."

Ms. Rohan looked shocked. She made me realize that this was not normal. It'd be best to share these concerns with our supervisors.

4

Bilingual Education

The morale of the school appears to be exceedingly high; good manners were everywhere apparent. During the recess, as well as during lunch, the boys are left without supervision, and the outer gates are wide open. No disastrous results follow, nor do the boys ever quit the grounds without permission. The principal of the school says it is wiser to put the boys on their honor than to place them under supervision. The Principal is a wise man.

—Professor W. A. Appleton, after visiting the school at Eighth and Lehigh, in 1907.

Rodolfo had a thick neck, a buzz cut, and a few light freckles across his button nose. And I hated him. He didn't so much arrive in class one morning as invade it, in his XXX-tra large football jersey and jeans. He was twelve going on skid-row eighteen. He was the tough kid, boisterous and unpredictable, as likely to punch his best friend as risk his life for him. The class reacted. The girls looked slightly terrified. The boys looked thrilled. High fives went all around amid a murmur of, "yeah, Rodolfo."

As though some unseen twine had been untethered, my students stopped being good one day. The honeymoon was over. I couldn't reel them back in.

The day began badly. That morning, the main office sent up my students' scores from some standardized test they'd taken the prior year. "Oh, look, everybody. Here are your test scores," I announced. I should have looked at them first. Instead, I read the numbers to myself as I handed them out. They were lower than even I had expected. Many students, including Rodolfo, scored a 1, meaning the bottom 1 percent of all test takers in the state. No one scored higher than 15 percent. A bad feeling sunk in as I went round the room.

Rodolfo snatched his and shouted, "Yeah! One!" thinking it meant first. The other students were shouting, "What this mean?" Caught off guard, I didn't know what to say. Later, at night in bed, I would play this moment over in my mind. Should I have hidden the painful truth from him? Or should I have capitalized on it to encourage him to do better? Or should I break the news to him gently, and then discuss how he could improve? I didn't want to dump failing scores on their impressionable minds. Burned into my own brain were the Ss for "satisfactory" I'd received in elementary school, instead of Es for "excellent." At that moment, I panicked. So, I ducked the issue. I explained the scoring in a cryptic way that they wouldn't understand. Being eleven, they were accustomed to feeling confused by adults and let it go easily. Then, I steered us onto something else. This did not exactly feel like the right thing to do. Later, I noticed Rodolfo staring at the score. He had a confused, unhappy look on his face.

Then I tried to teach.

A few days earlier, Mrs. G. delivered our English books. I thought we were waiting for new books. In fact, these texts were from the early 1980s, making me think that they had been in a nearby closet the whole month. The first chapter was titled "The Four Types of Sentences."

This was completely impractical. I tried to teach it, but my students didn't even know how to make a sentence. Shouldn't we at least start with subject and predicate? They didn't even really know English. The night before, I had tried to sketch out a lesson plan tailored to their specific needs, but in reality it looked more like a list of my thoughts, hopes, and possible activities strung together. When I reviewed it in the morning, I barely understood it myself:

MS. ASQUITH'S LESSON PLAN

I. Writing complete sentences.

What makes up a complete sentence? How do we know when to stop it?

A sentence has a subject and predicate. Everything else is decoration.

Combine lesson 2 and 3 in book. Subject is person or persons, the thing or things doing the action. Predicate is the action or actions.

Follow activity by everybody looking at Pedro. Describe Pedro or write down what he is doing and circle the subject and predicate.

Turn to page xx in book and we'll go over it together. (Read aloud everyone for practice.)

Do exercise in the book. Change with partner, go over together, give a grade and note it down like you're the teacher.

Point out that the subject can be more than one thing.

Student notes should read: Complete sentences. What is a complete sentence and when stop it?

A sentence has a subject and a predicate.

Remember, every sentence must have a subject and verb (predicate).

Later, combine what we learned.

What?

I hadn't gotten far. Several students didn't know English, so how was I to teach them about predicates? And the others either didn't get it, or didn't care. Some couldn't form sentences, so trying to explain what a predicate was useless. Often, I would corner myself.

"Someone give me an example of a popular sentence?" I said, chalk in hand, poised at the board.

"What's up?" said Vanessa.

"Okay. That's true. That's a sentence," I said, trailing off. Where was the subject and predicate in that? I struggled to explain the verb "to be" and confused myself. I'd have to look that one up. Student attention began to wane and I thought, "Who am I kidding? I don't know how to teach." Many students tried to follow along, but forcing this lesson on them was like mixing oil and water—this lesson didn't go with this class. Rodolfo was about to let his dissatisfaction be known in a loud and disruptive way when the door flew open.

It was the school police officer.

"Get me some boys!" he shouted.

They returned with reading textbooks. Finally. This had to be easier. Why the school policeman was delivering them was a mystery. They hauled out copies of the reading textbook *Vistas*.

He, Rodolfo, and Big Bird dropped stacks onto the floor next to my desk with a *thwap!* Rodolfo began tossing them on desks, like Frisbees. Desperately, I scanned the table of contents and found a series of short stories and poems, followed by questions on theme and foreshadowing. Most teachers spend hours preparing their lesson plans. I did, too. But none of my lessons ever worked. I decided to start right away with a short story in *Vistas.*

"Read pages seventy and seventy-one, and then answer questions one through five at the end."

I forgot to write the page numbers on the board, as I knew I should. After two minutes, they lost interest again. Ten minutes later, only a handful of girls were still reading. That was it. Everyone else—most of the class—had given up. Ronny, a seventh-grader who had been held back, flipped through the book searching for lewd graffiti from past students, which he whispered to the class. A chorus of "ewww, Miss!" rose up. Vanessa, who had finished the story, looked up at me expectantly. I felt my authority sliding. The story was too easy for her, but the Spanish-speaking students were at a complete loss.

"Just try your best," I said to Valerie, who spoke only Spanish, and I quickly swiveled around to the next crisis before she could point out that she didn't understand English, so how would *trying* help?

Rodolfo kept kicking the wire shelf under Ronny's desk until Ronny swung around and pushed Rodolfo's papers onto the floor. For two painful hours, I cajoled, and then tried outwitting, then begging, and finally threatening them in an attempt to get them to pay attention. Any brief respite in arguing allowed me to see myself losing my dignity and becoming that mean, shouting teacher I would have criticized as a reporter. Yet I felt powerless to stop it.

I copied an essay out of some teen magazine on drug testing, hoping that would catch their interest. My "lesson plan" was for them to read it and then discuss it. To be safe, this time I read it aloud. They listened quietly.

"So, what do you think?" I asked at the end.

Two boys raised their hands. For a brief moment, we all listened as Daniel gave solid, logical arguments against drug testing.

"It's a violation of our rights to search our locker," he said. But then Ronny must have said something to Rodolfo, because he swirled around and shouted, "Shut up man! You a drug dealer!"

"Rodolfo, please raise your hand," I said.

"It's true, Miss!" he yelled. He slammed down his books and cursed at me.

"You're in detention," I said.

Ms. Rohan had been sending students to Mrs. G.'s office, but I refused to do that. I promised to handle problems myself because I wanted to show the students that I was the ultimate authority. My ears rang. Then a spitball whizzed through the room. I quickly looked away, knowing that everyone saw me ignore it. I didn't have the energy to confront it. The trouble was that whenever I traced a spitball's origin, it led back to Rodolfo or Ronny or another boy, all of whom denied it angrily. Confrontation sapped time and energy away from the rest of the class, and I personally felt embarrassed to challenge a student and lose. No one ever told me how physically tiring teaching was—and I had run the Boston Marathon. How did the older teachers manage? By 11:30 AM, I had already punished Ronny with lunch detention and Rodolfo with after-school detention. When was lunch?

Relinquishing the drug debate, I pulled out my copy of *Chicken Soup for the Kid's Soul,* an idea borrowed from another teacher. Hoping to calm them, I opened to a story about a boy whose mother was addicted to heroin. The morose tone of the story and the sadness that welled up in my students' expressions reminded me how tough their lives were. Leaning on the desk, tears came as I read, mostly from nerves. I coughed to cover up my choking voice.

At lunch, I dismissed the rows one at a time, specifically instructing Ronny to stay put. Big Bird approached my desk. Behind him were Vanessa and some girls.

"Miss?" Big Bird said, with raised eyebrows.

"Not today, okay?"

He loped out the door with his head down. They wanted to stay and have lunch together. Eating lunch in the classroom with the teacher was, for some reason, a big treat for sixth-graders. But I had no time for the well-behaved kids on this day. I had to discipline Ronny, who was leaning back in a desk wondering aloud why Rodolfo didn't have to stay, too. This was one of the many small ways in which the needs of the well-behaved students were brushed aside for those of the troublesome students. Ronny sat in silence for a few minutes.

Ronny was thirteen and lanky, with long arms, milk-chocolate skin, and a fluid motion. He had grown up in the Dominican Republic and had moved to North Philadelphia only a few years earlier. His father ran a popular rice-and-beans eatery a mile north of the school, and a grocery store where Ronny worked after school each day. Ronny always wore stylish, expensive-looking gold chains. One day I was collecting $2 from everyone for a field trip, and Ronny pulled a wad of twenties from his back pocket and asked me for change, which I didn't have. While Rodolfo burst into anger unpredictably, Ronny was gentle and shy, but mischievous, nonetheless. They'd fight all morning, and then I'd see them joking around at lunch. This must have been their torture-the-teacher routine.

"Look Ronny, I know this isn't the best class right now. And that *Vistas* story was boring. But, you know you can't act this way in our class. What kind of class would that be? You have to be on the team."

His face softened.

"You can do it, you're bright."

Pete's advice had been: Don't take student misbehavior personally.

I suggested we read the story together. But once the book was open and Ronny stuttered through the first line, I realized the deeper problem. In the next few weeks, I saw that Ronny could read neither English nor Spanish. Ronny had already failed sixth grade once. Each lunch, he crossed the cafeteria to join his seventh-grade friends. When the bell rang, they went on to their seventh-grade classes, and Ronny returned to the same Room 216 as he had the prior year, with, in his eyes, a bunch of little kids. The prior year he had had the emergency certified teacher whom Mr. Marr called Jaime Escalante. How many emergency certified teachers had Ronny been subjected to?

"Miss, I don't want to end up in the store like my dad."

He told me one night a bunch of guys had broken in and held a gun to his head, and he saw his dad with a gun to his head. Sometimes he had nightmares about it.

"What do you want to do?" I asked.

"I wanna be a baseball player. Or draw."

"Oh, Ronny," I said. "No matter what you do, you have to be able to read."

He nodded. This was not a motivational issue, I realized. Ronny wanted to know how to read. No one was teaching him.

When we finished reading the story, Ronny had a giant grin on his face. He seemed thrilled that a teacher was finally going to help him. I sent him off to lunch and watched him race down the hall. Watching him go, I felt better at that moment than I had in any other job in my life. The feeling of connecting with a needy child, of giving him hope, of keeping the light on in his eyes, was so powerful it washed away every other frustrating aspect of the profession. Already, I understood my mission, here: Ronny wouldn't graduate from sixth grade without learning how to read. This would be the year Ronny learned to read. And I'd be the teacher to do it.

Checking the clock, I realized Ms. Rohan's class would be pouring in here in ten minutes, and they spoke even less English than T61. Once again, there'd be no time to eat. I returned to class and began to erase the blackboard.

***

The situation continued to spiral for days, and then weeks, until I was on the brink of exhaustion: a drowning woman. I could not keep up with everything thrown at me, and each day became not a day to teach but a test to survive. The kids were tough, but it was the administration that was killing me. Every period of every day they interrupted my lesson with a new memo, a new requirement, a new form to be filled out. One morning I counted eight classroom interruptions before lunch. How were we supposed to focus on the kids when Mrs. G. had so many needs herself? Then, one stressful Sunday night, Eppy called to check up on me. I spilled out the situation—I had no idea how to teach or what to teach them. I had no control. No one at the school was helping me. Some of my students couldn't read or write. He laughed knowingly, which depressed me even more. He told me Julia de Burgos was considered the worst middle school in the city. Indeed, Julia de Burgos's school-performance score—which measures test scores, student attendance, dropout rate, and other factors—was the city's worst. We ranked last among the city's forty-two middle schools. In reading and math, eighty-five percent of our students scored in the lowest category, "below basic." Translation? Almost nine out of ten students here couldn't read a book or do simple math problems.

He told me if the school didn't improve, the state would take it over. If that didn't solve the problem, then the city would completely disband the school and new teachers would be transferred in. Of course, no one would be fired, just spread out among different schools.

"You can't keep beating a dead horse," he said. "And you can't change the kids, because it's not their fault." He had tried to get me into a "better school," he pointed out, but I had insisted on teaching there, he said. Remember?

That night I lay in bed and cried. Each chaotic school day reminded me that I had given up my previous career to make a difference, and so far I had only made a mess.

When I looked around me, I saw a handful of good teachers, a majority of average ones, and a dozen really bad teachers, like Mr. Jackson, the seventh-grade English teacher who just shouted all day long. His students regularly burst out of his room, gasping in laughter and running down the hallway. Once they left his room, they became Mrs. G.'s problem, and she was unsettled about that. Something needed to be done about his class, she said. But with so many other classes without any teacher at all, it was hard to hold Mr. Jackson to any type of standard. As for me, as long as I kept the students inside the room, I was teacher of the year.

But I didn't want just to be better than Mr. Jackson. I didn't want just to be "doing well for a new, untrained teacher," because that low standard was why nine out of ten kids were failing. The students deserved a trained teacher like Mr. Rougeux, the sixth-grade teacher on the first floor. He was a twenty-three-year-old who wore rumpled khakis and a white shirt and tie to work every day. He was an inspiration. His sixth-grade classroom was a playground of science projects and math games—and raised hands. Students behaved because they learned. I observed them cleaning up the classroom one day before filing out calmly to lunch. I wanted that kind of classroom.

My students deserved that kind of classroom. If they failed again this year, some might drop out of school forever. This was their last chance at an education. Who could blame these kids for acting out when I kept giving them assignments they couldn't do? My effort to teach Ronny to read had been immediately undercut by the fact that I didn't have a spare second in the day, and he worked after school. So I tried putting him on the back table with some kid's books and telling him to read silently—that was hardly teaching. I stuck Spanish-only Valerie back there, too, with a Walkman singing the alphabet. That helped her for a while, but then a student broke into the classroom and stole my Walkman, so I was stuck. I was realizing that teaching wasn't simply putting worksheets in front of students and telling them "go." It was setting realistic goals, creating lessons, and guiding students to reach the goals. Who ever thought this could be done by any one person, and without any training?

***

"The thing is, I don't know what I'm supposed to be teaching," I started.

On the day of our meeting, Mrs. G. was all business. We were crunched into two opposing kid desks in Room 216. It was 3:00 PM. Both of us were exhausted, hungry, and cranky; the determination with which I—spurred on in my talks with Ms. Rohan—planned to ask the administration for help waned once I was face-to-face with Mrs. G. She looked annoyed, as though I were complaining. The meeting felt confrontational, and she intimidated me.

Mrs. G. was a pretty Puerto Rican woman in her thirties, petite, and given to moments of warmth and *cariño*. Yet when things weren't as she liked them, she barked orders like a military sergeant and was the only administrator to actually type up an agenda for after-school meetings. She dressed in business suits and kept a spotless desk. She was high maintenance, a perfectionist, someone Pete would have described as a hard-ass. This had its pluses. When she marched into a classroom, back erect and nose in the air, the students shut up. She described this strict behavior as typical of teachers in Puerto Rico, where she had taught until she was twenty-six, before she was recruited to be a bilingual teacher for a Maryland school district. Although our students thought of themselves as Puerto Rican, Mrs. G. always made the distinction between our students, who "would never be accepted back on the island," and real Puerto Rican students, who were neatly dressed, respectful of teachers, and would "never act crazy like these kids." Most of the Puerto Rican–born teachers held this attitude and wielded it over the students, who very much wanted to be considered Puerto Rican. However, these same teachers also pushed Puerto Rican and Hispanic pride only when it suited them (in grant applications and in hiring) and were quick to use it to separate themselves from any behavior they didn't like. Having grown up with foreign parents myself, I understood my students' struggle for identity. Kids need to feel anchored and accepted.

It turned out Mrs. G. was not only bilingual, but also trilingual: She had mastered a language called upon by school-district administrators when they needed to appear to be addressing an issue but, in fact, were not. We would have many long, disjointed conversations in which answers only appeared to have anything to do with the original questions. I was always left playing along as though she had helped me, while feeling vaguely unsatisfied and not knowing why.

"Are we supposed to be teaching bilingual education? What's the deal?" I asked.

"This school offers a bilingual program in all the main subjects, including a class in ESOL reading. It's designed to promote awareness among students as to the importance of retaining their native language as well as adapting to their new community."

"Well, do I get any books or anything?" I asked.

"The primary problem we face is that we don't have a bilingual teacher for the sixth grade."

(She looks at me pointedly, as though this were my fault.)

"So, how do I know what to teach them in English? I don't have any books; some students don't speak English."

"I gave you books," she said. "There are also some workbooks in my office. They are to be used as aids."

But I meant textbooks, real ones, and not one, but an entire classroom set of them. I wanted more than anything for her to crack, just a little, and tell me exactly what was going on, how it worked, and what I should do. But I received no concrete advice.

"You have to figure out what their needs are," she said. "We have many different levels at this school. It's a challenging position."

My frustration mounted. On paper, the designation "bilingual" required we follow all kinds of state and federal guidelines, and the main office kept harassing me to fill out the paperwork indicating that I was following them: Students were supposed to have a language test to determine if they needed bilingual placement. They were to be assigned to a level of 1 to 4 based on language mastery. They were supposed to get periodic language evaluations. They were supposed to eventually graduate from the bilingual program.

In practice, none of this happened. The main office secretary determined placement by asking, "Hablas Inglés?" None of my students were tested, and none of their files indicated a level. How could I give them one? Without tests, I could only guess.

Bilingual students were also supposed to receive special materials. In the spring I would learn that for each level a handful of textbook companies printed bilingual books and materials. None had been ordered for this year. The reason was not lack of money, but disorganization. Books had to be ordered in advance. At my sister's school, teachers met with their team in the spring or summer before the upcoming year, agreed on what everyone would teach, coordinated grade levels (so, for example, the seventh-grade teacher could build on what the sixth-grade teacher had taught), and created a budget for the principal. Supplies were then ordered accordingly, and the teacher began setting up the classroom and lesson plans in August. This was how it should work, and does, in many schools. That was impossible in our school because of teacher and principal turnover. With a new sixth-grade teacher every year, planning was impossible. Every September this school had to reinvent the wheel.

I would learn that our lack of a true bilingual program was considered a big problem—not because our students lacked the important services, but because Mrs. G. and others had millions in grant money from the Portal grant to account for. So, Mrs. G. couldn't acknowledge that we didn't offer a bilingual education program, either on paper or in meetings. She and the principal even forced Ms. Rohan and me to take time-wasting steps during the year to maintain the image that we did have a bilingual program, by meeting with a bilingual textbook salesman (to look at books I couldn't buy) and turning in weekly lesson plans that had stated goals of enhancing students' bilingual capabilities. One day someone even distributed a book titled *Arguments for Bilingual Education*. There was no advice for actual teaching. This was pure political propaganda. The duplicity was as exhausting as the teaching.

The night after our meeting, I called my sister, whose school was in one of the nation's most affluent areas, Potomac, a Maryland suburb of Washington, D.C. Given the real estate taxes, her school had more than twice the funding of Julia de Burgo. In her county school district, paid staffers spent years developing a curriculum based on state standards, educational trends, and pedagogical research. Updated textbooks were bought regularly and were ready in August. For example, the curriculum for my sister's government class was divided into units and posted online in June for teachers and parents to review. In August, my sister clicked on Unit One, and there were seventy pages of daily lesson plans, sample activities, and essay questions—specific goals and objectives and sample exam questions. All she had to do was print them out. Lessons were coordinated on a countywide level, like building blocks, based on what the students already knew, and prepared them for the next block. Tests and exams measured student mastery of content for promotion to the next grade. When I told Nikki I was making up lessons as I went along, based on whim, with no guidance whatsoever, she said, "No way! Get your curriculum from the vice principal."

The next day I went straight to the vice principal, Mrs. Jimenez. She was in her fifties. That year, the teachers celebrated her ten-year anniversary at the school. If she had particular feelings about the state of our school, she kept them to herself. Mrs. Jimenez believed in keeping a positive outlook, even in the most dire circumstances. She was warm and supportive, and in a properly functioning school probably would have been effective. Here, the students either treated her warmly, like a grandmother, or ignored her. After some pleasantries, I leveled with her.

"I don't know what to teach. Do I get a, um, curriculum?"

She smiled. "Oh yes, Ms. Asquith. Don't you worry. You should have a curriculum. I will look into that." She began lifting up papers on her desk like she might find it there. I knew the answer was no.

***

As a former *Philadelphia Inquirer* reporter, I'd been privy to the inner workings of the school administration. This led me to believe that I knew which levers to pull to get things done. One afternoon, after I had exhausted all other avenues and was beset with fear over what the next morning would bring, I dialed the Pennsylvania State Department of Education in Harrisburg and informed them of my situation. I was passed around until I ended up on the line with the top dog—the head of the state's Department of Bilingual Education.

I had interviewed this woman before as a reporter. While she had been high-handed and grandstanding during the *Inquirer* interview, faced with the practical questions of a new teacher she seemed at a complete loss. Worse, she was uninterested. She spoke harshly and sounded annoyed to be bothered by a new teacher with nothing to teach. When she asked the name of my school, I felt like I was a traitor, ratting on Mrs. G. by admitting I hadn't been given anything to teach. She suggested I call Hispanic organizations, such as NABE, the National Association of Bilingual Education. I had already tried them, and they had told me they were primarily a lobbying organization. She sighed audibly. "Wait just a minute."

She put me on hold. Then her secretary came back on. She gave me a phone number, which I dialed.

"Hello, Philadelphia School District." It was for the switchboard of the Philadelphia School District. They passed me back to the North Philadelphia cluster office, and guess who they suggested I talk to? Mrs. G.! Several months later, in a rare friendly moment between Mrs. G. and me, she told me all this had been reported back to her, in the vein of "Control your teacher."

"You go over their heads again, and they'll blackball your career, and you'll be stuck at this school forever," Mrs. G. warned.

In the end, Ms. Rohan stuck to English, and I taught in a weird hybrid of English sprinkled with Spanish directions. Sometimes I used both languages to make my point. The students soon starting writing in whichever language they felt comfortable with, and I didn't stop them. At first the students liked the classroom chaos, but soon became frustrated. They wanted a sense of accomplishment. No matter what assignment I drew up, at least half the class was always left behind.

Aside from the students, I began to worry that I was going to get in trouble. The principal kept threatening us with memos about her new policy that we turn in weekly lesson plans and write daily objectives on the board—or else. Clearly everyone preferred to pretend the students were doing okay instead of confronting the honest truth about the problem and the steps needed to solve it. Requests for support were stonewalled, and anyone who stepped out of line was threatened with disciplinary action. (No one would ever be fired, of course. But a bad review on file could block a teacher's efforts to transfer or rise into administration.) This corruption led many teachers to cut corners, give in to cynicism, or leave the system.

Thus far, I had had no relationship at all with the principal. To me and the other new teachers she was a faceless voice, barking demands on the loudspeaker. I had not yet seen the principal interact with the students, either. I only heard her voice. Each afternoon she bellowed her mantra over the airwaves: "Failure is not an option." "We will be the number-one school in Philadelphia," she'd announce (by late autumn, we were still dead last at forty-second). Did she really believe she could take students who were illiterate in English and Spanish and teach them to read and write in English at a sixth-grade level in just one year? Apparently not only teachers can experience "the Fantasy Stage." Not only did we lack the time and staff, but there didn't even seem to be a recognition among the administration of the absence of basic skills among our students. In my opinion, we ought to back up and teach basic, elementary skills to these students. Instead, we just plowed ahead with esoteric lessons about indigenous Puerto Rican Indians and the four types of sentences. In terms of student achievement, the principal didn't believe in slow and steady wins the race, but came from the shoot-for-the-stars camp. "Test scores will skyrocket." "Teacher absences will be cut in half." "Not one student will fail. Not one!" As for that final promise, it was indeed a pledge she intended to keep.

5

The Badlands

Most Philadelphians called it The Badlands, a four-square-mile neighborhood of crumbling row houses and abandoned factories with the highest homicide rate in the city. The deteriorating factories sat on every corner—Quaker Lace Company, the Stetson Hat company, and numerous carpet and paint companies. These days, the only legal industries were fast food and check cashing.

The Badlands's informal borders were Broad Street to the west and the Delaware River to the east. To the north lay Route 1. This linked wealthy suburban teenagers with The Badlands's open-air heroin corners run by Puerto Rican kids. In 1999, a *Philadelphia Inquirer* investigation studied police records and court documents to determine that The Badlands was the heroin capital of the East Coast. The *Inquirer* also documented how police and courts harshly prosecuted the Puerto Rican dealers. Their suburban buyers—the white kids—were left alone.

Julia de Burgos Bilingual Middle Magnet School sat in the heart of The Badlands. There were two other middle schools and a smattering of elementary schools also in the neighborhood. Serving the community was one high school, Edison, a five-minute drive from Julia de Burgos. It was considered the city's most dangerous and violent high school. From my tidy, manicured apartment building in downtown Philadelphia, I could be at my school parking lot in exactly eight minutes, a time I calculated precisely in order to maximize the number of times I could hit the snooze button in the morning. Driving up Broad Street, as City Hall slipped into the distance behind me, I would automatically push down the locks of my car doors. I lived only two miles away, but I should have needed a passport to get to work. The Badlands was like a foreign country. For two years I had lived in Philadelphia and could list every coffee shop, bookstore, and martini bar in Center City. This was "my world," and it was built to fulfill the hopes, desires, and expectations of people who had grown up like me. Most of us came from middle- to upper-class families, were raised in the suburbs, and spoke English.

Indeed, I had never strayed outside downtown Philadelphia into the neighborhoods before I began teaching. Few of my friends had crossed those invisible borders between downtown and the neighborhoods either. Why would we? Crime, heroin, stolen cars, graffiti—those were the images called to mind at the mention of The Badlands. Police suspected white people in North Philadelphia of buying drugs—why else would they be there?

Similarly, my students thought my downtown world was like another planet, and I would realize this much later on when I pushed them to think of colleges like Villanova and the University of Pennsylvania. All the best colleges were in "my world"—a world built for me that they simply didn't know. Inevitably, with my arrival, the two worlds began to crisscross, and when I projected onto them the same expectations projected onto me, these worlds began to collide.

***

The three most popular students in my class were Vanessa, Pedro, and Luis, and they all shared one characteristic: They were second-generation Americans.

I was learning, to my surprise, that class popularity was based not so much on money, looks, athletic ability, or personality, as it had been when I was eleven and twelve. Those characteristics factored in, but the strongest determinant for groupings was immigration. Where you were born and how long your family had been in the neighborhood were critical distinctions among the students: The more Americanized you were, the more popular you were.

Vanessa, Pedro, and Luis all hailed from families that had settled in Philadelphia as early as the 1940s. (A few families settled first in New York and then moved to Philadelphia for a more affordable cost of living.) Vanessa's grandma was one of the early pioneers to North Philly, following in the footsteps of the Polish and Eastern European immigrants before her, drawn by the jobs in textiles, hosiery, and shipping. She was part of a tiny migration of Puerto Ricans that trickled in throughout the '50s, '60s, and '70s, a small community alongside the much larger number of African Americans migrating up from the South. Vanessa's grandma spoke only Spanish, but Vanessa spoke only English, snubbing her nose at both speaking Spanish and most things Puerto Rican. Kids like Vanessa considered themselves Puerto Rican, but they barely understood Spanish. They spoke it occasionally to their grandmas and to bodega shopkeepers. Vanessa had never even been to Puerto Rico. She and the other second-generation students were raised speaking English and listening to hip-hop and rap, not salsa. They wore baseball caps, football jerseys, and Timberland boots. Essentially, they had adopted the style and accent of inner-city blacks. This group made up about one-third of my students, but their power over the class was overwhelming.

After them came first-generation students. They were either born in Philadelphia in the 1980s to recently immigrated parents or moved to Philadelphia when they were very young. This group was the largest because Puerto Rican immigration to Philadelphia surged in the 1980s when the neighborhood officially became a barrio. From 1980 to 1990, the number of white households in the neighborhoods surrounding Julia de Burgos dropped from 6,170 to 3,233, while the number of Hispanic households doubled from 3,922 to 7,336, according to census figures. These first-generation students walked a tightrope between both cultures. Their ties to Puerto Rico were still strong. They were raised speaking Spanish in the home and neighborhood, but had picked up some English in the schools. Many could not read or write properly in either language. Those who were schooled under Spanish-speaking teachers were really lost. Rather than bilingual, they were nonlingual—fluent in neither language.

Ronny, from the Dominican Republic, was like this. He arrived when he was nine years old, too young to have learned Spanish perfectly and too late to easily absorb English. He spoke Spanish at home, and also to most of his teachers at Julia de Burgos. Several times a year these kids returned to Puerto Rico for a month or more and constantly lived with the possibility that they'd move again. One of my best students, Iris, would go home to Puerto Rico at Christmas and not return to Philadelphia until late February—missing weeks of school.

The remaining third of my class, about a dozen kids, were the most recent arrivals; they were at the bottom of the class hierarchy. Students derogatorily called them hicks or FOBs for "fresh off the boat." They had been born in Puerto Rico and had arrived in Philadelphia within the past year. Kids like Valerie, Yomari, Ernesto, and several others had arrived only in the months prior to the start of school. They spoke only Spanish and were the least American-ized; they came from the Puerto Rican countryside and dressed more conserv-atively, without the brand-name sneakers, skullcaps, and basketball-player shirts. They didn't speak slang. They were shy and very well behaved. They deferred to teachers and rarely raised their voices. Mrs. G. and the other Puerto Rican teachers regularly pointed these students out as typical Puerto Rican children, who were much better behaved than inner-city black kids and the sec-ond-generation Puerto Rican students who mimicked them. Throughout the year, I would watch some "hicks" succumb to peer pressure and change the way they dressed, spoke, and gestured to fit into the neighborhood norm. Oth-ers couldn't adapt, hanging out with Spanish-speaking students and teachers all day. In the year I was there, these kids didn't learn English. Instead, they lived in the tiny microcosm of Puerto Rican life that was recreated in North Philadelphia—a world of Spanish-only speakers.

I'd come to realize that the main reason bilingual education was such a flop at Julia de Burgos was lack of organization. There was another reason, though: the popular kids associated speaking Spanish with backwardness. It was the language of their grandmas and so-called "hicks" in the neighborhood. While they celebrated Puerto Rican pride, they also wanted to assimilate into their new country as quickly as possible. They viewed speaking English as cool. Every time I tried to teach a lesson in Spanish, Vanessa would roll her eyes, and many others in the class did the same.

***

In late September the city hosted its annual Puerto Rican Day Parade in which ten thousand flag-waving spectators lined the Benjamin Franklin Parkway downtown to dance salsa and sing "Puerto Rico, Mi Isla Encantada." The city's Puerto Rican power structure—primarily made up of City Councilor Angel Ortiz and school board member Benjamin Ramos—led pride parades and gave speeches. The aim was to present a positive image of an ethnic group more often associated with heroin busts and homicides, not that many Puerto Ricans from North Philly actually attended the downtown parade.

I was attending the parade this year for the first time and bringing students who'd also never been. I'd invited Vanessa, Pedro, and Luis on the pretext of rewarding them for good behavior. I also thought the downtown parade might give them Puerto Rican role models. In reality, it was mostly a tactical decision. They represented the class power structure, that is, they were the popular kids, and I wanted to win them over. My invitation was more like a bribe.

Class queen Vanessa had real pull over the students. Girls measured their own popularity by their proximity to her at the lunch table. Boys didn't even bother talking to her—at twelve years of age they wouldn't have a chance in her world for another five years, if ever. Only Big Bird openly stared at her, much to her annoyance. Vanessa was pretty, but what helped propel her to goddess status was that she was also a year older. (She had been left back twice.) The seventh- and eighth-grade boys liked her, too, which counted for a lot. She ignored them. For most of the year, she remained steadfastly disinterested. Vanessa was not the bitchy popular girl who marked the elite girl clique in my middle school. She was likeable. She giggled a lot and spoke in a soft, lilting voice that made everything she said sound like she was teasing. She also was the teacher's pet. She pleaded to sit in the front, and she finished every assignment. She'd decided that she wanted to eventually attend CAPA, the creative and performing arts school, Philadelphia's premier arts high school. Only a select number of eighth-grade graduates across the city were allowed in. I had promised to help her get there.

She climbed into the car with her silky black hair pulled into a high bun, wearing a red V-neck T-shirt, a gold *Vanessa* necklace, jeans, and Timberland boots. Pedro and Luis immediately shifted uncomfortably, as though aware of being in the presence of someone important.

I knew less about the boys. Pedro's parents were divorced, and he lived with his grandmother and his sister in North Philadelphia. His mother lived with her new husband in the suburbs. He was clever, easily distracted, and needy in a vulnerable way that made me think he didn't get enough attention from his mother. He would spend the morning angling to stick a "kick me" sign on my back, then sulk all afternoon if I didn't let him sit with me during lunch.

Luis was bespectacled and diligent. He had owlish eyeglasses, and when he knew an answer he'd shoot his hand in the air and slowly turn beet red from holding his breath until I called on someone. He was from North Philly, but he'd spent the prior five years in a public school in suburban Florida, where his dad had been transferred temporarily. This taste of life outside The Badlands gave him a perspective on Julia de Burgos similar to mine. He knew what a functioning school was supposed to look like and would say things to me like, "This school," and shake his head.

The sunshine gleamed on the pavement as Luis Rollerbladed to the front of the procession and snapped a picture with the mayor of Philadelphia. A half-dozen schools participated in a cheerleading competition, and we lined the concourse to watch the Julia de Burgos cheerleaders march past with a salsa step. Our principal held half of our school banner and marched up front, wearing a Julia de Burgos T-shirt. Teachers had stayed late into the evening the night before, stitching Puerto Rican flags onto their pleated skirts. Our girls had won in the past, but this year they would come in second.

After the parade, Vanessa, Luis, and Pedro walked across City Hall to the Hard Rock Café. We ordered cheesesteaks and Cokes, and then we played trivia. After one hard question, Luis shouted, "Oh, Miss," raised his hand, and held his breath, like in class. We all laughed, and Vanessa shoved him.

"Why you raise your hand, stupid?! We in a restaurant." Luis turned bright pink.

Glancing up at the bar, I realized I'd been to this restaurant many times with my *Inquirer* friends. How odd to be back in the same place as such a different person. That felt like a lifetime ago. I hadn't talked to my old friends in ages—I didn't have the time for anything but teaching. From 6:00 AM until 4:30 PM I was at school, and after eating dinner I had to correct papers and plan for the next day. Phone messages collected and went unanswered. My family thought I had disappeared. Pete and I barely had time for each other. I didn't even have time to open my mail on some days. Yet, if God forbid I didn't spend two hours planning the night before, the school day would be true hell. This table of sixth-graders was my world. Even though their lives were such the opposite of mine, I'd never felt so at home with myself. I was interested in every little thing they said. We laughed a lot, and afterward Vanessa gave me a hug. Then it was time to take them back to North Philly.

Each year the *Inquirer* and *Daily News* cover the Puerto Rican Day Parade. Later, I would read back issues and see that in recent years there'd been two stories: the happy feature about the P. R. pride parade downtown, and then a crime story, filed out of North Philly, about a violent event, such as a shooting, car burning, police assault, or murder. This was the paradox of Puerto Rican society in Philadelphia. Second-generation Puerto Ricans orchestrated one image to present to downtown residents. Those living in the neighborhood celebrated in their own way, as I was about to find out.

On the taxi ride home, a block off Broad Street, police had closed Lehigh Avenue in front of our school. They waved us north, up Seventh Street, and we came to a full stop in what looked like miles of traffic. North Philly is laid out in a grid, with a few central, four-lane avenues, like Lehigh and Allegheny, and lots of side streets and alleys that cut across. Usually I stuck to Lehigh and Allegheny Avenues, but on this day we had to inch down back streets and into the parade, with people pushing against our windows on all sides. We watched a man holding a beer stumble and fall against a stoop. A few houses down, several chickens pecked around in a fenced-off garden. We were still two miles from my students' homes and had moved no more than three blocks when the cabbie said, "You're going to have to walk."

"Oh, no," I said.

We weren't getting out here. I wanted to explain that this was The Badlands—one thing to experience from a passing car window, another from the ground. I wasn't from this world! I didn't know if I could survive it without the pretense of a classroom and a plastic badge labeling me "teacher." My watch read 5:30 PM, and the sun was setting. I had not planned to be walking the streets with three sixth-graders during a street party.

"Miss, we're not moving. This is the closest we gonna get," the cab driver insisted. We could either get out or go back downtown. I stuck a $20 bill in his hand, and we climbed out. Within minutes we were sucked into throngs of people lining the streets, celebrating, blaring salsa, and throwing confetti. My students wavered in and out of sight as people pushed past.

"Luis! Omigod, stay with us!" I shouted. From just five feet away, he couldn't hear me. Lines of cars jammed each alley. Puerto Rican flags were everywhere, sticking out of sunroofs, tied on as dresses, draped around the fronts of car hoods, and even attached to swinging windshield wipers. Women shimmered in glittering evening gowns from atop sunroofs as though they were in a beauty pageant. On the sidelines, old ladies relaxed on lawn chairs. I felt lost in a maze with no idea which direction to walk in. I tried to assess if we—or I—was in any real danger. I gathered Pedro, Vanessa, and Luis to formulate a game plan.

"Chill, Miss," Luis said.

They looked at me as if I were overreacting. They lived here. Over the deafening roar of the crowds, Luis yelled something to me and pointed to a truck bucking through an open intersection at forty miles an hour. Leaning out the window, cheering at the top of her lungs was my eleven-year-old student Juanita in a low-cut evening gown. My mouth dropped open. Before I could say anything, the crowd swayed, and I grabbed the handrail of a stoop to steady myself.

"Hey, Miss!" Down the block Josh sat in a deck chair in a circle with his mom, his aunt, and several cousins. He tossed a handful of rice at me. I'd never been so grateful to see someone. Sensing, though, that everyone else was having a fun time, I covered up my panic. "Oh, hi!" We did quick introductions with his family. His mom was a smart, well-dressed woman in her thirties. She asked me how Josh was doing in school. We chatted for a while, and a few more of my students passed, all looking surprised to see me. Next to them I felt protected. A rice fight nearby got out of hand, and Josh's mom looked annoyed, but didn't say anything. I heard glass breaking.

"There's gonna be shootings tonight," Luis said nonchalantly. He looked at me. "We'd better go."

The sky deepened, reminding me that nightfall wasn't far off. Reluctantly, we said good-bye. At first I was worried about my students. Forget that—I should worry about myself. This was way outside my safety zone. I didn't even know where I was anymore, but I did know that I looked like the only person not from this neighborhood. Soon, my students were leading the way. By 7:30 PM, I had walked at least three miles to three grandmothers' row houses. I peeked inside Vanessa's and saw a pretty living room decorated with mirrors and smiling family photos. There was also a huge television with cable. I told her mom that Vanessa had straight As on every assignment. They invited me to stay until things quieted down, but I was trying to keep up this facade, acting like I was a teacher in charge and knew exactly what I was doing.

"I'll be fine," I said, waving good-bye.

Hardly. At least I seemed to be on the outskirts of the party. I headed toward the main drag and tried to phone a cab. The dispatcher laughed. "We're not sending anyone up to North Philly tonight," she said. Pete was off in western Pennsylvania on residency. A man on the corner gave me directions in Spanish to the train fifteen blocks east on Allegheny Avenue, away from the noise. The sun was setting behind an abandoned factory. I wondered what life had been like for immigrants one hundred years ago compared to today. As I walked, I read the prominent names still hanging among the rubble: Pomerantz and Company Office and Products, Pine Tree Silk Mills Company, Keystone Dyeing, Canvas Makers, Delco Metal. If they were all empty, where were the residents supposed to work? Was it possible to have hope when surrounded by despair?

A car bucked past, packed with people and blaring salsa. They must have been heading into what would be an all-night celebration. My overwhelming emotion was no longer fear or pity, but admiration and a strange longing to belong. So much was shared here—my students may not have money, but they grew up with the support of their entire extended family. This neighborhood had traditions and celebrations, and a shared history. Yet the suburbs and all it embodied—college, high-paying jobs, cars—was my vision of success for my students. If I could only get them out of the ghetto, I thought, they'd have a chance. That was a goal that would be a great deal harder for them than it was for me. Was that what I wanted for my students? What they wanted for themselves? Was that what it took for them to "make it"? I felt as though I was finally seeing my own prejudices.

As these thoughts swirled in my head, three Puerto Rican girls pushed a baby carriage down the sidewalk toward me. I thought of Vanessa. I wondered what she thought when she saw girls only a few years older than her with babies. Was this her future, or would she somehow wrench herself from her neighborhood's norms and attend a good high school and a good university—my vision of her future?

Attempting to blend in, I pulled my hair back into a bun. Maybe my Julia de Burgos T-shirt and the P. R. flag that stuck out the back pocket of my jeans would give me a day pass to be walking around here. I braced myself for the encounter. Did I say hello or ignore them? I didn't know the neighborhood rules. They stopped talking when they saw me, and while passing, one said, "Look, even white people come out." They laughed.

A few minutes later a young guy sitting on a stoop shouted at me "You're not Puerto Rican. What you doing with that flag?"

The flag went in my bag. I flushed with embarrassment and quickened my step toward the distant lights of a dollar store and a Dunkin' Donuts. I felt like I was leaving behind this image I had that my students would easily glide toward college and the suburbs with the help of a caring teacher (me). A train approached. The two-mile ride would take me back to Center City, my world. I stepped off the platform, checked the map, and slumped into my seat. At least I had had clearly defined goals. Suddenly, my anchor felt wrenched out, and I was adrift. What did success mean for my students?

***

Later on, I would look back at the Puerto Rican Day Parade as one of my most humbling and liberating moments as a new teacher. After being told for so long that I was going to "make a difference," I realized that my time with them represented just a tiny fraction of the overall experiences and influences that would ultimately determine their outcome; the largest one, by far, being their parents. Of course, this may seem obvious to a regular person, but at the time, the prevailing new-teacher fantasy was something out of Hollywood—from *Dead Poets Society* to *Lean on Me*—that we would make a major, significant difference and change the course of our students' lives. This kind of unrealistic thinking leads to teacher burnout. The parent is always the major factor in a child's life. In fact, my sphere of influence would be no greater than my short time with them in the classroom. The best thing for me to do was to focus my energy on the time that I had with them in school and create the most powerful lessons I could. I couldn't worry as much about trying to influence what happens to them after 3:00 PM. After all, it does take a village to raise a child, and a teacher must see themselves as one person in that village. That was a less romantic notion, but a more practical one, and the right one. When I realized that my role in that village was simply in the classroom, instructing them in English, social studies, and reading, I became a much more focused teacher and a much more effective person in my students' lives. If I could be a good classroom teacher, that was hero's work.

6

The Two Percent Factor

Oh let my land be a land where liberty,

Is crowned with no false patriotic wreath

But opportunity is real, and life is free

Equality is in the air we breathe.

(There's never been equality for me

Nor freedom in this "homeland of the free.")

—Langston Hughes,
from "Let America be America Again"

A fight broke out in the school parking lot between the friends of a pregnant girl and Baby Daddy, as they called the father-to-be. I wasn't there, but I'd heard what happened. A pulsing crowd of students circled the melee and began chanting and whooping. The principal raced out of her office and jumped right in the middle of it to break it up. She was punched in the face and knocked down. I saw her the next day, a beleaguered fifty-something-year-old woman, pushing her eyeglasses up against her face with a bandaged wrist. This scared me, but then I heard even worse news. The third-floor team leader, Mr. Whitehorne, said that the student who hit her was never even expelled or transferred.

"What else do you have to do after you punch the principal?" he joked.

***

The principal had a theory. She called it the 2 percent factor, and she explained it to the teachers in a speech in the library. "We have eight hundred fifty kids on roll, and the majority come to school, go to class, and cause little or no disruption. There are, however, about two percent, or seventeen students, who cause the majority of our problems. Unfortunately, these students also tend to upset other classes and increase our discipline problems." Most teachers agreed, but some estimated the number of troubled kids to be closer to 5 percent.

I agreed with this idea. Even though almost all of the students in my classroom were misbehaving, only two students—5 percent of my classes—were causing 95 percent of the chaos. Not kids like Ronny, the Dominican boy who I'd promised to teach how to read, or Rodolfo, Mr. XXX-tra-large football jersey. They were a challenge, but I felt that with sufficient effort I could win them over. I categorized their bad behavior as "mischievous." My truly disruptive students were much more troubling than that. "Threatening" was a better category.

To put this theory in proper context, I call up the popular book and teacher movie *Lean on Me*. It's based on the true story of Joe Clark, the New Jersey principal who tried to clean up his school by kicking out all the drug pushers and violent offenders—the 2 percent. Once they were gone the teachers were able to take back control of their school, and all the students listened and learned.

In real life Joe Clark was attacked by teachers' unions and politicians, called a racist and elitist, and run out of the school system by lawsuits. But I understood what he wanted to do. On many days I dreamed of doing what Joe Clark did.

I had my "5 percent factor": Jovani and José R.

***

"Good morning everyone," I said with the forced cheer of a teacher who knew she was in the eye of the storm. The day always started out well. "Okay, uh, here's a story. Read it and finish it, please." I passed it out.

Still without reliable resources, I was making up my own lessons. On this day, I had written out a story and questions. My "story" was about a twelve-year-old named María leaving her fishing village in Puerto Rico to immigrate to Philadelphia with her family. "What will life be like for me there?" she wondered. I wrote the story myself and translated it into Spanish. The assignment was to "finish the story."

Afterward, I wrote on the board five words I'd picked out of the dictionary. The kids were to define and use them in a sentence.

After that, they were to answer this essay question: "What would you do with $1 million?"

This was my typical day, a loose cobbling together of self-created activities. There was no English or social studies period. The only "classroom objective" was to keep the kids from killing one another—and me.

Before I could even get started, I heard a soft knock at the door. A new student stood in the hall, and from his smirk alone I knew he'd be a handful. He laughed and said, "Hiii, Misss," in this slurred way that made me wonder if something was wrong with him. He had a shaved head and looked like a collection of balls stuck together—wide eyes set in a beach-ball-shaped head, baggy shirt, and puffy pants. "Hii, Miss. I want to be in your class." He held a slip of paper in his hand from the main office. Behind me the noise level mounted. I heard several cries of "Hey! It's José R.!"

My heart sank, and my first thought was No way! In only a few short weeks, my attitude about teaching had adjusted. Back in August, I wanted to reach every child, to be like Jaime Escalante and leave no child behind.

Actual teaching was hardening me. Each day was like a struggle that began before the students arrived. First, I had to battle with the other teachers for use of the copying machine, which was locked in Mrs. G.'s office. Some days, Mrs. G. would arrive late and the veterans muscled past me. Then the bell would ring, so I'd have to rush to class with only one copy of the morning's assignment and anywhere from twenty-one to thirty-five students, depending on the day. To avoid the panic attack this caused, I started my day at the copy shop in my neighborhood, sucking up the cost. The copy shop was always overflowing with harried young teachers, and I found comfort in knowing I wasn't the only desperate one.

Desperate was putting it mildly. For a full month I'd plowed on, but it had felt like a full year. I was exhausted and looked worried all the time. My skin was breaking out. I thought I'd detected my first under-eye wrinkle. Several weeks of eating corner-store Cubanos and Dunkin' Donuts was not helping matters. Nor were my clothes. After my back started aching from standing for five-hour stretches in heels, I shelved my vanity and bought ugly-yet-sensible flats. They were comfortable, but made me feel old. One afternoon while sitting in a student desk correcting class work, I thought of my girlfriends working for magazines and Internet start-ups in New York City. They had boyfriends who were earning six figures on Wall Street. They were still so young and glamorous. Their lives were fun, while I stood in a classroom wearing ugly, rubber-soled shoes, shouting at eleven-year-olds. I felt I had aged twenty years in two months.

At night, after grading and planning, I wrote in a journal all I was learning in this new world. Stepping inside the classroom made me realize how many of my education stories in the *Inquirer* had missed the mark. Once, I had written about financial awards bestowed by the state education department on schools for improved attendance. As a teacher, I saw how attendance could fluctuate depending on what time it's taken, whether in-school suspended students were counted absent and whether a school includes excused absences. Teachers could also easily fudge the numbers if they had a reason to, such as a financial incentive.

I had also written a good deal about computers in the classroom, and I had assumed that was a positive expense. The past week Mrs. G. had given all the bilingual education classrooms a $1,200 iMac computer. Mine was wheeled in every morning and sat there for most of the day collecting dust. I tried to use it, but one computer was not helpful with an entire classroom of kids. Most of the other teachers used games to keep the tough-to-control special education students busy. That was a newspaper story I never would have gotten from a school board member or union rep—my typical sources for stories.

Pete occasionally helped me check homework, when he wasn't on seventy-two-hour shifts at the hospital or sleeping. Most days, I was holed up in my apartment alone. We'd begun arguing a lot about stupid things. My friendships at the *Inquirer* felt as distant as my high school friendships. I faced ten more months of this. I remembered the Venezuelan teacher circling the holidays and telling me, "You'll be doing this." I couldn't deny how desperately I wanted a day off.

Faced with the reality of teaching, all I could think of was that I couldn't handle another difficult student in my classroom.

"Just one moment," I told him, racing for my class list. He was not on it.

I phoned the main office, and they said José R. was in seventh grade. Why was he with me, they wondered?

"Let's just say, he's not," I replied. Technically, he was still in the doorway. I scribbled a note to the seventh-grade advisory teacher: "José R. belongs with you!"

Just before I handed it to José R., I thought twice and scratched out the exclamation point. Still, I couldn't believe my luck. Problem solved or at least pushed on to someone else. Good-bye, José R.

My impeccably planned morning went smoothly for a grand total of eight minutes. That was how long it took the kids to "finish the story." I quickly discovered that half my sixth-graders knew nothing about dictionaries. A few did not know the alphabet. Many of the rest announced they didn't feel like looking up words if the other students didn't have to. We entered into negotiations: Would they do it for a prize? How about a ten-minute break afterward? Some agreed, but others refused to bend. Remembering I wasn't supposed to attach material rewards to learning, I changed my mind and tried to demand they do the work for their own enlightenment. It was too late. Small conversations broke out, like the first thick splatters of raindrops before a downpour. I tried to have a heart-to-heart.

"Please, just get quiet a minute. I'm sorry that the class isn't better prepared. I know it's not your fault. Let's just do the best we can with what we have," I said. After that mini-lecture, most of the students obliged me and politely answered the essay question "What would you do with $1 million?" Almost every student said they'd buy their mom something, such as a house. Josh wrote:

> I would buy a big house with 35 rooms for my family could live with me. I will buy a car, dirt bike, Hummer limo, and games to play with all my family. I will have eight TV in the Hummer and a pool in the Hummer with girls.

No sooner had they scratched out a paragraph or two than they started tapping their pencils. This hammering of ten-minute activities, unconnected to any broader learning goal, just wasn't holding their attention.

Then I heard a soft knock at the door . . . again. José R. was back, with a goofy grin, and a note from the seventh-grade teacher: "Readmit, I'm looking into this."

I didn't know the seventh-grade teacher. I only knew she was more senior than I was. I stalled for time.

"Okay, José. Um, go to the main office and explain what happened."

He disappeared and then reappeared eight minutes later with another readmit note. I had a sinking feeling that no one wanted José R., which meant the new teacher was going to be stuck with him. He must have picked up on my true feelings, because this time José R.'s grin was gone and he was staring at me. Suddenly, I felt deeply ashamed. Did he see the truth—that not even his teachers, who were paid to take him, wanted him? Just three weeks ago I had vowed I would never push a problem student onto another teacher. Looking into his face, I felt the cold calculation of what I'd done. I'd promised myself I'd help all the kids in my class—so what if he was really supposed to be in seventh grade? I was a teacher, and he seemed troubled, needy—yes—but blameless, and here I was secretly trying to keep him out of my class.

"José, I'm glad you're back in our class," and patted him on the back. "Please take a seat." A wave of murmurs spread through the room, like the soundtrack of a horror movie. He grinned, and he stayed. How bad could one student be?

***

Jovani had been in my classroom since early September. At first he was shy, even sweet. In the first week of school, he'd affectionately drawn the two of us in a house, labeled it "Jovani and Ms. Asuith," and sweetly pined for my atten- tion. The trouble was that he couldn't read, write, or follow instructions. When the other students teased him, he'd pick a fight. What's more, the main office had no record of Jovani. His file was missing. None of the phone numbers he gave me worked. He told me once his mother was a bartender in the neighbor- hood, and I had left a message for her at the bar. Whenever I tried calling her at home I got a message saying it was disconnected. Even though Jovani was nearly thirteen, he had the skills of a kindergartner. I had wondered if he was one of those crack babies born in the late 1980s that one heard so much about then. I thought kids like this were supposed to be in special education.

Jovani wanted my attention. Yet each morning that didn't revolve around him, Jovani grew bolder, angrier, and more bitter. Sometimes he would sit in silence for hours. Other times he would demand I help him. If I was helping other students, he would slam his books on the floor and have a tantrum. The other boys—especially Rodolfo—began to pick on him. When this happened, Jovani turned mean. He lashed out to defend himself and began picking fights.

I guessed he was a special education student. These kids had legal rights to tutors and individualized learning plans, all of which Jovani clearly needed. It didn't seem fair to push him to do work that was beyond his capability and then punish him when he acted out. It also didn't seem fair to the rest of the class to have one student constantly ruining the lesson for everyone.

Jovani was bad enough on his own. When José R. arrived, he had a partner. I couldn't stop them.

Only a few days after I accepted José R., he and Jovani returned from lunch on the verge of hysteria. They burst into the classroom chasing each other and then darting back out and running down the hallway. The weather was just turning cold. They threw their big puffy coats across the room.

"It just doesn't matter!" Jovani chanted, mimicking the cry of a TV wrestler.

Vanessa made a beeline for my desk, her entourage of admirers huddling around her. The little connection I had made with Vanessa at the Puerto Rican Day Parade had paid off. She insisted on sitting in the front row, and finished all her in-class assignments with a studied attention to detail. She wasn't necessarily advanced, but the rest of the class was so far behind an average sixth-grader academically that she was well ahead of her classmates. I began to worry about how to challenge her and not lose the rest of the kids.

"Miss, she pull me out into the hall and start acting real tough because her friends were with us," Vanessa said. An eighth-grade girl had just accused Vanessa of flirting with her boyfriend. "I told her, 'If I wanted to get with your boyfriend, I would.' She said, 'Yeah, right.'"

The rest of the class slammed their binders down on their desks. José R. ran back out of the room. I bumped between desks chasing down Jovani.

Class was supposed to begin immediately. It was fifteen minutes before we got going.

"Today we are learning vocabulary words for parts of the body," I said in Spanish. I drew two stick figures on the board.

"One person is from Philadelphia and the other from Puerto Rico. Who can tell me what this part is in English?" I asked, pointing to the neck.

This was my first bilingual lesson, and I was enormously proud of creating something that, finally, did not leave the Spanish speakers behind. For weeks I had been trying to personally tutor Ronny in class and during my prep periods, but finding spare time was a challenge. He looked at me with puppy-dog eyes—he clearly wanted to learn. So I thought a lesson like this—that the whole class could do—would be an appropriate measure of their willingness to learn. It worked. The students listened and raised their hands enthusiastically. All their energy channeled into class work, and we rhythmically worked, laughed, and learned.

Not for long. Jovani drew a stick figure as I had asked but then quickly gave up. He didn't understand what I wanted. He fell behind everyone else and began to shout out, "wait for me." And "Miss, help." I gave him personal attention, but the second I left his desk to help someone else, he jumped out of his seat, sang songs, and ran down the aisle to the back.

"Jovani, please sit down," I said, starting out nicely.

He ignored me and began throwing himself onto the floor in an imitation of a wrestler executing a body slam. The girls in the class complained.

"Miss, he boddering us." The boys wavered between concentrating on me and laughing at Jovani. Ronny, who had been labeling body parts, put his pencil down and craned his neck to watch.

Meanwhile, José R. was poking his pencil into the girl in front of him, and whispering dirty words.

"I got a part," Jovani shouted, striding with gangly legs to the front of the class and pointing to his crotch. "Dick!" He knew the word in Spanish, too, which made everyone laugh. They looked at me to see what I'd do.

His insolence was more than just personally embarrassing. If I didn't do something he'd destroy class for everyone. Each time he trod over me, he eased the path for other students to act out and ignore me.

"That's it, Jovani," I announced. "You're getting a pink slip."

The class looked stunned. The pink slip was the most severe form of discipline. Below that was the white slip, which was detention. But few teachers gave those out because they had to be taken home, signed by a parent, returned, and then submitted to Mrs. G. Few students ever returned them with a parent's signature. Among those who did, even fewer actually showed up to detention. If they missed detention, Mrs. G. or the vice principal was supposed to issue an in-school suspension, but they were so snowed under with bigger discipline problems that they soon forgot. Other times, the in-school suspension room was filled.

Most teachers relied on the pink slip, which sent the student immediately out of class to Mrs. G.'s office. From there, she decided what to do. Pete warned me not to use the pink slip too early in the year. It had to be a last resort. Sending a student to Mrs. G. for discipline gave the message that the teacher needed help with discipline. It made the teacher look weak. Also, every time a teacher used a pink slip, it weakened its fear factor.

This, however, was a last resort. Jovani left. I tried to return to the short story, but then Valerie, who was ten, complained that she didn't understand a single word. "You're not teaching me any English!" she demanded in Spanish. Valerie had arrived from Puerto Rico only two months before. The earnestness of her comment stopped me.

Some time later, Rodolfo teased her about her shoes, a pair of oversized red high heels. She screamed at him in Spanish. He hurled insults back. "Silencio!" I shouted over my shoulder. I was tending to another raging emergency involving Ronny and a big, hairy lewd body part drawn in his textbook when, out of nowhere, Valerie burst into sobs. As the tears streamed down her cheeks, I raced to her side, but she had completely lost control. The room fell quiet, and I watched her face go pink, her shoulders heave, and her heels shake inches off the ground, looking tiny and helpless surrounded by big kids. Again, I wondered why I had a classroom with both ten-year-olds and thirteen-year-olds— they didn't go together. Valerie was a little girl, and sixth grade wasn't supposed to be like this. My sixth grade had science experiments with Bunsen burners, reading classes with book reports, vocabulary words, and gentle, nice Ms. Mercer, who baked us cookies and made her classroom colorful and fun. Sixth grade for ten-year-old Valerie was a daily struggle with bullying, humiliation, and frustration. For a moment, we all felt guilty. I kneeled at her desk and protectively wrapped an arm around her gasping frame. "Valerie, just go to Mrs. G., okay?" I urged. She wriggled out of her desk, her high heels landing on the floor with a clack. She stumbled right out of the classroom. Everyone snickered.

At 10:00 AM the phone rang. "Shhhhh," I told the students. It was the main office calling again. Where was my paperwork? "What?" I pressed the phone against my head and plugged my finger into the other ear. I looked at my desk, covered in half-finished student assignments. "Okay, okay. I'm sorry." Every day the office interrupted class looking for attendance sheets, students' home phone numbers and addresses, behavioral reports. This time they wanted the emergency lesson plan they had requested in the event that I was absent. It was due last week. The principal herself asked for it. I hung up, pressing my head briefly against the phone before turning back to my class. I didn't even have a lesson plan for when I was present. Every day was an emergency.

***

Later, I found out the music teacher, the gym teacher, and Ms. Rohan had also been sending Jovani to Mrs. G. I was the last holdout. She sent him home with a letter saying he could not return without a parent. For days his desk sat empty. Then at 10:30 am one morning Mrs. G. knocked on my door.

"Jovani's mother is here," she said.

My hand was resting against the chalkboard. "I'm in the middle of a lesson," I said.

She shrugged. "This is your chance to talk to her. I'll watch your class." So I apologized, and left them for a few minutes.

Jovani's mother stood by the windows, with light reflecting off the back of her small shoulders. Jovani stood with her. She was barely older than I and had a petite frame. Jovani's clothes were always several sizes too big, and dirty. Her jeans and shirt were skintight and her hair and makeup done perfectly. She was pretty, with a soft array of colors on her face, blue eyelids, tanned cheeks, and rosy lips.

"Hi, I'm Jovani's teacher, Ms. Asquith. Habla Inglés? Español?"

"Yes," she said. Her voice and expression were gentle, and it took away some of my fear. I thought she would be intimidating, but she seemed more unsure and meek.

We stood awkwardly in the hallway for a minute, with Jovani between us, her hands resting on his shoulders protectively.

I searched my brain for some positive things to say about Jovani. I thought back to September. "He used to try really hard, and raise his hand," I praised.

Then I tried to be as formal as possible, and I read off Jovani's offenses. "But, lately we've had a lot of trouble. Jovani refuses to work, he gets out of his seat, he starts fights, he sits on the windowsill, he curses in class. . . ."

She glared down at her son. I was surprised to see Jovani biting his lip. He backed against the window and seemed to shrink into his clothes. He tucked his face under his armpit and then looked up from his lowered head into his mother's disappointed face.

"The teachers scream at me! They hate me! The other kids bother me! They beat me up!" he cried. Then he burst into tears. Jovani looked utterly small and helpless cowering, there, in his oversized, unkempt clothing. I wanted to defend myself. Even though Jovani couldn't articulate it, I knew what he meant: The teacher doesn't give me work I understand. She doesn't help me. I want attention.

I tried to jump in, but his mother had seen this before.

"No, Jovani," she said sternly. "The teacher say you bother everyone else."

He dried his tears with the long sleeves of an oversized turtleneck, and she talked to him until he agreed he would do better. "Okay," he said, nodding. "Okay."

We made him accept that his bad behavior was his fault. We convinced him that he wasn't completing his work because he was a "bad child;" our message was "try harder," even though I couldn't shake the feeling that Jovani had tried. His bad behavior was born of frustration. No one had taught him how to read or write. He was smart enough to see that he was years behind his friends academically and too proud to let them make fun of him. But if I said that, and had we began a frank discussion about Jovani's needs, we'd have been forced to admit that his mother had not prepared Jovani and I, as the teacher, had not provided for him. Both Jovani and José R. needed to be in special education class. Jovani looked ashamed and he went home with his mother.

***

The Bilingual Team met each Tuesday. Ms. Rohan was having the same problems with Jovani and José R., so we devised a plan to request Mrs. G. place them in special education. After school, I rushed over to the team meeting scheduled for that day. I was feeling desperate. We were approaching the two-month mark and my students had learned almost nothing. The six of us sat around a table snacking on cookies and juice. Mrs. G. ran these meetings with military precision and a typed agenda we rarely veered from.

I jumped in with my own problem. "I'm having a lot of trouble with Jovani," I said.

"Oh, I think that boy got dropped on his head as a child," Mrs. G. said, granting that I sent him to her the least. "He's the one I'm most worried about. He should be in special ed so that he would get transferred to another school and not be our problem."

I glared at her, but she didn't seem to notice or care. The other teachers veered back to their personal conversations as I struggled with what to say next. Clearly, Jovani was a special education student, or he needed to be designated as such. We had several special education classrooms at our school, and I suggested placing him in one.

"The mother has to push for it," Mrs. G. declared. It was probably illegal that he was in a regular class without more assistance, she said, but as long as no one said anything, we weren't obliged to do anything. "If a parent doesn't advocate for their rights, then the school lets it slide. That's how it works here."

My face must have fallen because the Venezuelan teacher, who was in her second year teaching, was slapping Ms. Rohan on the back, grinning.

"Welcome to the Philadelphia School District," she chimed knowingly. "Now you are beginning to see."

"I'm going to talk to his mom, then," I replied.

"Don't suggest special education," Mrs. G. warned. "You're not allowed. You're a school district employee. Your allegiance is with the school."

Mrs. G. had her reasons for letting things slide. One reason was the time-consuming, burdensome process of getting José R. and Jovani into a special education class. She was correct—a parent did have to push for special ed placement, because it required dozens of meetings in which the parent, the teacher, Mrs. G., the principal, and a psychologist had to be present. If any one of us didn't show, the rest would be sent home and the meeting rescheduled. How would we do this? I couldn't even get Jovani's mother on the telephone. I didn't have a home phone number for José R. The process required the teacher to fill out pages of paperwork outlining teaching strategies attempted and failed. Both boys would have to be evaluated several times—by not only a regular psychologist but also a bilingual psychologist. Needless to say, our school didn't have either. Typically, the process took from months to years.

As early as October, Mrs. G. was accusing the other teachers of using her bilingual program as a "dumping ground" for the special education students. She said special ed kids were intentionally misdiagnosed as "limited English ability" and sent into bilingual education classes in her section. At other schools, the reverse happened—immigrants who couldn't speak English were often misdiagnosed as having a disability and sent to the special education teacher. More often than not, both special education and bilingual education were federally funded cash cows that teachers used as dumping grounds for whatever students didn't fit into their classrooms. At our school, the bilingual program was a stronger program, with more teachers (largely because of Mrs. G.'s efforts) so it became the dumping ground.

Throughout the year, at least a dozen students would show up at my classroom door with a note from some teacher in another section who was clearly trying to fob them off on the new young recruit. Some stayed permanently. Others would stay only a few days before Mrs. G. would successfully argue to have them sent back to the third floor. Sometimes the supervisors would strike a deal: You keep such-and-such "bad kid" if we take your "bad kid."

Really, none of them were bad kids, and they certainly weren't impossible to teach. In fact, they could have been the easiest of all to manage, as they were the type of students who most craved borders. They needed a smaller classroom, with a trained teacher who could give them a daily routine and work that they could succeed at. Was that too much to ask for?

7

The New Teacher Exodus

*If well-trained, competent, caring teachers were present in every classroom,
we would witness a staggering increase in student achievement, motivation, and
character improvement, along with a marked decrease in discipline problems.*

—Annette L. Breaux and Harry Wong, from *New Teacher Induction*

The assistant principal at Bartram High School, ten minutes away in West Philadelphia, was shot. The *Inquirer* and the *Philadelphia Daily News* plastered the violence across the front page for days. Fifteen-year-old freshman Eric Coxen had taken a .25-caliber pistol to school as protection from a bully. A scuffle broke out in the hallway, and when the assistant principal, sixty-one-year-old William Burke, intervened, Coxen fired the gun, shooting him in the thigh.

The *Daily News* did an in-depth look at violence in schools, and ran this cover story: WHY THE SCHOOLS ARE STUCK WITH TOO MANY BAD KIDS. The doctored cover photo showed a shadowy figure lurking in a school hallway, and the editorial message was clear: the students were to blame. I felt the opposite. It should've read, WHY THE KIDS ARE STUCK WITH SO MANY BAD SCHOOLS. Bartram High School had 3,120 students. (Julia de Burgos had eight hundred kids.) It wasn't a school—Bartram was a factory.

Then the predictable outcome followed. First, identify a scapegoat. Shortly thereafter Bartram's principal was transferred to another school. Second, pretend to find a quick-fix solution. Seven days later the Philadelphia school board voted unanimously to install walkthrough metal detectors and X-ray machines at every high school. According to the *Daily News*, two metal detectors had arrived at Bartram in August, but no one had bothered to install them.

To the public, these actions gave the appearance that something had been done. However, inside the schools the teachers on the front lines saw the writing on the wall and reacted with their best survival instincts. Teachers began to quit, en masse.

In Philadelphia one hundred new teachers resigned in September—that meant 8 percent of new hires had given up in the first month on the job. By the end of the school year, the percentage of new teachers who had quit rose to 25. Sixty percent of new teachers hired at the time I was, in September 1999, had left the profession entirely within three years.

At Julia de Burgos, the first to leave was the woman who taught English for speakers of other languages—the one who, on my first day, had told me I wouldn't last. She transferred, through a connection, to an administrative position overseeing ESOL programs downtown, even though her departure left us without a program for her to "oversee." The school district began to pay Ms. Rohan an extra $250 a week to give up her prep period and cover the class until a replacement arrived (who never did).

Then one of the special education teachers departed on a mystery sabbatical. No one knew the reason. She just disappeared. On the third floor another special education class constantly cycled in new victims. The special ed teacher down the hall from my room was transferred after choking a student. (If a student couldn't be expelled after hitting the principal, why should a teacher be fired for choking a student?) I was in the hallway during lunch when Ms. Rohan sidled up to me and nodded toward two armed police officers standing at the doorway of P68, the special education room. They stood casually, feet spread, in their stiff police uniforms. Light streaming through the windows reflected off their shiny black shoes.

The writing teacher left. The school psychologist left. I couldn't keep track. No wonder those veterans were so cold to me that first day. They assumed I'd be gone by now.

The other new teachers were barely hanging on, like the nun on the third floor. She had been overheard saying something less than pious about the students. Then there was Mrs. Soleimanzadeh, a former actress, who was twenty-six and taught seventh-graders, also on the third floor. She was trying as hard as she could, but she had thirty-three students, and she was actually attempting to use the 1982 social studies textbooks we were given—without much success.

The exodus at Julia de Burgos came to a head one Friday afternoon. I was heading off to meet teachers for happy hour at a neighborhood bar, which third-floor team leader Mr. Whitehorne called the weekly meeting of the Pedagogical Society. It was really just a bunch of teachers getting drunk and celebrating forty-eight hours without any students. On my way out the door, the Spanish teacher was hurrying down the empty hallway toward me, his arms loaded with posters and boxes from his classroom. He looked unusually sanguine.

"Ms. Asquith," he called, gesturing me over with his elbow. "Could you give these keys to the vice principal?" He passed me what looked like classroom keys.

"She's right in her office," I said, motioning down the empty corridor.

He looked sheepish. "Oh, I don't want to interrupt her. She's with people," he said. "It's my last day, so have a good year." And he swiveled and hurried down the hallway. Puzzled, I carried the keys into the vice principal's office. She was leaning back in her chair, laughing with the classroom assistant at a joke.

"The Spanish teacher just gave these keys to me and said it was his last day."

The vice principal stopped laughing. She stared at me until I put the keys down on her desk. Then she flew forward in her chair and dashed out of her office after him. The click-clack of her heels faded down the corridor. The classroom assistant laughed. "They droppin' like flies."

I never saw the Spanish teacher again, but around that time an article appeared in the *Inquirer* about the shortage of foreign language teachers in the New Jersey suburbs, where pay was higher and classes were smaller. Maybe he went there. I'd heard that it was especially tough for the Spanish teacher at our school. He saw a different group each period and he couldn't form a bond with his students, making discipline impossible.

For a long time the principal tried to fill the gaps by forcing teachers to substitute, or "cover," for a class during prep periods. This was the worst thing in the world. Not only were we struggling with our own classes, but now we had our prep period taken away and had to teach during that, too.

In our school, the teacher most affected by this exodus was Ms. Vinitzsky, who ran the in-school suspension room. She took the kids who'd been given a day's suspension or tossed out of class with nowhere to go until 2:43 PM. Or if there was no teacher, she often had to take the entire class. Ms. Vinitzsky was a brassy, tough-talking blonde in her fifties. No matter the time of year, she had a deep tan, a big, sprayed helmet of hair, and a sweater that slipped off her shoulder. She spoke with a strong South Jersey accent. I loved her. Everyone in the school did. She was tender with the kids, but also tough so that she could handle any of them. Even though her room housed a good many of the 2 percent factor, the ones no other teacher could handle, it was always quiet. The kids were always busy doing something. Some days I didn't think the school could have held together without Ms. Vinitzsky.

Our school was struggling from day one. By October we had an additional nine teacher vacancies—meaning that at any point during the day as many as 150 kids arrived at classes with either rotating substitutes or no teachers at all. Mrs. Liss, a nice lady in her sixties who'd been working at the school for forty years, began walking around the main office shaking her head and saying, "I don't know how we're going to open the school each day."

***

Unfortunately, what was happening in Julia de Burgos, and in Philadelphia in general, was typical of inner-city schools across the nation. This wasn't the first year cities had struggled with teacher shortages, but the situation was worsening in the late 1990s because the booming economy drew teachers into other fields. In general, teaching suffered from one of the worst turnover rates of all professions. Violent, low-income schools in particular tend to turn over a quarter of their staff each year.

Some tried financial rewards to solve the shortage. The State of Massachusetts offered new teachers a $20,000 bonus to be paid over three years. After the first year, one-third of new teachers had quit. Four out of five reported that the bonus had little or no effect on whether they stayed or left.

In our school system, I would receive an extra $1,500 in the spring as part of the promised sign-on bonus. By the time I'd received it, however, not only had it been whittled down to $750 after taxes, but I couldn't have cared less. I would have paid double that in return for a sense of success with my students.

In Philadelphia, as in most urban school districts, a bonus could hardly compensate for a serious discrepancy in salaries between rich schools and poor schools.

A new teacher's salary in Philadelphia was $30,000, almost twenty-five percent lower than that paid in nearby suburban schools, where teachers earned

$38,000. In fact, not even a $20,000 bonus could make up, in the long run, for the salary discrepancy between school districts. In Philadelphia, the median teacher's salary was $51,104; in some suburban schools it was $85,395.

My first paycheck had been a shock. At the *Inquirer* I took home about $650 a week. My teaching pay after taxes was about $367 a week. When applying for the job, I had anticipated a $30,000 annual salary, and for that reason rented a $700-a-month apartment. What I hadn't planned on was that the state, city, and union would take out a total of 40 percent in taxes and fees. After I subtracted the $3,000 in annual tuition I had to pay for required classes at the local university—and not counting all I spent out of pocket for teaching supplies—I estimated my earnings at less than $275 a week. This wasn't a competitive salary for a college graduate, which made me think that, really, solving the teacher shortage wasn't so complicated. The reason schools pay varying salaries is because schools are funded by local property taxes. Hence, in the case of Pennsylvania, the rich towns with the big, expensive housing have a much greater tax base to invest in schools and pay teachers. They jack up the salaries to compete with other schools to attract the best teachers. Naturally, the best teachers would gravitate to the best salaries, leaving behind the worst teachers in the poorest schools. In places like the United Kingdom, schools are funded by the government based on need. In some cases, teachers in poor urban areas could be paid more than their counterparts in suburban schools.

Instead of raising the salaries of teachers in low-income schools to be at least equal to those of neighboring schools, though, cities launched publicity campaigns to boost recruitment. Working in poor urban schools was suddenly considered doing a good thing, or "making a sacrifice." Teaching poor children was no longer a profession, but charity work.

Around the time I started teaching, the New York City school system spent $8 million to hire a top-notch Madison Avenue advertising company to launch a recruiting campaign. Former New York City Schools Chancellor Harold O. Levy had originally asked for $16 million, but the school board shot him down. Posters went up all over the subways challenging people to "make a difference." These campaigns told new teachers that even without any background or significant training in education, they could "give a child a chance" and "save a life."

New Yorkers responded. The recruiting office met its quota and hired 8,334 new teachers that year. By the end of the first year, 1,875 of those teachers had quit—24 percent.

Randi Weingarten, the president of the United Federation of Teachers, was a voice of reason when she said: "It's not honest to have a glitzy marketing campaign and then have teachers end up disillusioned because they don't get the resources or support or salary they need to do the best job."

Clearly, inner-city schools didn't have a problem with teacher recruitment. They had a problem with new teacher retention. In *The First Days of School*, Harry and Rosemary Wong calculate that every time a new teacher leaves, a school district and its taxpayers lose $50,000 in lost training, recruitment, and administrative costs. I wondered what the school districts could look like if only they invested half that much in training and supporting the teachers once they were hired.

By October, I needed to call my parents and ask them for a few hundred dollars to help carry my rent, supplies for the students, and occasional Friday-night pitchers of Budweiser. I felt ridiculous asking for money when I had a full-time job, but $350 a week was not enough. Married teachers could lean on their husbands, but single teachers, like thirty-something English teacher Ms. Ortiz, lived in poor neighborhoods and scrimped. Few could afford downtown apartments in Center City unless they lived with boyfriends, as Ms. Soleiman-zadeh did.

With no husband, no time to look for one, and school loans to pay, Ms. Rohan had it really rough. She shared an apartment forty-five minutes outside the city. She packed a lunch everyday. And, still, she took a second job as a waitress at Applebee's to make ends meet. She went straight home from school on Fridays to sleep because on Saturdays she bused tables until 2:00 AM. When Ms. Ortiz and I invited her out, she declined. Some Mondays she arrived looking more exhausted than she had on Friday. Nevertheless, when it came to her students, she dug deeply into her own pocket. She bought decorations for her class and music CDs as rewards for good behavior. She bought workbooks for the special ed kids. After we lost our prep periods, she used her free time to grade papers and to plan. I knew she took students' phone calls at home when they had problems, and drove to their row houses to meet with parents. Her devotion was unlimited, and largely unrewarded.

8

The Pedagogical Society

Mkono Mmoja Haulei Mwana.

One hand cannot bring up a child.

—Swahili proverb

Mr. Rougeux ordered two more pitchers of Budweiser and spit tobacco juice into a can. Mr. Rougeux and Mr. Whitehorne had invited me to their weekly meeting of the Pedagogical Society, which was held at the J Street Bar and involved, as I was happily learning, a lot of drinking.

Mr. Rougeux was Philadelphia's number-one teacher, a twenty-three-year-old who had the top score on the city teaching exam and had been featured in a front-page *Inquirer* article the previous year. The piece was about the city's "efforts to hang on to their best teachers." He was famous, and we had become friends.

This was nice because I felt lonely. From the moment I arrived at 7:45 AM until I left at 3:30 PM, kids surrounded me, but it wasn't the same as having company. I felt like a theater actress: Despite the packed audience, I was still alone, on stage. Teachers had to keep on guard in front of students. When students were around, for example, the teachers used Mister and Miss and spoke in formal tones. We couldn't talk about our personal lives or gossip about the principal, and lately there was always a story about some way she had angered a teacher. Students weren't allowed in the teachers' lounge, but it was a dreary, dark place where only the secretaries and school police milled. I usually ate lunch at my desk.

Then one day Mr. Rougeux came by to check on me, which no one else had done. He waved through my door window. Soon I was observing his classroom daily and learning from his lessons. He taught sixth grade on the first floor, and I marveled at his skills. Kids in his room behaved. He had already set up a technology lab in the back of his class, getting computers as donations from his alma mater, Villanova University. What's more, he was building an ecology center with a real pool and fish. By spring he even had a duck in there. He had sandy hair and was an amateur boxer. Unlike most young, white teachers in the city, Mr. Rougeux was conservative, practically right-wing. He drove a pickup truck, chewed tobacco, and came from a rural, blue-collar family. His grandfather had been a railroad worker in Altoona and a big union advocate until he was injured and the union turned its back on him. Mr. Rougeux hated the union and didn't mind making his views public. He rolled his eyes every time a union issue came up and never went to any meetings. In fact he seemed to shun the entire school. He was popular with his students, but unpopular with the rest of the staff.

Mr. Whitehorne was Mr. Rougeux's best friend and political opposite. He taught seventh-grade science, and he was also an administrator—the equivalent of Mrs. G., but on the school's third floor. In his late fifties, Mr. Whitehorne had devoted his life to neighborhood activism. He was a Marxist and an intellectual. He had moved into North Philadelphia in the 1960s to foment revolution among the industrial workers. Having joined the Cohn Clothing factory, he pressed hot irons for years while huddling with fellow workers on lunch break, during which he'd lecture on the bourgeoisie and repression. Mr. Whitehorne had become a science teacher at Julia de Burgos in 1988 and had risen to union leader and team leader of the third floor. He was well over six feet tall with a mass of snowy white hair and baggy pants that rode low on his hips. He had a no-bullshit manner and a terrific sense of humor about the job's darker moments. Mr. Whitehorne and Mr. Rougeux argued about most everything, but held a tremendous amount of respect for each other.

Ms. Ortiz also came out on Friday nights, but not just from pedagogical interest. She liked Mr. Rougeux, I suspected. Her eyes clung to him when he vented about the liberal school administration, pausing to spit tobacco from his cheek. She was Puerto Rican, raised in Chicago, and had blond hair, a button nose, and a pearly-white smile. She dressed up for class in miniskirts, black boots, and makeup, so at first I thought she was in her twenties. She was actually in her mid-thirties. She taught seventh- and eighth-grade English and had been at Julia de Burgos for a decade. All the girls loved her. When she found out I knew how to salsa, she would call me in my classroom Friday afternoon. "Hey bitch! Wuz up? Are we going dancing tonight? Let's get me a man!" Sometimes students sitting in the front row could hear her through the phone. "That Ms. Ortiz, again?" I tried not to laugh.

There were awful teachers, too. They didn't join our drinking society, but were common conversation fodder: Mr. H. took his class on a field trip to Hooters; Mr. T. liked to stand up at union meetings and make intelligent speeches littered with legal jargon because he was once a high-powered attorney until he acquired a costly cocaine habit; Mrs. B., the special ed teacher, had yet again finagled herself a paid sabbatical/leave and would be gone all year. Then there were the long-term substitutes who were a rung below emergency certified teachers and were paid by the day. The most colorful was Ms. D. on the third floor, a fussy, cardigan-wearing schoolmarm type, who put an apple on her desk every day until the kids started taking it. A former substitute in the suburbs, she constantly compared our kids to suburban students in a racist way. "They don't act like this in Lower Merion."

Throughout the year, "Ms. D. stories" became legendary—the highlight of our Pedagogical Society meetings: Ms. D. gave 120 of her 140 eighth-graders an F in science; Ms. D.'s eighth-graders locked her in her classroom for two periods, forcing security to remove a windowpane to unlock the door; the eighth-graders stole Ms. D.'s purse; Ms. D. told Mr. Whitehorne she'd decided on a policy to "teach only the students who want to learn"; some guy stormed into the main office complaining he'd almost been clobbered on the sidewalk by a flying textbook—from guess whose class?

The nun always got a laugh, too. This week, Ms. Ortiz had heard that a student ruined the nun's overview with white-out, and she started crying in front of her class—again.

"She needs to toughen the fuck up," said Ms. Ortiz, balancing a buffalo wing between painted fingernails. Mr. Whitehorne said she had petitioned her church to teach as part of her "mission." This made everyone laugh.

"Man, she didn't realize what she was getting herself into," Mr. Rougeux chimed in. "Not even God would ask this of anyone!"

Then there was Mr. Jackson, the new seventh-grade English substitute on the Bilingual Team, whom Mrs. G. called a "ticking time bomb." He was black which everyone thought was great at first because he could be a real role model for Hispanic and black boys, many of whom had fathers in jail. He stood over six and a half feet tall, and kept his back straight as a board from his days in the military. He was posted to the Bilingual Team because he thought he spoke Spanish. At meetings, he insisted on communicating in broken, grammatically creative Español, even while we spoke in English. This took forever and made the veterans cringe.

One time I asked him what he was teaching in seventh-grade English, hoping that would help me design my lessons. He sized me up suspiciously.

"Okay," he said. He picked up some papers off his desk and looked through them. Then he walked to the back end of the room near the windows and took an English textbook off the shelf. He opened it up to chapter one.

"We're learning how to make a sentence," he read.

"Really?" I was having the same problem he was! I explained to him that chapter one in the English textbooks Mrs. G. had given me was titled "The 4 Types of Sentences," which was ridiculous. How could I teach them the types of sentences if they hadn't been taught the necessary English to even write a sentence? The bell was going to ring, and I had T62 for two hours in the afternoon, and nothing planned yet. Each day they grew more frustrated and less compliant. My voice became tinny and desperate.

"Well, do most of your students already know how to write sentences?" I asked.

He didn't say anything. I tried to explain myself. "Well, I mean, it says in my book that I'm supposed to teach them the four types of sentences. You know, declarative, exclamatory, etcetera. But, I think it's above their heads, don't you?"

He put the book back and straightened even taller, looking down on me in an arrogant way. "Well, this school doesn't give us anything to teach them."

I looked around Mr. Jackson's room, which was barren and uninspiring. The walls were bare, and the bulletin boards empty. It was clear that Mr. Jackson had no more of an idea what to teach than I did. Later on, I would find out that Mr. Jackson wasn't teaching them anything at all—it was a "free period." When I passed his room the following day, I heard him screaming at them, "SIT DOWN! BE QUIET!"

I thought: This was the English teacher I was to send my students to next year?

On most Fridays we stayed at the bar until 6:00 or 7:00 PM, and then I went home and usually fell immediately asleep, unless Ms. Ortiz called me to go to The 8th Floor, a dance club downtown. (Sometimes I found the energy.) Occasionally, though, the Friday-night Society meetings stretched out from 4:00 PM until almost midnight. On those nights the happy hour tables would clear out and the regulars would line the bar by around 8:00 PM. We would order cheeseburgers for dinner and settle in for the night.

If there was only one thing that kept me going those first few months teaching, it was these evenings and these kind teachers. They were my support group. They loaned me lesson plans, taught me discipline tricks, and explained how the school worked. They listened and sympathized. Simply knowing I had friends down the hall was a tremendous source of comfort. When the times got really tough, it was all I had.

9

Special Education

Rogia was a ghost. She looked about twelve, was black, and on school records, had an address, and even grades. No teacher at Julia de Burgos ever actually saw Rogia, though. She was one of the students labeled "educable mentally retarded" (EMR). Of the three special education categories, EMR was the most grave—the most severely dysfunctional.

The first was emotional support (ES). These students were mainstreamed into regular classes and supposedly given extra assistance in the form of personal tutors and special classes during the day in which trained special education teachers helped them with their course work. The second group, learning disabled (LD), was more challenging. They were supposed to have their own classrooms and teachers.

Rogia belonged to one of the vacant special education classrooms, so she spent most of the day roaming the halls, trying to avoid being yelled at. Every day she lingered after school in the hallways, following the janitors from classroom to classroom. Sometimes a janitor let her help wipe down desks. Other days she was screamed at. "She just don't wanna go home," one janitor would say. I let her sit in my classroom after school, but then a janitor saw this and told me, "She gonna steal your stuff." After that, Rogia didn't come back after class.

The day I met Rogia I was hurrying down the hallway to Mrs. G.'s office during a prep period, carrying Jovani's paperwork under my arm. A week after I met Jovani's mother, they'd both returned to school to tell me Jovani was leaving for good. "He's transferring to Jones Middle School," his mother said, her arm wrapped around his bony shoulder. This time she was cold and treated me like the enemy. She wore glittery silver eyeliner and glared at me from half-slit eyes. Jovani skipped down the hall to collect his drawings from our classroom, delighted at having the full attention of his mother, teacher, and Mrs. G., who came by my classroom and spoke demurely to his mother, acting sad that

Jovani was leaving. No sooner had they left when she cheered, "Thank God he's someone else's problem! He's out of our hair!"

A few weeks passed, and Jovani reappeared. He showed up in class like a sucker punch to my stomach. "How was Jones Middle School?" I stammered.

"I didn't go there," he said. No note. No explanation. Class had to begin, and there was no time for a follow-up. I didn't even know if he had reregistered in the office. This time he was much, much worse. He ran around all morning, and Rodolfo had threatened to beat him up. Vanessa was falling asleep from boredom, and Ronny needed my help—not to mention the other twenty-five kids in the class. They had to learn this year; some of them didn't read or write English yet, and they didn't have time to waste. I decided to make a strong push to move Jovani to special education, for the sake of the other students, no matter how much time or paperwork it required.

***

My students were banging away on keyboards in the music room and looking bored. Vanessa stared glumly into the distance. A few of the younger girls tapped away delightedly. Despite the instruments, this was not music class. This was their English language class, or ESOL. This was the class dumped onto Ms. Rohan after the ESOL teacher transferred to a cushy administrative post. Mrs. G. put the students with the music teacher, although she continued to refer publicly to the class as ESOL. Vanessa saw me and started waving, so I ducked and hurried on.

Mrs. G.'s office was empty of students—a rare, rare occurrence. "I need to talk about Jovani," I explained to her. "He needs special education, I think." Before I could finish, a security guard started bellowing down the hall. We ignored her at first. Then it became impossible. Mrs. G. stormed out into the hallway: "What is going on here?" That's when I saw Rogia.

She hung halfway off a stair, arms wrapped coyly around the banister, and watched us with big, lingering eyes. Most of the girls at the school meticulously slicked their hair into fancy buns and wore sparkling makeup and gold jewelry. Rogia had on a ratty T-shirt, and her short, choppy hair stuck out in all directions. She looked as though she had slept on the couch, woken up, and walked right out the door for school.

"Rogia, I want you in class—now," Mrs. G. said.

Tears welled in Rogia's eyes. She looked desperate but didn't budge. "Rogia, get outta my hallways!" the guard yelled. She sniffled a little and started to whimper. The screaming in the hallways descended on her from all directions. "I'll take her to class," I said. The security guard stalked off.

I followed her down the stairwell, where she leaned on the banister and peered up at me.

"Hi, Rogia," I said, pronouncing her name Rue-gee-ah. "Can I talk to you a sec? Don't be scared. I'm not going to yell at you."

Her tear-stained cheeks puffed up as she sniffled. I put my arm around her. "I'm Ms. Asquith. I teach sixth grade. What grade are you in?"

"Seventh," she said.

"Hon, why aren't you in class where you're supposed to be?" She shrugged.

"Let's go to your class together," I said. "I'll take you, Okay?"

She leaned into me as we walked together and chatted. I tried to make her smile. Some special education students, I suspected, suffered from problems beyond low IQs and learning disabilities. Many were victims of physical and sexual abuse, or had been abandoned or bounced between foster homes. They came from broken homes to a broken school, where the special ed designation that aimed to help them served, in fact, only to hurt them. Special education for these learning disabled kids was like a scarlet letter, leading to taunts from other students ("Hey, LDs!")

Rogia's class was at the far end of the top floor. We wound around the stairwell and climbed up to the third floor, which had a mural depicting life on an island. We passed Ms. Soleimanzadeh's room. She was writing on the chalkboard. The door to Rogia's classroom was separated from the hallway by three steps, and the windows had bars across them.

As we walked up, I had her smiling. The door was locked. "Here we go," I said, rapping at the window.

The door swung open from the inside. About seven kids stood staring at us from different sides of the classroom. There was a pungent mothball smell mixed with another smell—rodent droppings. Dim sunlight filtered through a dirty window. A few desks were turned over. Everything had been put aside and forgotten, as in an attic. The blackboard had no chalk; the bookshelves had nothing to read on them. Someone during a previous year cared enough to tack bulletin boards on the walls, but they were now void of student work.

A man jumped up from his desk as though he'd been caught doing something he shouldn't. He was the long-term substitute. Oversized Coke-bottle glasses framed his beady eyes, and he was wearing a tightly tied backpack. Before we could say anything, someone yelled, "Yo, Rogia be back!" Then I understood why Rogia preferred the empty solitude of the hallway to her seventh-grade room.

A fat boy charged at her, causing her to break away from me. She dodged him, cursing back, sticking out her small chest, and threatening to punch him. The remaining handful of kids picked sides and chanted them on. A boy with long arms covered in a super-size flannel shirt threw down the magazine he was reading and pushed the fat boy. "Don't be talking 'bout my sista," he shouted. He grabbed the boy's shoulder and threw him to the side, knocking him against a desk. The noise rose to a thunder, and suddenly desks were being overturned and pencils thrown. Rogia stumbled to the radiator near the opposite wall. She stuck her hand into a box of crayons and flung them across the room. I ducked and a spray of crayons hit my back.

The creepy substitute stalked from behind his desk and pushed his Coke-bottle glasses up to his eyes two or three times. He moved toward Rogia and another boy to separate them, but immediately backed away when their waving arms whizzed past his glasses. He turned to me, his face sallow.

"Do you see this?" he said. "They're animals in here. I can't do anything." He turned to them. "You're animals!"

The mothball smell was nauseating. Something in me snapped and I lunged forward to help. "Stop it, stop it!" My words spilled out, but were muted by the shouting. I tried to pull the boys apart and knocked into a desk. My hair was strewn across my face, and my heart raced madly. Edging backward, something caught my eye: eight long nails jammed through a long wooden board pointed sharply to the ceiling. Two inches of the nails protruded from the board like a barbaric stick. The kids pushed each other back and forth several feet away. One of these children could easily pick it up and beat the other to a bloody pulp. I screamed for them to get away, but no one listened. Any minute now teachers would come running into the classroom and take control of this, I thought. But no teachers came. I shouted for help.

"Hey, Ms. Asquith," someone said. Juan, a school security guard, was crunched into a desk, his muscular arms stretched out in a lame effort to separate kids jumping around him. I hadn't even noticed him when I walked in. Juan was the school's most hulking, formidable member of security, the kind who charged headlong into the riots that started in the parking lot or cafeteria. His size alone intimidated most students. "Just leave her here. We'll take care of her," he said.

The screaming and fighting continued, but it was Juan's presence here that hit me the hardest. He wasn't rushing in to break this up. He had been here all along. While I sped around wildly, his steady expression was completely devoid of any sense of urgency. His uniform made him look all the more powerless. He waved his arms around in a vague gesture to break up the fight, but he wasn't alarmed. This was the normal state of affairs here. I realized: The only difference on this day was me.

As I backed away, I caught the eye of a lone figure in the middle seat. He had a word puzzle on his desk and a pencil in his hand. He was maybe fifteen, soon-to-be handsome, with intelligent eyes that followed my every move. He looked trapped, like a man imprisoned. His eyes said, "Get me out of here." I wanted to pull him out right then and there, and enroll him in my class. He apparently understood the injustice and craziness around him. I looked away. Rogia's face was streaked with tears.

"Rogia!" I shouted. "Come with me." But she wasn't budging.

"Fuggedaboutit," Juan said.

"Rogia, I'm in room 216. Two-one-six. If you ever need to see me, come there."

I stumbled down the stairs. The door swung shut and locked behind me. Across the hallway, Ms. Soleimanzadeh and the other teachers continued their lessons, undisturbed. I felt, of course, like I had to do something. But what? Who did I tell—the principal, Mrs. G.? They already knew. I took the long route back to my room, so I wouldn't have to pass Mrs. G.'s office and see the janitor. I was sure they would laugh at my naivete.

The bell rang, indicating my prep period was over. I hurried, still shaken, back to my room. The students were arriving for my next class. I hugged the first child I saw, who happened to be Jovani.

"What's wrong, Miss?" he asked, in a soft, childlike way. The rest of my class stumbled in, the boys with their baby cheeks and the girls with their sparkly butterfly hairclips. They were so young, so little. Given their sharp tongues, it was so easy to forget that six months ago they were in elementary school.

"Nothing." I hugged him tighter. Jovani was staying with me.

***

Dead leaves piled on my car windshield in the parking lot and crunched under my feet as I popped my trunk and unloaded crates of supplies. Late each afternoon I dragged my crates back to the car and went home to work all night, alone. Time slipped by. Winter had arrived.

One Monday afternoon I felt flushed in class. As the students in T62 ran around, I held my head in my hands. My throat burned. The doctor diagnosed laryngitis. For the next three days, I lay in bed.

Shortly before I had gotten sick, my relationship with Pete could no longer stand up to the demands of my job and his busy schedule. Neither of us had any energy left to talk about our problems. We decided to "take a break," which was a nice way of saying break up.

Pete had pushed me to teach and had been my main support. Now he was gone. Strangely, after we ended it—we were in his car—I crossed the street and looked up at the moon, feeling a pressure lift: one less emotion to deal with. My classroom was an emotional nightmare every day. The prospect of another week in the classroom without a solid lesson plan filled me with anxiety. Yet the troubles with Pete ran deeper than our busy lives. I was shutting him out intentionally because I was changing, and I wasn't sure I liked the person that I was becoming.

I'd set out wholly single-minded to learn to teach, and suddenly my failure became a real possibility. I'd personally staked everything on succeeding. I'd given up my career, my *Inquirer* friends. I'd rebuked my parents and taken on the trust of and responsibility for fifty children. If I was failing and wasn't making a shred of difference, what was the point? How could I answer the question: How was your day? "Well, I saw a group of special education students locked in a classroom with no teacher and I didn't do anything about it."

I called a lawyer friend of mine and told him what happened. We'd sue the school, I said. Could you do that? Sure, he said, but most special education lawsuits came from parents, not teachers. Then Mr. Whitehorne told me a lawyer was already investigating our school on behalf of a special ed parent. In the 1980s the entire city had been sued for lacking a bilingual program, which was why we had so many bilingual education mandates that required so much paperwork. What good could a lawyer do?

Next I considered calling a reporter I knew at the *Inquirer*. What would a big story on the failures of special education solve, though? Hadn't I left journalism because I wanted to have a more direct impact? Education had seemed so black and white from the newsroom. We had only to figure out what the problem was and who was to blame. Fixing it was someone else's job. Now that someone else was me—I was the teacher who was supposed to solve the problem.

I thought about calling the school district for help, but then remembered the last time I called the bureaucrats. What would I say to them? "I'm a teacher, and I'm calling to tell you that some classes in our school don't have teachers. And these classes are violent and dangerous." They knew what was happening.

What a fool I was ever to have thought that I was the only one who cared, as though a lack of caring was the missing ingredient to improving the schools. Mrs. G. was probably like this in the beginning. Every new teacher probably went through it—a time when they believed they could solve the school's problems; a time when they thought all it takes is courage to stand up to the problem. Now I had courage enough only to push me to show up every day. Solving the problems required . . . well, what did they require? More teachers? Less corruption? Better parents?

A few weeks later, Rogia's teacher left. Replacements were cycled in—all untrained babysitters who would spend a few days screaming at the students and then march out in the middle of the day, perhaps giving up for good their dreams of making a difference, too, and leaving a classroom of thirteen-year-old special education students in their wake. I don't know what happened to Rogia in there, but I hate to imagine the worst. Later in the school year, when I was almost numb to these things, I saw an eighth-grade boy try to fondle a female student in a class I was subbing. I stopped him and sent him out for the remainder of the period. Who's to say what happened the next day? In the spring, a thirteen-year-old special education student at a school a few miles away was raped in the stairwell, and the newspapers displayed it on the front page. The principal expressed relief that it "hadn't happened at our school," but I wasn't so sure. Rogia was the only girl in her classroom on some days. By spring, the pool of substitutes ran out, leaving Rogia with no teacher at all. That's when special ed students started roaming the hallways and the fires began.

How could I show up at a school each day in which girls as young as thirteen were being routinely abused and possibly raped while we all looked the other way? Yet faced with the reality that we each as individuals could not solve the problem, should I quit in protest or continue to show up each day and do my best, even if it meant teaching under conditions I deeply objected to?

How could I be part of a school that allowed such wrongs? But how could I walk away and condemn another classroom of students to the same fate?

10

Rebuilding My Classroom

The day I returned from my laryngitis sick leave, I made a decision not to abandon my class. I'd do the best job humanly possible each and every day. My first Monday morning back in the classroom, I knew this was the right choice. It was wonderful to be back. I had missed my students. Ms. Rohan had passed around a card for the students to sign. "Why we missed Ms. Asquith":

— She smart and like's to teach us. She rather spend her time to teach us instead of being home. Likes to do fun things with us.

— She give the class chances. She is pretty and nise.

— She always come to class in a nice mood.

— She is very kind nice and young.

— She nices person that you can have in your live.

— She is pretty and she has a nice smile everyday when she comes to school to teach.

— Her clothes match.

I hung it up behind my desk. After a week of reflection and rest, I felt invigorated and prepared, as I'd spent days on the computer creating lesson plans. Even though I was more alone than ever, I felt surrounded by love and affection, and that would be more than enough.

Seeing as I was keeping Jovani and José R., I'd devised a strategy to take control of my class. It would unfold on two fronts; classroom management and improved content. My first challenge was to truly take control of my classroom. I was being too easy on them, and letting too many minor infractions slide. They were running all over me. On the way to school I had chanted my new mantras "You must sit them down before you can teach them," and "I am in charge. They must do exactly what I say." Content would stop temporarily as I focused on teaching them classroom management. I created sample lessons with the point being to enforce order. One of the first orders of the day was to stop the spitballs.

Indeed, on my first day back, Rosalia was hit with a fat, dripping wad, right in front of me. Rosalia was one of about ten girls I called the Hello Kitty girls because they always carried colored pens and neon erasers in Hello Kitty carrying cases. The spitball made Rosalia look petrified and instead of ignoring them like I usually did, I had to defend her. The disrespect had gone on long enough. I put down my chalk and walked to the center of the room. This was my opportunity.

"Everyone stop what you're doing," I said.

It was time to step back and teach them to be my students. And they didn't need to be coddled. They needed a teacher with the backbone to get them in line. They needed high expectations, not low ones, from someone who believed in them. In Ms. Ortiz's words, I needed to "toughen the fuck up."

As students exchanged cavalier smirks with Rodolfo, these lessons gurgled together in my head. I wouldn't ignore the problem anymore.

"Somebody in this class just threw a spitball," I said forcefully. I waited five seconds, using their surprised silence as a tool. "Somebody obviously thinks spitballs are funny." Another ten seconds. "Someone obviously thinks spitballs are important enough to interrupt this whole lesson. Well, I spent a long time planning this lesson, and I don't think it's funny at all."

I walked slowly up and down the aisles, glaring at each and every student. This was not acting. I had devoted hours the night before to preparing my own lesson. I had dropped $50 at Barnes & Noble for grammar books and spent an hour typing up Spanish-English worksheets and inventing activities. I had invested a lot of my time and energy because I cared that they learn something.

As I paraded through the room I realized why I hadn't stood up to them before. I was afraid they wouldn't listen to me. My confidence wavered. What about Pete's advice? "Never enter a showdown you can't win." Rodolfo might ignore me like the boys in the hallway always did. Then what would I do? What if a student told me to fuck off? Why would they listen to me? I didn't know. This could be humiliating.

Then, I heard a student murmur, "tell her, Rodolfo," and I felt emboldened. I walked over to the back of the room, looking as strict as I could.

"Now you want to talk too, is that it?" I asked, raising my voice a little. "In what classroom is a student allowed to talk while the teacher is talking? Not in mine. I'm not going to teach in a classroom where there are spitballs. You all have too much at stake to waste our little time together. Now, I want to know: WHO THREW IT!?"

I remained in front of them all, hand on my hip. I didn't blink. Don't be scared. Children need boundaries. Nothing is personal. I waited. Who would imagine living in fear of sixth-graders, but what could I do if they ganged up against me?

Thankfully, the taller I stood the further they backed down. Most of them stared into their necks. They didn't look very rebellious anymore. They looked chastened. Still, no one came clean. I upped the stakes. "We will all have lunch up here," I said.

Students swiveled around to check Rodolfo's reaction, but he stared at his desk. Seconds passed. Finally, when I moved to sit down at my desk, his voice rose up.

"Yeah, whatever," he blurted out, his face as pink as the tip of his eraser.

That was good enough for me. I hid my relief. We finished the lesson, and just for good measure, everyone stayed five minutes in lunch detention to show I meant business.

When the class left, I sat in the desk next to Rodolfo's. Despite his problems, I liked him. He reminded me of my older brother Jon, who, for dealing fireworks or bullying teachers, was a regular in the principal's office of our private school. Both Jon and Rodolfo were weak readers and hated school. They would have been best friends. The primary difference was that my parents hired an expensive SAT tutor for my brother while Rodolfo would most likely drop out. Now one was a Wall Street stockbroker, the other undoubtedly heading toward much less attractive options.

I reminded myself that my end goal wasn't to punish Rodolfo or to get even, but to teach him. Classroom showdowns weren't about winning, they were about getting the student to learn. Again I thought of Pete's advice: It's their job to act up. It's not personal.

The personal battle became instantly defused when I readjusted my view: it was the students' role to act up, and mine to manage them. Rodolfo slumped in his chair, arms dangling to the floor, feet propped up on the back of the desk in front of him. He stared straight ahead at the midday sunlight reflecting off the windowsill. He came directly out of central casting for the part of juvenile delinquent. When I met his eyes, though, he looked away. He was not angry; he was nervous.

"Rodolfo, I kept you after because I can't teach when you throw spitballs in class."

Silence. "Rodolfo, look at me." He glanced at me. "Do you understand what I mean?" He looked down. "I know spitballs are funny," I said. "Rodolfo, look at me. I don't think you're a bad student. But I'm the teacher, and it disrupts our class, and obviously I can't ignore it."

A student knocked on the door with our lunch. We ate in silence together. I didn't need to say anything else. I wanted to sit there, the two of us together, for fifteen minutes, so he would see I cared. I didn't know if this was the right way to discipline or not, but I followed my instincts. I knew little about Rodolfo, but it helped to think of him as simply a boy trying to hide the fact he couldn't read. He was looking for some attention, or being a spirited kid. Anyhow, yelling would have no effect on Rodolfo. Giving him a bad grade was not going to matter much to him, either. The punishments had to take time, be personal, come directly from me, and have a positive side that he wanted to work for. All children sought approval and attention from someone they respect.

A few minutes before lunch ended, I had them clear their desks, and I reinforced my message. I was careful to adhere to another teacher adage: Treat each kid with respect. Understand where they are, and see why they did what they did. Acknowledge.

"Rodolfo, I know it's fun to throw spitballs. I used to do it, too. But now I'm the teacher, and so it's my job to get you to stop. It disrupts the class and all we're going to learn. I don't want to see any more spitballs, Okay, hon? Anytime you want to spend lunch up here with me, you just ask, and we can have a nice lunch together. But if you choose to throw spitballs again, we're going to have some problems."

"Okay, Miss," he said.

I checked my grade book. "I'm going to get your home phone number so I can let your parents know if anything like this happens again."

He gave it to me.

"Is that your mom's or your dad's, or both?"

"My ma's."

"Do you know your dad's?"

"My dad's dead. He got shot gambling."

***

For a week I continued to devote all my energies to classroom management. Each morning we reviewed the class rules, and did exercises on them. We practiced lining up to leave for lunch. We practiced throwing away garbage. We ran drills on pencil sharpening and what to do if you had a question. One morning I devoted an hour to practicing passing back papers. My class didn't turn around all of a sudden and completely, as in that movie *Dangerous Minds* when Michelle Pfeiffer teaches her students a karate kick and then suddenly they're her angels. Nor was there one big meaningful moment when my students and I finally "got it," as in *Lean on Me*. The spitballs returned the following day, in fact. Once I was consistent with the lectures and detentions, though, the Rodolfos and the Ronnys left the dark side and joined my team. It was more like working on a painting—if you come back every day and keep at it, the image you desire starts to take form on the canvas. You have to keep at it, and if something isn't working, you have to make corrections and then come back and try again. You can't ever give up, no matter how desperately you want to start teaching actual content. After a few weeks, the spitballs stopped for good. Confronting the problem had worked and lessened my fear of confrontation. I realized there was no point in plowing through a lesson when no one was listening. Before I could teach them the difference between j and g, I had to train them to be students. My students.

I began calling them at night, visiting their homes after school to meet their parents. One visit helped create a well of trust that I could draw from when trouble started. I also realized that each time I lifted my demands, they rose to meet them—so I really started to get picky. At the slightest interruption, teaching stopped and we addressed the problem. One day I had a record twelve students in lunch detention. When half my class didn't show up in the cafeteria, Mrs. G. scolded me with a note: "You cannot keep students during lunch." I scribbled back, "Okay, next time I'll send them to your office," but then tossed it in the garbage.

For so long I had been focused on getting my students into college and cramming as much teaching in as possible, but it was the little micromanagement flare-ups that caused the big problems in class. Usually a disaster day didn't happen suddenly, but began with one student acting up and the momentum building. I learned to stop that from happening by addressing the problem immediately instead of looking the other way and letting it smolder. Soon, I was stopping the class for small infractions, like passing back papers incorrectly. Everything I taught them I reviewed three times. I used up a lot of days in the beginning, but I believed that I would be saving myself months in the end. One day I was walking down the aisles collecting homework. I balanced homework in one hand and tried to check off my grade book with another.

"I don't have my homework," Pedro called out. Neither did the next three students. Only half the class had been turning in homework regularly, and I wondered if I should stop giving it. It crossed my mind that the students here weren't used to doing homework.

That night I conducted an experiment. I called every student. At Pedro's house, his little sister picked up. When I said it was the teacher, there was a long silence. "Ooohhh, Papi, it's your teacher." Pedro arrived at the phone breathless and wary.

"Hi Pedro, this is Ms. Asquith. I'm calling to remind you to do your homework," I said. "No excuses. I want you to have it in tomorrow."

"Okay, Miss."

The next day, Pedro turned in his homework before the Pledge of Allegiance. So did everyone I called. Jovani pulled a piece of paper out of his back pocket and gave it to me. He had written his name on it. Miguel burst in panting, as if he had run straight from the bus. In his hand he clutched a piece of white paper with ten sentences written on it.

"Wow! That's great, Miguel," I said.

He smiled, reminding me of the first day when he lost his front tooth. I smiled back, and patted the special spot on my desk for Miguel's homework.

In the beginning, I had to call a lot, but soon the expectation was there, and they assumed they had to meet it. My energy gained momentum. I really wanted a good class. I invested myself physically and emotionally. I started to believe I had something important to teach and felt indignant when they didn't pay attention. I kept attendance on the board, and when students were absent, I complained. One day Valerie was absent. She lived across the street from the school, so I pulled out my cell phone and called her, in front of the whole class. "Valerie, we're counting on you being here." Five minutes later she bounded in the door, explaining that she had been helping her mom with errands. On the board I changed our attendance to 100 percent, and everyone cheered. That month we won a pizza party for best attendance. I felt proud of their accomplishments—and I told them so all the time. I felt my class coming together, albeit slowly. This was teaching, and as long as I had them nothing else mattered.

Even Rodolfo came around. He began to act out only once or twice a morning, instead of the entire time. Once, he didn't do any of my punctuation exercises, so I kept him in class for lunch. "C'mon," I said, dragging a desk up next to his and opening his notebook. "Let's do these together." He glared at me unwaveringly until I dropped the act and spoke from the heart.

"Rodolfo, if I were just trying to punish you, I'd have you copying the dictionary. Okay? I want you to learn. I have you in here practicing these because it's important to both of us that you can read."

He didn't say much, but when I pointed to the page he scrawled down the number one. And we began. That was when I understood Rodolfo's resistance: He didn't want me to know he could barely spell. I noticed him checking my reaction, and I breezed along. As we finished the exercises I told him how proud I was of him. The next time he acted out in class, I shot him my new teacher look, and it carried enough of a connection to settle him. The personal contact had been established, and now my opinion of him mattered. By giving him attention, I gave him an interest in behaving well. A few weeks later the entire class wrote letters to the *Daily News* about the city mayoral race. The paper chose Rodolfo's to print.

"If I were mayor, I would build a new school and buy food in the lunchroom, new teachers, a schoolyard, new buses, new classrooms with heaters and air conditioners, a store in the school, new desks, a big library. I'd stop the fighting and put the good students in a good school, with new computers for every student and big lockers. It will help this school a lot and the world. Rodolfo, 6th grade, Julia de Burgos."

I dropped a dozen copies on his desk, and his face lit up when he saw his name in the newspaper. His friends surrounded his desk where the paper was opened in a V. He couldn't stop smiling at me. This was what Rodolfo wanted—a taste of victory. I knew I'd won him over, at least for now.

***

As classroom management slowly improved, I turned my attention to improving the content of my lessons. I had tossed away the social studies textbook; it was useless, boring, and difficult. Mr. Rougeux didn't use it. Only the lame teachers did. I was spending a lot of time observing Mr. Rougeux's classroom. He was so talented and so kind to me. He subscribed to a weekly periodical run by *Time* magazine called *Time for Kids*. It cost less than $100, which Mrs. G. approved. Each week, twenty-five copies showed up in my mailbox with cover stories from the Pokémon phenomenon to the U.S. elections to school violence. On the back were lesson plans and project ideas. I invented many of my own. *Time for Kids* was my textbook. Forget about the Egyptians, the Incas, and the Native Americans, all of humankind's history that sixth-graders across the country were learning. I didn't have that luxury. My textbook authors weren't professors; they were the reporters and editors of *Time* magazine.

Still, that wasn't enough to fill three hours. I browsed the children's section of Barnes & Noble and found a flurry of social studies workbooks for fifth- and sixth-graders. They cost $20 each, and I bought three. I mentioned this cost to Mrs. G., hinting that I'd like to order some for my whole class.

"You, you always want books," she said to me disapprovingly.

Then she waved me away, saying the school had no money, and she had just bought me *Time for Kids*, and what would we do next year? So instead, each morning, once she'd finished her class work, I sent Vanessa to Mrs. G.'s office for fifteen minutes of photocopying and stapling pages together. Sometimes I made forty copies of five different pages and stapled them together. Mrs. G. saw this but never said anything. Pretty quickly, I had copied the whole book for every student. I imagined the photocopying costs to be far greater than the cost of actually buying the books. For some reason, this point was lost on Mrs. G.

My night class at Temple University, which the school district required of new teachers, also helped. I no longer covered material mindlessly, but learned to decide beforehand what my goal of the day was. Then I'd teach to that. So instead of writing on the board "Today we will do pages 30–33 in the workbook," I would write, "Today's Goal—To answer the question 'Why Do We Use Map Scales?'"

I also learned to start class with something snappy that grabbed their attention. In September, my lessons always began with the same, dull "Open up to page . . ." That turned off students. Teaching was like writing a newspaper story. You had to have a jazzy lede that grabs the reader's attention.

One late afternoon I reached pedagogical nirvana. The class was social studies; the lesson was mapping skills. I began with "Tell me about a time you were lost." I took a few answers.

"Now, what would have helped you find your way home faster?" Hands shot up.

"A compass," said Josh.

"A cell phone," said Vanessa.

"A helicopter," said Luis.

Gee, those were pretty good answers. "Ummm, what else?" I asked hopefully.

Finally, Pedro called out "A map!"

From that, I segued into an explanation of what a map is and how we use them. I explained what a map scale is and why people use them. Everyone was paying attention and interested, so when I asked them to open up their social studies books no one groaned. They each took turns reading aloud a short passage from the textbook that dealt with map scales.

Then I handed out a worksheet from the workbook I'd bought. The worksheet was titled "Winter Wonderland," and students were to measure distances between winter-related activities in a park. One question it posed was "How far is it from the sleigh to the ski poles?"

Every child was working, in fact, a mini competition brewed to see who could figure out the solutions first. Finally, the class reached a rare and perfect mix of challenging but doable work. Those who finished early tutored other students. Daniel helped Nilsa, who didn't understand the English. I asked Vanessa to peer-tutor Yomari. As I moved among desks, checking work, I felt a rush of exhilaration. I was teaching! They were learning, and I had got them there. There was only one slight hitch.

"Miss, what's a sledding hill?" and "Miss, what's an igloo?" No one in my class had been skiing or sledding before, so I stopped class, and we reviewed the new vocabulary.

The lesson lasted for an hour. I gave them four review questions for homework, and we moved on to reading class. I felt so proud of T61. Some of my most challenging students were soaring. They all did their work because everyone else did. When they acted up, I said things like "Do you see anyone else acting like that?" For once, the answer was no.

I kept my lesson plan on my desk:

My Weekly Lesson Plan for Reading

Reading Harry Potter

TEST on Friday: Students should know basic characters in the story, as well as setting and plot, author, date written, number of chapters. Question them about cause and effect and foreshadowing and vocabulary.

VOCAB: mysterious, tantrum, owls, cloaks, spectacles, emerald

CHARACTERS: the Muggles, Dursley, Petunia, Dudley, Mr. Dursley, the magicians, Harry Potter, Dumbledore,

OBJECTIVES: Predict outcomes, draw conclusions, make inferences, interpret cause and effect.

- Make inferences and draw conclusions about events, characters, and setting.

- Identify one-dimensional characters as opposed to fully developed ones.

- Predict outcomes, draw conclusions, make inferences, interpret cause and effect.

- Review and assess.

- Recognize organizational features in text: table of contents, chapter headings, subheadings, glossary, index.

- Write a persuasive response to work, with a point of view, judgment, reasons why, supporting evidence from text or personal knowledge; anticipate reader concerns or counter arguments, provide closure.

- Analyze literary elements (plot, setting, character, theme, and foreshadowing).

- Make perceptive connections among the texts, personal experiences, and prior knowledge.

After class Josh approached my desk and asked, "Hey, Miss, remember when you used to keep us for lunch detention?" I stopped. No, I didn't. I had a flashback from the days of lunch detention of seven students, and I realized how far we'd come in only a few weeks. This was it—I was teaching.

Teaching most of the class, that is. The challenge had become the smart kids. What did they get out of my lessons? Vanessa's dream was to attend CAPA, Creative and Performing Arts school, the city's top performing arts high school. CAPA was one of a handful of highly selective public high schools that only 2 or 3 percent of students were accepted into. I had pushed her constantly to keep believing she could do it, but by the middle of the year I needed more convincing than she did.

11
Visiting Villanova

Grassy banks. Student unions. The dark oak of dining halls. Villanova University.

Leaping out of the bus, Vanessa threw her arm around me. "Miss, this place be bangin'."

"If you work hard, you can make it to Villanova," I told her.

Several cries went up. "I want to come here, Miss!" said Mariely, one of the Hello Kitty girls.

Excellent. This was exactly the reaction I wanted. Mr. Rougeux, a Villanova alumnus, had planned a class trip to Villanova University and had said there was extra room on the bus if I wanted to invite a dozen of my students along as well. The timing couldn't have been better. I specifically invited the one group of students in my class that wasn't benefiting from my new teaching strategy: the advanced kids, such as Vanessa.

Each day, Vanessa finished her work in a few minutes, and then she waited. And waited. Attentive at first, she would then begin to tire, and her head slowly would begin to fall, followed by drooping eyelids. By 9:30 AM, as the other students struggled along, she would drift off to sleep on her perfect worksheet. I would have to maneuver around her forehead to press a "100 % !" sticker on her paper.

The longer she stayed in class, the more obvious it was she wasn't learning anything. Sometimes she tutored other girls. Other times she wrote love letters to a boy she and her friends referred to as Bebe. He was a ninth-grader at the nearby high school. She and Yahaira had met him at the arcade earlier that month. She spent a lot of time reading books I brought in for her or making up her own assignments.

"Miss, this work is baby work," she'd say. "We already done that work in third, fourth, and fifth grade."

She wasn't alone. About a dozen students, mostly girls, read and wrote at sixth-grade level, yet I had stopped giving out sixth-grade-level work because the slower kids couldn't do it. I tried to invent separate assignments for them, but that wasn't really teaching; it was keeping them busy.

This was happening throughout the school. The tough-to-teach kids absorbed all the teaching time. The bright kids worked independently or not at all. I estimated the smart, well-behaved students received less than half as much face time with teachers as the disruptive, disrespectful ones. Fair? No way. Yet the smart, obedient children would endure their boredom in silent deference to the teacher as the less-skilled kids went berserk. So who does the teacher have to cater to? While I was aware of this, I hadn't thought of a way to do much about it. In the meantime the only challenge Vanessa was receiving tested her ability to wait, endlessly—an untold number of hours each week—for the rest of the class to catch up. Perhaps a trip to college would help keep their interest alive. Only two students in my class had someone in their family who had attended college. Vanessa had an aunt who went to community college, and Big Bird had an older sister who went to Temple University. A place like Villanova would be a completely foreign concept to them.

I was secretly pleased that Mr. Rougeux would invite me instead of any other teacher, and although I tried to act professional and distant from him, my students immediately picked up on the day's subplot. Every time Mr. Rougeux and I were within more than a few feet of each other, a murmur would spread that swelled into "Oooohhhh Mmiiissss, you and Mr. Rougeux!" I shushed them and tried not to turn beet red.

Mr. Rougeux had an activity planned for his class at the computer labs. I had organized a tour and then a meeting with a Villanova student who would tell them about college life. Once we arrived they ran up and down the hills, under trees, into the dormitories, and through the chemistry labs. I explained how students lived with their friends on campus, how they chose their classes, majors, careers. I even explained the cavernous dining halls and meal plans.

After lunch, we were going to meet with a student. Villanova University's nickname was Vanillova, because the student body was predominantly white and from suburbia, like me. In the 1990s they had made an effort to integrate the campus, and I had imagined we would be able to find at least one minority student with whom my kids would identify. I had suggested the week before that we call the head of the Latino student group. Mr. Rougeux balked.

When I met the head of the Latino student group, I understood Mr. Rougeux's lack of enthusiasm. The Latino president was Puerto Rican, but that's where his similarity with the Julia de Burgos students ended. He wore a collared, pressed shirt and preppy slacks, and he shook my hand when he introduced himself. He spoke English perfectly as he told me all about how much he "enjoyed his experience at Villanova." He had an upper-class air about him. His parents may have been from Puerto Rico, but he was not going to relate to my students. As nice as he was, I doubted he would see how Villanova might connect to a kid from The Badlands. I wiggled out of inviting him to speak.

Instead, Mr. Rougeux's contact spoke to admissions about finding a student. After lunch I saw a girl walking across campus toward us. She was an eighteen-year-old freshman from New York's Spanish Harlem. When I laid eyes on her the first thing I noticed was how out of place she looked at Villanova. She wore huge gold hoop earrings, a gold chain, and a puffy silver jacket. Her hair was slicked back into a bun. Her name was Vicki and her parents were from the Dominican Republic.

"She look like the people we know," my girls said.

We settled in a conference room in one of the science buildings. She took a seat at the head of the table and looked out at my twelve students. I had assumed she would make a small presentation, but she looked like a nervous eighteen-year-old who didn't know what to say. An awkward silence settled over us.

"So, um, what questions do you have?" she asked.

My students looked at her blankly, so I jumped in.

"Can you tell them why you wanted to come here?" I asked.

"Oh, yeah. I want to be a lawyer," she said.

"So, how do you like Villanova?" I asked.

"It's awright," she shrugged.

Vanessa raised her hand. "Um, how'd you get in here?"

Vicki leaned back in her seat. She didn't seem very comfortable playing a role model. "I worked really hard back in my old school. Nobody in my family's ever been to college."

Silence again.

"You see," she said suddenly. "I wanted to make something out of my life. My friends aren't doing anything back home, and I didn't want to be like that. They hanging on the streets all day wasting their lives."

My students nodded and the room relaxed a little. Other kids asked questions about the dormitories.

"So what do you all want to do?" she asked them.

Vanessa raised her hand again. "I want to be a journalist."

She smiled at me, and it dawned on me that maybe I was having more of an influence on them than I had realized. I knew only a little bit about Vanessa's home life. Her father was in jail on drug charges and her mother worked in a bottling factory. Her mother was only a few years older than me, about sixteen years or so older than Vanessa. They looked like sisters, and they would link arms and speak together in low, conspiratorial voices. I knew Vanessa's mom wanted her to go to CAPA. She had once told me: "I want her to go to college and do better than I did."

Listening to Vanessa, I realized how badly I wanted her to succeed and live up to her potential. Other students were asking their questions, and the conversation began to flow. Some were shy, and they whispered "Miss, can you ask her this . . ." I persuaded them to raise their hands. Lost-tooth Miguel asked in Spanish if Villanova was different from her neighborhood. She nodded, answering in English.

"You know, they don't serve *arroz con habichuelas* here," she said, and then paused. "It's real different. It's like, not so easy to make friends. The students here, they party a lot and I don't really drink, so I don't go. And the classes are really tough."

Vicki's face fell as she spoke and for a brief moment revealed how lonely she was. She talked about struggling to fit in with well-to-do suburban students who had grown up in huge houses and had parents who were well-paid professionals. These people would never dream of visiting North Philly. The twenty miles from Philadelphia to Villanova masked a cultural chasm. In the same way I didn't fit in at the Puerto Rican Day celebration in my kids' neighborhood, Vicki wasn't comfortable at Villanova. However, while I could avoid North Philadelphia forever and do fine, she had less of a choice. Villanova was her ticket to a career in law—her ticket to a better life. For most students at Villanova, college was an extension of their suburban life—a continuum of food, music, and people that they had grown up with. Vicki had to give up her identity to fit in here. And of course the classes were hard. If she had come from a school system that was anything like Philadelphia's, she would have been completely unprepared to compete against kids from suburban schools. A student from Julia de Burgos would have to be ready to master a culture built on a lifetime in suburbia within a few months. Vicki hadn't done that yet.

"It's not easy here," she said. "I take the bus back to Harlem every weekend."

She looked up at me, and I felt awkward. I appreciated her honesty, but I was crestfallen. I had wanted her to be positive and to encourage my kids to strive to get here. I had worked to set up this rosy day in which they would be wooed by free pizza, football, and a bucolic landscape. I thought, "This will surely motivate them to come here." As if motivation would be enough. What would happen when it came time for a hardworking student like Vanessa to take the SATs? She was being held back as it was in my classroom. What about the following year when Mr. Jackson would be her English teacher? She'd never be prepared for college. Vicki painted an accurate picture.

"It's expensive here, too," she added. Just as the tenor of the discussion was taking on a somber tone, a Villanova University professor who had joined us jumped in. He downplayed Vicki's negativity.

"Villanova is conscientiously trying to boost the number of minority students," he said. "Finances should not be considered an obstacle. We are willing to bend over backward to accommodate and help you to get in."

The students looked a little confused, and shortly thereafter we wrapped up the discussion. My girls circled Vicki, asking her questions, and I could see they looked up to her. She was laughing and talking back.

Then we met with Mr. Rougeux's class. The football game was next. I sat up in the bleachers and let the girls braid my hair. I had brought a friend to help chaperone. He'd watched us throughout the day. "They love you," he said. I felt an elated rush.

"Yeah, I love them, too," I said. The sun's reflection off the stands shone on us as football players zigzagged around the field. The girls had gone down to the track. They laughed as they practiced a cheer.

Later Rodolfo asked if he could join a football game on a patch of grass nearby where some neighborhood boys were playing. "Sure," I said. I watched him run up to a group of white boys who had recently arrived.

"You down to play?" he bellowed at them. I watched as they stared at him in his droopy jeans, oversized football shirt, and buzz cut, bewildered.

"Yo!" Rodolfo bellowed. "Y'all down to play?"

The boys looked at him and then glanced at each other uncertainly. Rodolfo saw that they didn't understand him. He thought this was funny. He started again, speaking in a mockingly slow and clear voice.

"Do . . . you . . . want . . . to . . . play?" he said with a smirk.

The kids shook their heads and ran off, taking their football with them.

Rodolfo returned back to Ernesto and his other friends. "Stupid asses," he muttered to himself. "They not ghetto."

***

Quietly, in my own mind, I started to distinguish between the students who I believed would "make it" and those who wouldn't. I wanted to believe all my students would succeed, but there was definitely something etched into the character of some that separated some from the others. It was intangible—like a drive and an ambition. It was an inner resilience that protected them like a force field from obstacles that knocked the others off course. I wanted Vanessa to have it, and to carry her toward CAPA high school. Yet I wasn't convinced she could do it on her own. There was, however, one student who I knew was going to make it. He had more resilience by far than all the rest: Big Bird.

Ever since the first day when he shook my hand and introduced himself it had been clear that Big Bird was different. His grades were average and his speech impediment made it difficult to understand him. Nonetheless, he showed up everyday and said the same thing, "I am going to college, Miss. I want to be a lawyer."

Big Bird was eccentric. Big Bird's massive frame and meaty arms meant he didn't look the part of a smart kid. Physically, he reminded me of Lenny in *Of Mice and Men*. His hands could crush a small animal, yet he was a gentle soul. He always asked, "Why?" For whatever I said, he'd gargle, "But why, Miss?"

Big Bird loved the library and begged me to take him whenever I could. He would read the strangest books and then try to incorporate what he'd read into the conversation. For example, I once saw him reading a book about the

Wild West. After that, he started calling himself a lady's man and opening doors for me. Sometimes, as we filed out of the classroom for lunch he would jump the line and smack his plump hand against the chest of whichever boy was rushing out.

"Ladies first," he'd say, and usher me out the door.

"What's gotten into you?" I'd ask.

"Miss, I'm like a man from the old century. They knew how to treat ladies."

Big Bird had recently started reading poetry. He would wander for hours looking at different books of poems, and would cradle the frayed books, slowly mouthing the words. Later on in the school year, I found he was secretly writing poems to Juanita, a twelve-year-old girl in our class. (She rejected him.)

One Saturday I offered to take Big Bird to the library so he could read books while I corrected assignments. Big Bird lived in the commercial center of The Badlands, close to dozens of other students. I parked outside his house and walked up a few steps. Outside on the porch, which was littered with old furniture, Big Bird's two little sisters huddled in the corner, whispering. When they saw me their faces lit up, and they ran inside. "His teacher here." Of the twelve row houses on either side of his block, only one was boarded up. The block was loud and transient, and it bustled with activity around the clock. The police department was four or five blocks down, but in between was a fairly well-known drug corner, marked by dangling sneakers. Big Bird said he sometimes saw some of my students out there dealing drugs.

Both of Big Bird's parents worked. His dad worked the day shift as a maintenance worker in one of Center City's fancy high-rise apartments. His mom cut and curled ribbons in a factory near Wilmington. She worked the graveyard shift, from 11:00 PM until 7:00 AM, so she could be home during the day. Aside from Big Bird, she had three younger children and an eighteen-year-old daughter to cook and clean for. On this Saturday, everyone was at home.

As the porch door shut with a thwack, my eyes adjusted from the bright sun to the dark living room, and I came upon Big Bird lying on the couch with a sheet of paper over his face. The row house has a common layout—the living room in front, the kitchen in back, and stairs placed directly at the entrance leading up to four bedrooms. The house was worn, but clean and nicely decorated. Two couches and a few chairs sat in a circle. Plants dangled in front of lace-curtained windows, and a photo of Pope John Paul and other religious icons were placed carefully about. Two Caribbean blue parakeets chirped from a foot-wide cage.

"What are you doing inside? It's such a gorgeous day," I said.

"No, no, no," his mother shook her head and spoke in Spanish. "The problem with Philadelphia is the kids can't go outside. It's too dangerous. They come up to you and ask, 'You want to make some money? Take this package.'"

His dad was reading a magazine next to him. "*Sientate*," his mom told him, but he shook his head. He wore an aqua blue button-down shirt with a Japanese animation character on it, open at the neck enough to show a white under-tank.

"My brother is a unique person," said his older sister Jocelyn. She had recently graduated from Edison, the local high school. She was going to attend Temple University. She'd be the first person in her family to attend college. "He's himself. He doesn't follow the crowd. He doesn't like black music. He's a romantic. But that gets him in trouble. Other people don't like that."

"Do you want your son to graduate high school?" I asked his parents.

His dad shrugged. "Oh, it's too soon to say."

"Oh, I want him to go to a good school," his mother said. "A school near the house."

"Mammy!" Joceyln protested. "There aren't any good schools near here. You gotta go out of this neighborhood."

The mother looked lovingly at Juan. "No, no, *mi hijo*. You stay close to your family. You go to a school near here. There are good schools."

Jocelyn rose and sauntered towards her bedroom. "No, there ain't, mammy," she said, and shut the door.

Juan didn't say anything. Finally, we left for the library. In the car Big Bird grew pensive. "I hate this neighborhood," he said.

"Why do you think so many kids drop out?" I asked him.

"Look around you, Miss," he said, waving at the abandoned storefronts and the guys on the corner. "Monkey see, monkey do."

"I have a math question. On a scale of one to ten—one being you drop out and ten being you graduate—what number would you be?"

"Twelve, Miss. I am going to graduate."

As we drove, I could see Big Bird had something on his mind. He started to say things like "I want to be a writer, too. I'm gonna write a book about my life. It'd be a sad, sad story."

My months of teaching trained me to pick up on big hints like this. I started asking questions that gave Big Bird an excuse to open up. This finally happened when I lied and said, "Your dad seems nice."

He shook his head. "Miss, my dad got two faces." Long pause. "You saw one."

I remembered Big Bird said the first thing he would do when he got a job and money would be to buy his mom a house so she could get out. I thought about how Big Bird just took the bullying from smaller kids and never hit back, and how he hated violence. Big Bird hated his father. That was his motivation: to save his mother.

"I'm so proud of you," I said. "Tanks, Miss," he said, as we headed up the steps into the library. A few moments later, Big Bird was absorbed in his books.

***

A week later a posse of eighth-graders jumped Big Bird in the hallway and beat him up badly. He stumbled in from the vice principal's office with a black eye and didn't say anything all morning.

The vice principal told me that she had been worried about Big Bird for months. He had stopped taking the bus home. He hung around the classrooms after school. He even complained once to the vice principal that eighth-grade bullies were after him. I'd suspected he'd already been jumped once because he came into class with a giant, dusty footprint on his back. Big Bird completely denied that he'd been fighting, saying only, "Ayy, Miss, *tranquilo*." Later, I heard he had written one too many love poems—he sent one to the girlfriend of an eighth-grade thug. Some students in my class accused him of acting like he was "better than everyone else."

After he was jumped, I had him stay after school with me every day. Pedro caught on and swaggered up to my desk one afternoon claiming that eighth-graders were targeting him. He, too, wanted extra time with the teacher.

At my desk they were helping me grade papers when we heard the principal's heels clicking down the hall. She was speaking with the vice principal.

"Big Bird," I leaned over conspiratorially. "Go ask them to look at our census projects and vote for the best one," I told him.

"Why, Miss?" he asked.

"'Cause we worked hard. Just do it," I said, pushing him out the door.

That week *Time for Kids* magazine was about the U.S. Census, so I came up with a project in which each kid would create a four-part package: an essay on why the census was important, a story about the first man to be counted in the census, a persuasive essay convincing people to take part in the census, and a graph showing population growth. I was so proud of this project—our first one—I'd laminated their work and hung it outside the room, along with a sign saying, "Vote for the Best One!" The principal never checked in on my classroom—no one did—but my class had done something right, and I wanted them to feel proud. Our census project was the best thing we'd done all year. No one had noticed except Mr. Rougeux.

Big Bird bounded out of the room. Pedro and I huddled behind the wall near the door and grinned at each other as we heard the principal's heels clicking toward our doorway.

We leaned in to try to overhear her muffled voice. "What'd she say, Miss?" Pedro asked.

"Shhhhhh," I whispered, shaking my head. I felt so proud standing in the classroom knowing that she was reading our projects. Two minutes passed. She called my name.

"Ms. Asquith?" I stood up straight and moved away from the door. This was the first time the principal had ever addressed me directly.

"Uh, Ms. Asquith. Why are there posters up here with mistakes on them?"

We raced out of the classroom. The principal had a pen poised in the air and had circled the word censes on Pedro's project.

"Why is there a spelling mistake on this one?" she admonished.

"Oh." My face burned, and I leaned in to double-check. Pedro's project had a graph, and—even though he hates to write—several essays. On the tenth line of his profile, on the first man to be counted for the census, he had scrawled, in small, messy, semiscript letters, censes.

I looked up at her and said, "Well, I'm sorry that got by me."

Ignoring me, she leaned in with a felt-tipped marker poised in the air and pressed it against the poster, making a big, indelible circle. Then she applied an eagle eye to the rest of the students' work. She would be here all day. Some of my students didn't know basic English yet, I wanted to say. She circled another word. I cringed. Vanessa had spent days on hers.

Instead, I turned to Big Bird and said, "We should only have perfect papers out here, don't you think?"

"Oh yeah, Miss. What do you think of mine, Miss?" Big Bird pointed to number four, one of the best. The principal studied it for about ten seconds, then said, "Your graph is statistically incorrect because you show means on a curved latitude, and you fail to make up for the discrepancy in measurement in the north-south bar."

He looked at me confused.

"I don't understand," he stuttered. She repeated something similar, but with equally pedantic phrasing. She used a bored singsong voice. Both of us stood there, wondering how to reply when she blithely announced, "Well, I'm voting for two different ones because I'm the principal." With a smirk, she scribbled down "Vanessa" and "Big Bird," then rushed off.

12
The Principal

The principal was growing more unpopular. She abruptly canceled Ms. Vinitzsky's after-school program for at-risk kids. She brushed aside the class schedules Mrs. G. and the Bilingual Team had spent the summer organizing. She didn't speak Spanish. She was never in the halls. She was arrogant. She was filled with bad ideas. Worst of all, she forced them on the teachers sporadically and unexpectedly.

Little good comes without controversy, particularly in the face of change-resistant, routine-oriented groups like teachers. So at first I rooted for the principal, as did Mr. Whitehorne. While she had no visible natural leadership qualities, she was willing to work hard—so much so she always looked haggard—and she clearly had ambition. "Let's give her a chance," Mr. Whitehorne said one Friday at the Pedagogical Society. I trusted his judgment.

As November approached, all we had were platitudes like "Failure is not an option" and "We will be the number-one school in Philadelphia." As teachers jumped ship, students grew bolder, and the veteran teachers snubbed their noses at her reform efforts, since the principal never gave us any concrete tools or advice as to how, exactly, we could become the best city in the school. Under these circumstances, failure seemed the only option.

They say the great thing about teaching is that with each new year a school gets a fresh start. Educator Harry Wong has a theory that it's the first days of school that matter the most. This is the time when kids are sussing out how much they can get away with—feeling out the teachers for what's acceptable and what isn't. These are the critical times. If you don't get them then, you lose them for the whole year. Early on, our principal became a victim of her own inexperience. Similar to how I lost control of my class those first few weeks, the principal lost control of the entire school, and she'd never get it back.

One late autumn afternoon, shortly after seventh period, the principal came over the loudspeaker announcing an all-school assembly. I rolled my eyes. Every week we had a different, unannounced assembly.

Veterans later grumbled that she should have consulted with them. They would have suggested she specifically not bring the entire school together. Break it down by grades. She didn't have the clout or authority to control eight hundred kids. The principal thought this was the opportunity to demonstrate that she did.

Our auditorium was the school's original, built in 1905. The floor sat about one thousand people and faced a raised stage, cloaked with heavy velvet curtains. A second ring of wooden seats encircled above, and the kids liked to sneak up there. Behind the auditorium was a condemned wing of the original building. Over the years it became a dumping ground for bent desks, broken windows, and trash. It was off-limits to all of us. The ceiling leaked and plaster crumbled onto the floor.

The "assembly" never stood a chance. Before the principal could begin, the special education kids arrived. They kicked open the heavy auditorium doors and barreled in, shouting, whooping, and pushing one another. They sat where they chose, kicking up their feet and leaving empty seats and empty rows between them. Onstage, color drained from the principal's face. My students sunk down and covered their ears with their hands.

"Sit down, everyone!" the principal shouted. She watched a boy lean over his row and smack another boy across the head. "Stop that! On the count of three, we'll have total quiet. One, two, three!"

The students, many of whom were already on their fifth substitute teacher in as many weeks of school, had stopped listening. One group filed in behind T62. A frumpy-looking teacher with round spectacles motioned at them. More students poured in. Paper balls flew. Small fights brewed and fizzled and then flared up again. We waited and waited. The principal gestured wildly into the microphone. I could barely hear her.

"This is not how the number-one school in Philadelphia should behave!" she shouted. "Let's show how our school can come to an assembly."

A boy wearing a bright yellow jacket showed her his middle finger. She pointed at him. "Detention! You will spend one hour after school with me in my office." He turned to talk to his friend. The principal turned her attention elsewhere.

So many were talking and shouting that it was impossible to blame any one student. As momentum grew, I prayed a fight wouldn't break out, which could've turned into a brawl, then a riot. The principal's poor planning was jeopardizing the safety of the entire school and staff. She was also sending out a message that would reverberate for the rest of the year: the principal does not have control. This was clear. Any initial shot she had at earning the respect of students evaporated. Then she implicated the rest of the teachers in her power-lessness. Unable to make herself heard above the din, the principal raised her splayed hand, with her palm facing out, and motioned for the teachers to copy her visual plea for silence. Mrs. Tooley, the science teacher, reluctantly placed her hand in the air and pursed her lips tensely. Ms. Soleimanzadeh, the other new sixth-grade teacher, was making her way down a row, trying to reach some rowdy boys. Mr. Rougeux had his hand in the air; his students looked into their laps quietly.

The situation was too far gone to rein back in now. Our open palms just exposed our failure, and all my students were watching. The longer I held it up, the more we felt ignored. I let it slide down, and shortly after so did everyone else. The principal, on the podium, was angrily gesturing to Mrs. Jimenez.

In the row behind us, seventh-graders began to fight. Two huge girls were threatening the skinny boys behind them. They held up their notebooks as if they were going to smash them in the boys' faces. Toward the end of the aisle, some boys were flicking the butterfly hair clips in Marianna and Sayara's hair. I had to protect them.

I leaned forward and swatted their hands back.

"Where is your teacher?" I asked.

"She gone, Miss," said one of the students.

"What do you mean?" I asked. I had seen her earlier.

"She left," said another girl. I scanned the auditorium, and sure enough she was nowhere to be seen.

"What's her name?" I demanded, thinking I was going to report her to the principal. I wrote down "Mrs. Humver."

At least fifty minutes passed before the noise finally lulled. The principal squeezed in some words. "I called this assembly to congratulate the three hundred students who had perfect attendance in September," she announced breathlessly. "I'm going to call each student's name by section. Please come to the stage to receive your certificate. Anthony Rodriguez."

A gawky boy, whose baggy pants barely hung on his hips, stood up and looked around uncertainly. His middle seat meant he was forced to push past eight students, giving the audience ample time to train their eyes on his every step. A low whistle spread. He broke free from his aisle and loped forward. By the time he reached the foot of the stage, several students catcalled and booed. Perfect attendance didn't exactly make a student popular.

The principal plodded ahead, undeterred, with more names. This was what she pulled us out of instruction for? She listed five more students, when noise drowned her out. She lost control again, and this time permanently. This mass of hormones was not going to sit still for three hundred names. For the next forty-five minutes, the idea spiraled to a painful death. Angry, the principal began dismissing classes that were misbehaving, and soon half the audience was gone.

We stayed, along with a handful of other classes, and watched in disbelief as the principal suddenly beamed upon us and continued handing out awards as though nothing had happened. My class cheered as I got my award for perfect teacher attendance. At 3:05 we left.

The last message of the day was an angry one from the principal over the loudspeaker. She told all the team leaders to "Report to my office immediately." From the tone of her voice, she planned to place blame elsewhere. The failed assembly was her bad idea. I dug the scrap of paper out of my pocket that read "Mrs. Humver" and tossed it in the trash.

***

After the assembly, whatever shred of fear the students might have experienced had been washed away, and the illusion of teacher authority went with it. Whenever a fight broke out in the hallway, and it always did, teachers thought twice about intervening. Into this power vacuum stepped the teacherless special ed students. They rowdily proclaimed victory over the hallways, freely running through them.

The principal decided to crack down further. She tightened the rules about using lockers and wearing jackets so that students could no longer access their lockers during the day or wear jackets anywhere inside the school. Anyone who disobeyed was suspended. Then she started hall sweeps.

One morning I was getting my students seated when over the loudspeaker the principal barked, "We will be having a hall sweep in one minute. Anyone caught in the hallway will have an automatic detention." The hallway filled with sounds of shuffling as kids ran past and school police gave chase. As a show of solidarity with the new school policy, I harangued a late student, demanded his name, and gave it to Vice Principal Jimenez, who raced from class door to class door jotting down dozens of names.

As the boy raced off, I returned to class feeling more stupid than emboldened. Mrs. Jimenez couldn't give all those students detention. She'd have to fill out detention slips for every caught kid and track them down to give them the slips to take home for signature. They'd then have to bring back the slips and return them to Mrs. Jimenez, who would fill out more paperwork, assigning the kids to detention. The paperwork alone would take hours, and if students didn't show for detention, and Mrs. Jimenez checked to see, then theoretically, the next step was to start filling out the paperwork for in-school suspensions. There was barely room in Ms. Vinitzsky's suspension room anymore. It was filled with the special education students who had nowhere else to go.

The school's disciplinary strategy was antiquated and ineffective. The students saw this and manipulated it. After a few weeks of her "cracking down," the result was not order, but apathy. Soon, students were given so many suspensions that they became meaningless. From many students' perspective, in-school suspension was a day with Ms. Vinitzsky, who had a tender toughness that wild kids craved—and at least they would have a teacher.

**

In many ways, principals are set up for failure in Philadelphia, and our principal was the perfect example. After twenty years working in the Philadelphia school system, this was her first chance to fulfill her career dream to be a school leader. Unfortunately for her, rather than train and cultivate its leaders, the school district treated new principals as it treated new teachers, with a sink-or-swim attitude. She was hired by the school superintendent in August—giving her only a few weeks to prepare. Then she was abandoned by the school district and threatened with dismissal if she didn't do a good job.

What's more, she was white and in charge of a bilingual school that was 90 percent Puerto Rican and entirely poisoned by Hispanic politics. Our principal reported to one of the twenty-two clusters of administrators running the schools. All of the administrators in our cluster were Puerto Rican. To the principal's credit, she took Spanish lessons, but to the teachers, Puerto Rican children had to have Puerto Rican principals. To them, the position of school principal was booty too valuable to be given to someone from outside their political network. Being Hispanic was more important than being able to lead a school.

While our principal was responsible for our school's outcome, she had no power of input. She wasn't permitted to hire her own staff. She couldn't fire her staff. If there was a vacancy, she had to sit around and wait for downtown to send teachers. She had few tools available to motivate her people, such as financial rewards (a teacher's salary and status ascended automatically, independent of effort or performance). As long as teachers did not break the law, they were almost impossible to fire or punish. In fact, a teacher needed to be rated unsatisfactory for two years in a row before they could be fired. Most teachers requested a transfer before they were fired, anyway. This was all because the teachers' union held principals in a vise grip.

Here's what the *Philadelphia Inquirer* had to say about school principals in an editorial that ran that school year:

"To read the Philadelphia teachers' contract, you'd think there wasn't a principal in the city who knew how to run a school. It specifies when public-address announcements can be made. It lays out all the rules for faculty meetings, including that teachers be notified two weeks ahead of time. And it dictates an elaborate system for how teacher vacancies must be filled; neither the judgment of the principal nor anyone else at the school plays a part."

Teachers could basically thumb their noses at their principals, but they were held solely responsible for the success or failure of their schools.

***

The snow began falling sometime after Thanksgiving and didn't seem to stop until Valentine's Day. A glistening layer of ice coated my car each morning, and—being without a boyfriend—I spent the first twenty minutes of my day digging my wheels out and scraping my windshield. I wrapped my head in the scarf one of my students, Frances, gave me and wore layers of clothing because the heat didn't always work at the school. My car slid up Broad Street, past Lou's Pest Control Cockroach and the Chinese takeout place. I flipped between Howard Stern and National Public Radio. I stopped at Dunkin' Donuts for a breakfast croissant when I had time. I would wait in a long line and then call out my order: the Asian employees, the suited office workers, the police officers, and me in my Julia de Burgos spirit-day T-shirt, with the pen necklace I'd invented in November. Teachers hung silver stars from the ceiling and put evergreen trees with white paper flakes on their desks. Flashing lights dangled across chalkboards. Outside, neighbors zigzagged Christmas tree lights from one row house across the street to another and back. Blocks had Christmas parties. Community centers handed out gifts.

In early December, the principal announced a school-wide reading contest. She called it THE ICE CREAM SCOOP CONTEST! Each class had one month to read and turn in as many book reports as possible. For every five book reports a class turned in, it would receive a cardboard cutout of an ice-cream scoop. The class with the most scoops would win. I recruited Vanessa to be in charge—of course, she liked to read.

During the previous two months, reading also had become a flashpoint of pride in T61. It was the only subject we consistently worked at for forty minutes and that everyone enjoyed. We had read *Bridge to Terabithia*, *Iggie's House*, and were beginning *Where the Red Fern Grows*. When I cracked a book, a spell was cast across the room, and we'd forget we were in Julia de Burgos, where it grew worse by the day. During silent reading, we could hear the whoops and screams of other students echoing throughout the school. Tucked away in room 216 behind a locked door, I grew more relaxed and loosened up standing in front of my kids. I would dramatize scenes and read characters in voices. I could stand in the middle of them, whispering dialogue, and look up to see each and every pair of eyes clinging to me. Mr. Rougeux had lent me his raccoon-skin hat for *Where the Red Fern Grows*, which I put on every time the hounds hunted a raccoon.

The ice-cream-scoop contest could be a feather in my cap—evidence that I truly was beginning to teach. It was something we could all work on together, because the kids could work at different levels. I was very conscious that this was December, and I wanted my learning curve to flatten and my teaching to get under way. The principal promised the winning class a set of reading books, a reading rug, and an ice-cream party. As I set out to prepare my class for victory, I could almost hear our name over the loudspeaker. When I dropped Vanessa off at her house that evening, I told her, "We are going to win those books—I promise."

Several students took books home, bringing back reports every two days. The principal was due to announce the winner in January. Our tally was posted on the blackboard: a whopping twenty scoops—one hundred book reports. I was already vowing to let the students who turned in the most reports be the first on the new reading rug, in our new reading corner.

I had gone to the bookstore and bought books for Ronny's level, but he seemed embarrassed when I gave them to him. "These baby books," he said, but he took them anyway, carefully tucking them into his binder so the other students wouldn't see them.

One morning, I rushed inside the school only to feel just as cold as I had been outside. I could see my breath in the hallway. In the main office, I heard the news. Someone had broken into our school . . . again. Over the blustery, freezing night, the third floor was ransacked and the windows busted. I ran upstairs to look around. In Ms. Davis's class, the special ed classes, and many other rooms, the decorations had been ripped off the walls and the desks rifled through. Each year the school was broken into several times, most often by student dropouts, who in addition to teachers' Walkmans and candy would also steal their old files—the last remaining record of their failing grades.

All third-floor students and teachers had reported to the auditorium, so the floor was still. I stood alone up there, surveying the destruction. I wasn't sure whether I should feel angry or sad that the students hated our school so much.

Because of the snow, Ms. Rohan and Mrs. G. were absent. My room was like an icebox because the heater was broken, and despite the extreme circumstances the "no jackets in class" rule was being enforced. I brought in my high school and Boston University sweatshirts so that the kids didn't shiver all day. Therefore, we moved into Ms. Rohan's room, where the centrally controlled heater was on full blast.

The "two percent factor" students, like José R. and Jovani, were absent, which caused attendance to dip by 60 percent. I did not miss them. Jovani and José R. were still tearing up my classroom, but because they were always being suspended, they were rarely in class. By the end of the year, José R. had received so many pink slips that he had experienced in-school suspension eighty times. (That's almost half of the one hundred eighty days in the school year.) He was also absent a lot. When José R. wasn't in class, Jovani would often settle down with crayons or play on the computer. Later in the school year I would run into a teacher who had known Jovani from elementary school, and she told me he had been diagnosed EMR, educable mentally retarded. With no paperwork on him, I couldn't move him into special education; not that I would until there was an assigned teacher—which there never was that year. Once he had earned a reputation as one of the 2 percent, no other teacher would take him as a trade. I can't say he learned a thing that year.

Ms. Rohan's room, it turned out, was so hot and swampy I had to open all the windows. It was a miserable day, a day in which all the school's shortcomings bore down on us at once: teachers too apathetic to show up, students so angry they lashed out and destroyed the place, a building so ill maintained we either froze or sweltered. During my planning period, I stared out the window, watching the icicles melt and run down the frosted window pane. I scrapped my lesson plan and made up activities on the spot. I read Harry Potter for forty-five minutes, and I let Vanessa and a few other girls write songs and poetry. The boys played a CD-ROM game I had purchased. Fortunately, I had brought my laptop to motivate the kids who didn't like journal-writing but did like computers. Josh, José M., and Yomari took turns. Normally, I gave them an assignment, but instead I told them to "just journal. Write about your feelings; what made you happy or sad lately. Whatever you want to talk about."

This was what came out.

— Eddie was selling drugs and a girl was standing on the corner. eddie was crossing the street and he said what's up with you and me. I was concerned about her becuase everytime he gets a girl he rape's them.

Love, Josh

— DEAR UNCLE JUNIOR

I just want to tell you that i love you, when you come out of jail that you will do fine out here beacouse I don't like were you are now. when you come out I hope that me and you do alot of fun things.

LOVE,

JOSE.

— PARA; MS ASQUITH

MS ASQUITH YOU ARE A GOOD TEACHER

BECAUSE YOU ARE THE ONE IS MAKING

ME LEARN THE ENGLISH AND I LOVE

WHEN YOU TELL ME TO DO MY WORK

AND SOME TIME YOU GIVE ME

A PINKSLIP YOMARI

***

When report card sheets arrived for me to fill out, my students cheered and whispered wondering anxiously about their grades. I told them they couldn't see them until their parents arrived. In truth, I was stalling because I had no grades. We hadn't done much serious work, and we hadn't even had a quiz yet. I hadn't even started teaching social studies until November.

My grade book was frayed and thinning from scrubbing it with different erasers. Nearly half the names had changed from those heady first days of school, and almost everything I'd scribbled in my grade book had been erased and rewritten. I had never learned how to keep a grade book; my system just evolved through trial and error. Next to the subjects and student names were a mess of stars, letters, zeroes, dates, X's, and checks. I'd wondered how I would decode what I had marked. The seventh-grade teacher, Mr. Pautret, advised that I should simply make my best educated guess about grades.

Mostly, I graded the students on effort, not ability. The "level-one" students received A's or B's and the "level twos," like Rodolfo, got C's. It was the rest I worried about, specifically, tiny Jovani, who presented me with the greatest grading dilemma. Aside from the house he drew during those halcyon first days, neither he nor José R. had done any work. The question was, could they do the work, or had it been too difficult for them? I didn't know how to assess them. I could hardly imagine passing students who had done no work in three months. Failing them wasn't fair, either. So I gave them C's. As I slowly penciled in 75 percent it dawned on me that if I did this again next term and then the next, I would be passing them onto seventh grade. I suddenly realized how kids floated through the system.

I had other troubles. First and foremost, the report cards were wrong. When Mrs. Liss had dropped them off, the subjects listed were Spanish, ESOL reading, and social studies. However, I'd been actually "teaching" English, reading, and social studies. I almost cried for fear that all these months I had been teaching the wrong subjects. I looked for my mentor, the seventh-grade bilingual science teacher whom I rarely saw. I raced down the empty corridor, past candy wrappers and Mr. Jackson's room, where I heard him shouting at his students again. I arrived at my mentor's room and explained it all to her. She studied the sheets quizzically for a minute and then shrugged.

"Mark W for the Spanish and combine everything else." W meant "withdraw."

"But they didn't withdraw from Spanish. It was never offered to them," I said. "What are my kids going to think when they get a grade for social studies and no grade for English? I've been telling them since September how important their English grade would be."

She shrugged. "I wouldn't worry about it. Most of these kids don't even pick the report card up."

"My students do care," I told her.

"See Mrs. G. about it," she said.

In her office, Mrs. G. immediately informed me she had nothing to do with whatever my concern was and directed me to see Mrs. Liss, the attendance lady and all-around administrative person. When I finally found her, she sent me back in a circle: Mrs. G. was in charge of report cards, she said.

"Look, Mrs. Liss," I said, panting. "Can we get this changed in time?"

Mrs. Liss was a sweet, absentminded veteran teacher who'd been in the Philadelphia school system since the early 1960s, the days when it actually worked. "It's too late now for this term," she answered. "Oh, Ms. Asquith, I wouldn't worry. The students don't even look at them."

Later that day the principal called an after-school report card meeting. "From the beginning of the year," she said, "I've said that failure is not an option at Julia de Burgos. Yet, I've seen that many of you have not only failed students, but given grades as low as the 30s and 40s." She gripped the podium like a shield. "Failing a student, any student, with a grade as low as a 50 this early on in the year virtually eliminates their chances of passing the year," she said. A student's final grade was cumulative, based on a total of four grades, each given every few months.

"I'm not saying that you should automatically pass a student. I am not saying that." What she did say was that she wanted us to raise this first grade up to at least a 64 so that, despite the failing grade, there was still a chance to raise the mark by the end of the year. This, she stressed, was in accordance with school district policy. "Let's give them a chance. It's only fair," she added.

No one said anything. Her curt, no-nonsense tone implied that this was not open for discussion.

"Additionally," she said, "I saw that a lot of the special education students had been failed."

She told us that, by law, special ed students had to have an individualized education plan (IEP), which was an analysis of their disabilities, along with strategies for teaching to those disabilities. I wasn't sure whether our students had IEPs. Mr. Whitehorne complained that they were incredibly labor intensive to create. The student had to be screened and tested. A parent had to come in for a meeting. Some students might need extra test-taking time or a personal reading tutor or a bilingual text.

How could we possibly evaluate every special ed student for an IEP? We had only a few guidance counselors for eight hundred students. There were only two full-time special ed teachers left for one hundred special ed kids, and one of those teachers worked full-time on "paperwork." Even if the students had IEPs, there was no teacher to follow them.

The rule was if we couldn't provide an education that fit their special needs, we couldn't hold them responsible for their performance. So, education or not, we had to pass them all. I wondered who in my class was officially labeled special education.

Mrs. G. raised her hand. "And since we have no ESOL program, you can't fail ESOL kids, either."

Wait a minute. I thought every student in my class was labeled ESOL.

The principal nodded her head in agreement. The atmosphere thickened into a palpable quiet. Most of the teachers remained expressionless, fixed in the wooden chairs like robots.

"Shut that off," the principal said.

There was a student in the corner with a video camera. Earlier they had been filming a portion of the vice principal's ten-year anniversary celebration. The kid had kept the camera on, recording everything the principal had said. She strode around the library card catalogue toward him, but he continued to film her.

"Uh, let's turn that off," she said. "I mean it. Off."

The student squinted through the eyepiece, backing away from her. He refused to put the camera down. "Let's have it," she said. "Okay, Okay now . . . we don't want this on film. We don't want to be on *Hard Copy* tomorrow."

Several teachers laughed. The principal attempted to chuckle along, like she was in on the joke. A few teachers whispered animatedly and smiled. Then Mr. T., the former lawyer, stood up from his seat in the center of the room.

"Headline," he shouted, spreading his arms: "SCHOOL FAILS SPECIAL ED STUDENTS!"

With that, the whole room erupted into laughter. Teachers were doubling over, making more jokes. I laughed, too. What she was telling us to do was so unbelievably wrong, yet she had been doing her best to normalize it. No one had the guts to stand up and challenge her, but now we didn't have to. A student had caught her.

The principal forced out a few more chuckles, making sure everyone saw that she was also in on the joke. I couldn't stop laughing as she calmly walked over to the student with the camera, plucked it from his hands, and shut it off.

***

The principal announced that Mr. Rougeux and I tied for first place in her Ice-Cream Scoop Reading Contest. We received school-wide recognition over the intercom. This was a huge victory, and my students encircled me, cheering and exchanging high fives. They were so proud of themselves, and we were on a high for the entire afternoon. Neither Mrs. G. nor anyone else on my "team" congratulated us, but I no longer expected it. I gave each student a "recognition" certificate to take home to their families. We planned out where we would put the library of books that the principal had said would be our reward.

***

There were no students on Monday. Imagine . . . a day with only adults—just like most people's jobs! The school felt both hauntingly abandoned and pleasant. I got two more awards for perfect attendance, and I could crack jokes, discuss world politics, and gossip about my weekend. God, I missed adults.

By the end of the day, though, I missed kids again. One of the cluster administrators droned on for an hour about a multimillion-dollar federal grant we just won.

"What has it been spent on so far at our school?" I asked.

"It has helped pay for the tutors from La Salle University. You know, so we could add a little boost to their salary to make the job more attractive. That's about it."

That didn't even begin to make a dent in the money. How about some more workbooks? Either the money was wasted, or this cluster lady was clueless, and why did we have to sit through this, anyway? Our days were so rushed, and the problems so time consuming, that a full day training with colleagues was precious. This wasn't a day for us to learn to better help students. It was a day for the cluster people to fulfill requirements of their grant-money salaries.

Then the principal took center stage. I wondered if she was still going to try to maintain this outward appearance in front of her bosses that our school was fine. How could she? I couldn't help but think about those first few meetings, and how I now weighed everything she said against the promises she made in the beginning.

"We are the lowest-achieving middle school in the city," she began. "There are forty-two middle schools, and we are forty-second. I don't want to say we have great teachers and a great program and are making changes, that despite these strengths we are still number forty-two. That just doesn't validate anything we do."

For the first time it occurred to me that this year had been a failure for her, too. It wasn't entirely her fault. How did she convince herself to come to work every day? At the end of the year, would she wonder if she had suffered through 180 days for nothing? I often wondered if certain kids would have been better off staying at home in front of the TV or roaming the streets, because at least then they wouldn't have been packed together like sticks of dynamite.

When the training finally started, the principal posted three large white pieces of paper on a blackboard. She listed "What Works," "What Needs to Be Fixed," and "What Doesn't Work." She steered us toward problems like lockers and agendas, but one teacher after another interrupted to complain that the principal was trying to pressure teachers into changing grades and passing every student.

"If the student fails marking period one, two, and three, and we've done some things to help, then the parent comes in at the fourth marking period and goes ballistic, why should we have to pass them?" George the math teacher asked. "Isn't that unfair?

Indeed—and illegal, too. Just last year, the school board had abolished social promotion. Social promotion meant that once students reached a certain age, they were to be promoted regardless of their grades. With social promotion, the city had the problem of illiterate twelfth-graders. So they abolished it, and now we had the flip side problem of fourteen-year-old sixth-graders. Who knew what was worse? The principal seemed to prefer the latter.

Mr. Whitehorne stood up and complained that the requirements were still too burdensome. "What we have is de facto social promotion. We've erected so many hurdles that they can't fail."

Ms. Davis, the science teacher, was nodding at Mr. Whitehorne. She was looking at a summer of paperwork if she stuck to her guns to fail most of her class.

The principal sounded defensive: "You guys have known since September what is required. I have parents in here that say 'I can't believe my child failed and the teacher never called me.' Parents are more informed than they used to be and they know their rights. As a parent you would be highly indignant if your child failed and you didn't know about it. I'm just saying, protect yourselves."

Soon, she would clarify exactly what she meant.

13
Changing Grades

Third-marking-period report cards were due in just a few weeks, and the complaints from that last meeting had now swelled into an uproar. "Failure is not an option at Julia de Burgos" became a sarcastic sneer among teachers, especially after the principal sent around the following memo:

1. *For all students who may receive a failing 3rd report card, please submit the following by Wednesday March 15th.*
   A. *A copy of all the grades upon which you base this decision.*
   B. *A list of all the times you contacted parents regarding the imminent failure.*
   C. *A copy of the complete CSP Tier 1 report that your team worked on.* [This was a four- to six-page paper that a teacher had to complete with her team. It documented the problem, strategies, separate work given, and outside sources the teacher arranged to help the student.]
   D. *A behavior performance review.* [This was a two-pager in which the child's behavior and all the teacher's responses were recorded and dated.]
   E. *A list of all supports and accommodations you used to pass this child.*
   F. *A list of the activities that the student needs to make up to pass.*

This list of requirements was intentionally impossible to meet. Failing a student would require a full-time secretary, according to this memo. The problem was not only the paperwork involved, but all the meetings with parents and other teachers. Furthermore, what happened to student accountability? Why did we have to have supports and accommodations for each and every child? Why did we have to give them second-chance "activities" they could do to pass? Plenty of students in my class worked hard to pass the first time around.

And where did that leave a student like Jovani?

The school hadn't provided Jovani with special ed, ESOL materials, a trained teacher, aides, a psychological evaluation—any of the supports he was legally entitled to. Jovani hadn't even received any textbooks. What were we holding him accountable to? The final result would be that I would pass him on to the seventh grade as a student who couldn't read, write, or do much else academically. Sadly, I could say the same for José R., Ronny, Yomari, and about six others. When I actually counted, I was astonished—that was 25 percent of my class.

That wasn't the end of the memo. Just in case teachers still had too much wiggle room, the principal added on these other requirements:

2. *No special education students are to receive a grade lower than "65" or a "Withdrawal" without written permission of the Principal.*
3. *No student is to receive a grade lower than a "64."*
4. *Students attending and completing satisfactory work in Saturday School will have the Saturday School grade count as 25% of their marks.*

Ms. Davis had been persuaded to raise all grades to 64, supposedly to give her students a chance to pass the year. The principal created this Saturday School, and even if a kid received a grade as low as 66 it was enough to eke by. The students would pass. The principal would boast a high-pass rate. Her accomplishments would be twice as impressive.

At the bottom of her memo, our call to arms:

Remember, failure is not an option at Julia de Burgos. We must make every attempt possible to help our students be successful.

***

During lunch one day, I visited the main office to look through my students' files. I was alone except for a few secretaries. The vice principal and the team leaders handled most of the discipline in their offices, so it was rare for a student to come in. A parent sat in the waiting bench by the door, his tough face tucked into the flannel lining of his scuffed jacket. Staring down at him from high on the wall was the melancholy face of Julia de Burgos, the Puerto Rican poet. I knelt on the floor, pulled open a cabinet door, and turned first to Jovani's file. I flipped through my students' names again and again. Jovani's file was missing. I continued to look and couldn't find several other students' files, either.

Behind me, a secretary clicked away at her computer. I said, "Excuse me, I'm looking for some students' files, and they're not in here."

"What's his name?" She typed Jovani's name into the computer and found him registered. "His records must be at his old school," she told me. "We'll call them and have them send it over."

Back in the files, I gazed at old class photos of my students. They looked so small and cute, with bows in their hair and missing front teeth. About half the class came from Cramp Elementary School, a kindergarten through fifth grade about one mile north of Julia de Burgos. There were state and city test scores, all of which were under twenty out of one hundred, and some were as low as one. There were old teacher reports describing some students as "wonderful in class but behind academically" and some as having "anger inside." Many folders were missing; others had missing information. José R.'s thin folder made no mention of special education. One student's folder didn't mention any special status either, even though Mrs. G. specifically told me this student was evaluated as special ed and that I should go read his folder.

The big surprise for me was the number of students in my class who had already been retained or left back. Scanning all my students' files, I learned half had repeated a grade twice. They weren't even in middle school and had been held back twice? I realized why there were so many thirteen-year-olds in my sixth-grade class. I rested my elbows on the cabinet in frustration. For months I had puzzled over why past teachers would promote illiterate students. They hadn't. In light of this, my question wasn't Should I pass or fail them? but How did I make them learn? Likewise, who cared whether Jovani was labeled special education? We didn't even have a working kitchen in our cafeteria. There were no special ed services available for him here.

It was true. Failure was not an option.

14
Arsons

Pick battles big enough to matter, but small enough to win.

—Jonathan Kozol, *On Being a Teacher*

By springtime, our school was so out of control, it was safer for most kids to stay home. Each morning, I would hustle everyone into the classroom and lock the door. Same thing after lunch. During class time, we would hear the screams and whoops of packs of students roaming the hallways, ripping things off the wall, and beating up other students.

One cold, sunny morning, three girls were stuffing paper into a bottle in Mr. Jackson's "Spanish class." Mr. Jackson wasn't watching. They torched the paper with a lighter, and dropped the bottle like a Molotov cocktail down a hole in the wall. It landed in the cafeteria storage room.

As the flames crept along, I played Multiplication Bingo with H77, Rogia's special education class. Eight students sat at their desks, but only one knew how to multiply. We switched to Addition Bingo. Rogia had her hand in the air when the fire alarm blared.

"Go ahead, Rogia," I continued. The fire alarm rang two to three times a day, so we ignored it. Rogia was upset because she'd missed the question.

"Murmur, murmur, murmur . . . fire alarm," came over the intercom, once, then again.

"Rogia, hon, let's just try this one more time," I said, holding up fingers to count.

The principal's stony voice interrupted me. "This is a real fire. Please evacuate the building."

Two kids bolted. I shut my windows, picked up my purse, turned off the lights, and lined up my remaining students. The hallways were packed. Everyone was charged up, almost to the point of panic. My students dissolved into the crowd on the stairwell. I pushed my way down to the fire exit, and crossed the street to my designated fire meeting spot, hopping over islands of ice and snow lining the curbs. Hundreds of students milled about, white blowpop sticks jutting from their mouths, hoods pulled over their ears. Within minutes, familiar faces reappeared. Rogia clung to my side. The principal rushed around, yelling orders at everyone, and no one was paying attention. Fire trucks arrived. I looked around for smoke. Was there a shooting, a suicide, a bomb threat?

"Hi, Miss! Miss, there a fire?" A boy with a toothy grin looked up at me.

It was Wilson, a boy I knew from a special education class I'd covered. "I don't know," I said.

Students encircled us, drifting in and out of conversation. I hopped around to keep warm.

"Miss, you still got that map game you gave us?" Wilson asked wistfully.

I nodded.

"We got a new substitute today, Miss," he said. I looked past his shoulder to see a brunette woman holding a lesson-plan book. She'd pulled her scarf over her chin, gritting her teeth. Around her, students pointed and laughed. "You got extra room in your class, Miss?" he asked.

Before I could answer, three other boys barreled into him from behind. Their vinyl jackets swooshed against each other.

"Yo, man, is that your new teacher?" asked one of them.

Wilson cracked up. "Yeah, man, we already kicked her out!" he shouted, jabbing his fingers at the lady. "We busted her out of the class on the first day."

Wilson was swallowed up by a whirlwind of boys. Everyone yelped and swooned, challenging the new substitute. She pretended to ignore it. They crowded around her, shouting, until she turned away. They regrouped around her. I went over to introduce myself.

She spoke a couple of words with a thick Eastern European accent, then stopped responding. She waved me away. I imagined her returning to her neighborhood, telling of her experiences with these inner-city "animals." She would speak from an isolated day or week, not knowing the months, or years, of neglect and abuse that created their behavior. They hadn't had a teacher all year.

After forty-five minutes we sought refuge in the cafeteria of a nearby elementary school that fed into Julia de Burgos. Four hours later we were speechless from hunger and cabin fever. No one had any news about the fire. Many students laid their heads on the tables. Others leapt up on the tables, danced, then ran out through the hallways. The elementary school teachers glared at us.

One hour slipped past, then another, and another. For a while I'd tried to have a class discussion, but the students lost interest without the books. Gossip trickled in: There was a lot of fire and water damage; we wouldn't be returning until the next day. The cafeteria's backless benches made sitting still uncomfortable. The light was dim and colored, and after a few hours, I felt sleepy and restless.

Vanessa sat next to me. She had been participating less in class lately, and I knew she was bored. Yet she showed up each day, the only student in my class with perfect attendance. She brushed my hair. We chatted, and a couple of boys played GameBoy. Two girls played with my cell phone. Then, finally, we did nothing—sat and thought, holed up for what turned out to be five hours with nothing to eat, drink, or do.

Vanessa began to nod off. As we sat there wasting learning time, I tried to see school through her eyes. Later, I would try to calculate how many days of the year I could describe as "wasted learning days." Nothing official, just my best guess as to how many days the kids learned nothing useful—days when they would have been better off at home watching TV than exposed to the dangerous influences at Julia de Burgos. There were the useless assemblies; pointless interruptions by Mrs. G.; botched lessons, given my inexperience; the entire botched month of September and most of October, given the absence of any materials or guidance while I learned to teach; Ms. Rohan's ten sick days; five weeks of disruptions from other seventh- and eighth-graders transferred temporarily into our class; and several dozen fire alarms. None of these factors were my students' faults. Then there was the entire month of January, spottily attended because of weather and family trips to Puerto Rico. It was impossible to do anything that month except one-day, time-filler activities. Vanessa and many others, like Pedro and Big Bird, suffered. For them, the reward was dozens upon dozens of days sitting idly, staring bored at the blackboard, wondering why they should bother going to school at all. I would have felt exactly the same way.

My final estimate of wasted learning days: at least 60, or one-third of the required 180 days.

For students like Jovani, who was suspended regularly, the figure was much worse. These students were nearly, if not entirely, illiterate in English and Spanish. This was a year in their life—one of the last years they would have in school. If I didn't teach them these things in sixth grade, they'd be gone in seventh and that would be it. It was their opportunity to learn English, to read, to add double digits, to tell time, explore, question, ponder, decide. And it was being wasted away, hour by hour.

Finally, buses arrived. Teachers were allowed back in the school. The building reeked of sodden ash. I wandered the hallways, looking for damage. Sometime that year, I had started calling Julia de Burgos "my school." I'd felt a growing attachment, a feeling much like family, but here among the ruins I resisted those ties. My room was fine, but three other classrooms had been almost destroyed. In one class, the windows were broken. In another, water stains had ruined the teacher's bulletin boards with her homemade class rules. I stood alone in the doorway, taking in the stench of smoldering plastic.

Ms. Vinitzsky's room was the worst of all. It had been used for in-house suspensions. The walls dripped with water. Chairs were blackened and up-ended. She shrugged and said, "I needed a bigger room anyhow." Other teachers arrived behind me.

The principal called a meeting in the library. She congratulated us whole-heartedly on a "smooth evacuation," even adding a thumbs-up. I didn't understand until I realized the cluster leader, her boss, was in the audience. She had rushed to our school in case the fire attracted TV news coverage (which it didn't). The whole incident was treated as an accident—as though lightning or a blown fuse had caused the fire. It was no coincidence that systematically neglected students, feeling bold and angry, could build a firebomb right under a teacher's nose. It was no coincidence that the teacher was Mr. Jackson, whose class had to be disbanded in November because he didn't even have a shred of an idea how to teach them. This was a culmination of seven months of "education." It might be a harbinger of worse to come. It was. Within six weeks, we had another major arson. No one would be hurt, but we were evacuated again for the day, and there was more damage.

One teacher commented that the kids were lucky. The fire could have been worse. He said that the part of our building behind the auditorium, which had been boarded up and condemned years ago, was filled with garbage, rotting wood, and broken desks. If the fire had reached that section, the whole place could have burned to the ground.

***

When school began, Mr. Whitehorne, one of our most popular teachers, played "La Bamba" on the guitar at the end of each school week. He played with a flourish of strumming, singing the Spanish words, after meetings in the auditorium, and at the end of most school events. The song rallied us and quickly became our theme.

Around this time, Mr. Whitehorne stopped playing "La Bamba" on his guitar and at some point the principal stopped saying, "Failure is not an option." This week, she called another library meeting. The topic might as well have been "Julia de Burgos Spins Out of Control!" because that's what we all felt.

"Maintaining meaningful content in your curriculum is the most important tool in discipline," she said. "I want interesting instructional material. I don't expect to go into any classrooms and see soap operas unless it is in your lesson plan and tied to state standards."

Cluster officials had caught several teachers showing soap operas during class time, and the principal had been reprimanded. Morale was low. Absenteeism was frequent. We needed more teachers. We were demoralized to the point of paralysis. No one cared anymore, and we hadn't even made it to spring yet.

The arsonists were eventually found and expelled. They were sent to Able Academy and Boone, both schools for delinquent kids. One of the girls, Gina, had been repeatedly suspended for fighting and drugs. The school had inches of paperwork documenting her reign of terror, yet we had never been able to expel her until this catastrophe. In this case, the paperwork was important to protect the teachers from administrators looking for a scapegoat.

The expulsion upset Mr. Whitehorne, not because it was the wrong thing to do, but because he had a long list of students he had tried to transfer to discipline schools throughout the year, only to be stonewalled by administrators.

"When it's a high-profile case, you see how quickly they can move," Mr. Whitehorne said.

The following Thursday, police were at our school again. On my way back from the sandwich store, I held open the front door for a boy being escorted out in handcuffs. A dozen boys had already been arrested at our school that year, yet it still shocked me. This boy in handcuffs was what the rest of the city heard about. A small minority of bad teachers and that 2 percent of lost students overwhelmed the good we did. Security told me he'd been arrested for having a weapon. I didn't ask if he had used it.

***

I hadn't had a prep period in weeks, and working around the clock was wearing on me. Teachers were supposed to receive at least one forty-minute period each day to correct grades, do administrative work, and rest. Every prep of mine was filled with a "coverage" for a special education class. That was forty minutes of grueling shouting and scrambling. I was coming to the end of my rope—we all were.

The teachers organized an emergency meeting. A student had threatened Ms. Fernanda, the seventh-grade English teacher, with eight-inch-long metal scissors. In the library, Ms. Fernanda stood in her billowing skirt and described what happened. "He walked up to my back and held the scissors, and then made sexual gestures. The scissors also touched me," she said. All the forty-five teachers in the room were quiet. This was bad, but worse things had happened this year without any teacher meetings being called. Would this be the final straw?

"In the thirteen years since I've been here, this is the worst it's been," our union leader said. "We had Ms. Johnson pushed on her back. We've had Ms. George assaulted. Now Ms. Fernanda, and it's not over yet. The warm weather is coming, and it's only going to get worse."

From a table in the center, Ms. Vinitzsky stood up: "What happened to the boy who assaulted Ms. Fernanda?"

"He was suspended for three days out of school," Ms. Fernanda said. "But not before I had to cover that class again with him in it. The students saw what he did. They see that we don't do anything about it."

Ms. Vinitzsky said, "That boy is the one the girls complained had his penis out in the hallways. I mean, why can't we do anything? That's a sex crime! He should be arrested."

Someone asked Ms. Fernanda if she'd asked to have the boy arrested.

"No. That kind of behavior tells me that he himself was probably sexually abused," she said. "He needs counseling, not to be arrested."

Looking around the room, I saw a lot of good teachers. There was Mrs. Tooley, the science teacher, who mixed strictness with love and won her kids over by inspiring them; Mr. George, whose teaching style was so clear, no-nonsense, and interesting that he had his eighth-grade math class already doing algebra. Ms. Vinitzsky, whose stern love could seat even the most angry special education students. (Mr. Rougeux, of course, had skipped the meeting.) We needed more good teachers like this—a whole school of them. All the vacancies and untrained teachers overwhelmed the rest.

The union leader stood up. "What we're considering is an informational picket."

Mr. Whitehorne explained that it was against our contract to strike, so an informational picket meant arriving early and protesting outside the school before 8:20 AM. All the teachers murmured. This was a big deal.

"Look," Mr. Whitehorne continued, "What we're talking about here is a protest, and it won't work unless we have support from everyone, and everyone is on board. If only fifteen or twenty teachers are going to show up, forget it. There can be none of this: 'Oh, that morning isn't good for me.' If we're going to do this, we have to do it right. We'll have signs and press releases and media coverage."

"What is it exactly that we want to ask for?" I asked.

"We want teachers for the special education students, and if they can't get them, then the kids need to be transferred somewhere they can get services," Mr. Whitehorne said. "Then, we want the paperwork for getting students into the discipline school expedited."

Ms. D. raised her hand. "Is this picket going to hurt my chances of getting hired in the suburbs?"

"No, no," Mr. Whitehorne answered. "But we have to be prepared to stand by each other. It doesn't mean there won't be recrimination or attempts to pick off those perceived as leaders. Brothers and sisters"—his speech was now like a sermon, complete a few "Amens"—"We have to put a stop to this. These are kids that haven't had a teacher all year. And you've seen what the bureaucrats want to do about it. They want to cover it up. They're not trying to solve it. If we get out there, and parents see us, it will say something. We've done it before, and it has reenergized the whole staff."

When he finished, we applauded. Thank God for Mr. Whitehorne. Here was someone who could command attention and make change—a true leader. Why he wasn't principal? The district's "Principal Certification" program required years of classes and tuition money, and he just couldn't afford it.

Mr. Whitehorne's words gave me strength. I wanted to believe that we could change things for the better. I felt this surge of confidence and gratitude. I wanted that protest. I wanted to do something to show that we weren't just ignoring what was happening here. I needed to act because I was aware of my growing complacency.

The protest never happened. The administration stalled us with promises, and then the school year ended.

***

I looked up to see *Time for Kids* twisted into a baton. Jovani and José R. were on the verging of pummeling each other to death. I took a deep breath and readied myself. My class had come together over the last few months, and I was teaching almost every day, with one exception: when Jovani and José R. were both in class. Together, they were too strong a force to reckon with. Lifting his magazine, Jovani hit José R., who then screamed, fell out of his desk, and faked dead. I ran through the routine—The Teacher's Laws of Least Intervention: I negotiated; I threatened detention, suspension, and phone calls home; I promised good grades, gum, and a certificate. Nothing worked.

"Just ignore him," I said to the class. "Don't get yourselves in trouble." They did ignore him for a few minutes, but it was too distracting. Jovani got up and tried to knock over the list of vocabulary words I had standing by my desk. I stopped the lesson.

"Jovani, go to Mrs. G.," I said.

"Good," he shouted back, and walked out before I could give him a pink slip.

He returned a few minutes later. Mrs. G. had sent him right back. I could see the students were frustrated. The louder I raised my voice, the louder José R. became. Then he buried his head into his desk and began whistling. It was impossible to ignore. I ordered him to leave.

Mrs. G. told me that a teacher sent José R. to her at least once a day, and the week earlier she had received ten pink slips on him in five days. Punishing him was a double-edged sword because he was suspended so frequently he missed out on projects and fell constantly behind. After three days working on a lesson, the gym teacher would have José R. suspended, and he'd miss the test. Or worse, he'd miss three days of lessons and then show up on test day. He'd cause such a distraction that he'd ruin the test for everyone. Mrs. G. was trying to place him in special education, but that process would take months.

"See ya!" he cheered as he shuffled out. Jovani, in the same oversized dirty turtleneck and sweatpants, tucked himself into a corner and gloated.

For two minutes, class returned to its serene cooperation and quiet. Ronny answered a question and offered to read aloud again. The girls underlined vocabulary words. Then the door flew open and banged against the wall.

"Mrs. G. n' the vice principal ain't in their offices," José R. mumbled. School security stood behind him, escorting him back to my class (i.e., making sure he was out of their hallways). My perfect lesson dissolved. Finally, I confiscated José R.'s magazine. While the rest of the class watched and waited, I got out the special workbook I had bought him. He pushed it aside. I tried to continue, but he was muttering in Spanish, distracting everyone.

José R., who weighed at least 150 pounds, was rolling his head back and forth and laughing as he swatted at tiny Jovani. I put my head in my hands. I was trapped—what good was another pink slip on José R.? The copies I kept in my desk were mounting:

Dec. 2: "José R. punched Dominique in the arm. I told him to stop and he raised his arm threateningly at her. He refused to move his seat and was disruptive all day long." (Mrs. G. gave him a one-day, in-school suspension, referred him to a counselor, and called his mom for a conference.)

Dec. 8: "José R. threw a ball of paper which hit me as I was talking." (Mrs. G. delivered a one-day, in-school suspension and set up a conference between José R. and me.)

Jan. 6: "José R. was continually entering and leaving the class. Finally in class, he was throwing into the air a soda bottle and making loud noises and ignoring me. When I passed his desk, all the students said he made an obscene gesture at me with the bottle." (Mrs. G. gave him a one-day, in-school suspension and called home for a conference.)

Ronny had put down his pencil and was talking again. I snapped at him: "Ronny, do your work, I'm not going to tell you again."

Ronny shoved his binder onto the desk. "Miss, can I change classes? I hate this class."

There was a growing list of students who wanted out of the class that Jovani and José R. were in, and they said so openly.

Ronny's future worried me the most of all. Ms. Rohan said she had met with his father the previous week, and he said if Ronny didn't learn how to read this year he'd be pulled out of school for good. Ronny's father ran several profitable bodegas in the neighborhood, and he felt that if Ronny wasn't learning in school, his time would be better spent at work. I knew Ronny wanted a better life for himself than that of a store clerk. His last chance at an education was drifting away.

While I tried to figure out what I could do that would be different from every other strategy I'd tried, the class snapped.

"Shut up, man!" Ronny yelled at José R.

"Yeah, sit down," another student called out. José R. didn't bow to the pressure; he jeered back. Soon, the whole class was yelling at José R. to shut up. Ronny, Rodolfo, the clique of little girls—Sayara, Marianna, Yazline, and Penny—all made themselves known:

— "We wasting all our time."

— "He always be ruining class."

— "I wanna change to T61."

I felt stunned, embarrassed, and pleased all at once. This was vigilante justice, and it was the last straw. I decided at that moment that whatever happened, I was going to teach—nothing could stop me. For the rest of the day, the class reviewed vocabulary, voiced their opinions, and wrote essays. José R. and Jovani waged battle, smacking each other as hard as possible with the workbooks I had bought them. It was a bizarre scene—90 percent of the class sitting angelically answering questions while two kids tried to kill each other. They fought, and we tried to ignore them. Ten minutes before school ended, from the back of the room, José R. shouted, "Miiiiissss, Jovani be hitting me. Help!"

"I don't care," I said. "You're getting an F for the day."

It was one thing for them to waste my time, but they were also wasting everyone else's time. I couldn't bear Ronny's helpless gaze at me, pleading for me to do something. Kids like Ronny were already so far behind in life that they were about to give up. Jovani and José R. were pushing their classmates' heads further under the water. No matter how they struggled, Jovani and José R. held them down. Back in September, I'd felt sympathy for the bottom-rung students, like Jovani and José R. Life hadn't been fair to them, either. Now my compassion had cooled. My attitude was hardening. They had transformed themselves in my eyes from victims to bullies.

***

I kept Jovani after school. If I kept both boys, they would giggle at me, so I let José R. go and promised to call his mother again. Jovani sat silently for fifteen minutes, withering under my glare. Technically, I was not supposed to keep students after school without writing them a detention the day before and sending a letter home to arrange alternative transportation. That system never worked because effective discipline had to be swift, and it had to be delivered personally. Alternative transportation didn't exist, so if I wanted him to stay I had to drive him home myself.

Mrs. G. had warned against this. "If anything ever happened, you'll be sued. They'll take your house." I knew Jovani would disappear en route to any other detention room. The school's discipline policy was effective only on paper.

I tried to call his mother on my cell phone, as I had a dozen times before. I had one phone number for him: his aunt's. Whenever I'd called her before she'd promised his mom would call back, but she never did. This time, no one answered. I had run out of consequences for Jovani.

After twenty minutes of silence and then a lecture, I swung my teacher bag over my shoulder and marched out the door. "Let's go."

"I'll walk home, Miss," Jovani informed me.

"No, I'll take you." I stomped along. I didn't have to pretend; I was furious, frustrated, and most of all, desperate. He skipped beside me down the long hallway, showing no sign of fear.

"I'm going to come inside and talk to your mother," I said. This time he would feel bad. I'd seen the way his mom disciplined him with a stare. Across the parking lot, Jovani yanked open the car door and climbed in the front seat.

"Oh, no!" I shouted from the driver's side. The front seat of the teacher's car was a major treat for students. "In the back."

Still expressionless, Jovani got out and hopped in the backseat. "I can walk, Miss. I live close," he whined. He was nervous. As we got in, I flipped open my grade book. Under Jovani's name, I had written "Third and Indiana." I wasn't sure where it was, but I figured I could navigate. "Seatbelt," I ordered, and he turned his entire body to grab it.

We cruised up Seventh Street for about a half-mile or so to Allegheny. We passed garages with big puffs of smoke coming out the top. Philadelphia had hundreds of cars stolen each year (including mine, last year), and here was chop-shop central. Toward the top of Seventh Street I remembered to lock the door. Certain areas in North Philly made me more nervous than others: a corner with too many guys lingering, a strip of abandoned houses. The second-to-last block on Seventh made me nervous, but locked in my car and driving quickly, I assumed I was safe.

I made a right on Allegheny, passed under a railroad bridge, and made another right, onto Third. Jovani giggled louder.

"Miss," he teased from the backseat. "Miss, I don't live down here. You goin' the wrong way, Miss. . . ."

The maze of streets in North Philly was easy to get lost in. I pulled over to double-check the address I had scribbled down, but then I realized I couldn't remember how I'd gotten that address. Who had given it to me? I pulled back onto Third Street. There was no sign of Indiana. I passed Cramp Elementary and pulled up beside a police car.

"Excuse me," I said, rolling down my window. "Can you tell me how to get to Third and Indiana Street?"

Later, I learned Third and Indiana was a notorious drug corner. How I must have looked—a white woman, with a Puerto Rican kid in the back, sweetly asking a police officer for directions to Third and Indiana. She stared at me like I was crazy.

"Oh, whatta you, a teacher?" she asked, then gave me what sounded like simple directions.

"But, uh, I wouldn't go down there," she said.

"I'll be okay," I answered.

"Just be careful down there."

Her directions lcd me into the worst neighborhood I'd visited yet. Cars, garbage bags along with loose trash, and cinder blocks were all dumped in the vacant lots that stood alongside almost every row house, many of which were empty and abandoned. Guys started walking up to the car and peering inside.

"This a dangerous neighborhood, Miss," Jovani said. He had stopped laughing.

"Jovani, where is your house?" I strained to make my voice sound calm. Then his giggles returned. Finally, Third and Indiana, but as I neared it an unsettling thought hit me. I didn't have an address, only a corner. This was not the place to start knocking on doors. I didn't even want to slow down. "Jovani, which is your house?"

He bopped up and down in his seat. "You say you know where it is."

It was getting darker. I turned off Indiana and began to double back. Jovani was bent over in the backseat. "You lost, Miss."

Where the hell was this house? I struggled to sound calm, but I couldn't get the fear out of my voice. "Jovani, this neighborhood is not safe for me. I'm getting scared. Tell me where your house is."

I checked the rearview mirror. He gazed out the window, lost in thought. Then he looked up at my reflection and smirked again. "Miss, I told you you don't know where it is. I told you."

I was back at Third and Indiana. The entire block was watching me now. Jovani was slouched so far down in his seat I doubted people could see him. "Jovani!" He had long missed the buses so I couldn't take him back to school, but I couldn't just drop him off at a corner, either. My voice had dropped to a whisper. "Tell me where your house is."

"I wanna walk. Now youuu losssttt!" He giggled.

I raced back to the school in silence. Jovani watched me raptly from the backseat. Three minutes later, I pulled into the parking lot. I locked eyes with him in the rearview mirror. "Good-bye," I said.

He looked shocked, and jumped out. As he walked back in the direction we came from, I prayed he would get home safely. If something happened this time, I'd be responsible. What if he told another teacher about this? I would be fired. That evil little monster. I wanted to kill Jovani. What had I done? I worried all night and slunk into school the next day. I held my breath until I finally saw

Jovani, unharmed, bounding into the classroom, beaming proudly over his victory. "Hiii, Miss," he taunted. He tried to get me to meet his eyes so he could gloat. I refused. All day he whispered to the others, getting all the mileage he could from it. It worked. Jovani had trounced me. He was untouchable.

***

One morning, as my class trickled in during morning announcements, I caught two unfamiliar faces in the crowd. They were special education boys.

"Miss, you covered our class," said the grinning boy in front. It was Wilson, the boy I had seen at the fire, and his friend Francisco. He stood in my doorway with a closemouthed grin that put me on guard.

"Miss! Miss, our new substitute is not coming back. We want to be in your class," said Wilson.

Other students were rushing past me, singing good morning. I heard them dropping their notebooks on their desks and chatting away.

"Please. Miss. We don't got no teacher," Wilson begged.

My first thought was to say no. Any teacher would say I'd be crazy to invite a special education student into my room; most jockeyed to send them elsewhere. I remembered how I'd taken in José R. that early October day. I had paid for that moment of weakness. Plus, a teacher couldn't just take in a stray student. Students belonged to someone. These students didn't. Something in Wilson's eyes made me pause. I had substituted for his class perhaps five or six times. He always did his work and insisted I correct it.

He needed a chance, and Mrs. G. was not in her office that day, so I didn't have to clear it with her. How could I turn him away? Wilson dropped to his knees and prayed at my feet.

"Pllleeeeeaaasse, Miss! Do you still have the map game?" Behind him, Francisco hopped around excitedly. "Why can't we stay, if you want us here, and we don't got no other teacher?" Wilson said.

"I would love to have you two here, but I can't just accept students without the rest of the school knowing," I said. "You need a note."

They disappeared. Five minutes later, as I was taking roll, they reappeared with a crumpled note and an indiscernible signature, probably a "good riddance" from a substitute. They settled into seats.

The students were working on structuring book reports. I was learning to give them a brief lesson each day, then set them off to work independently. I posted our goal for the project in large block letters on the board, and was specific about what they were expected to accomplish. My own report went up as a model. If they were confused, they'd get up and study the board. I was learning how they learned. When they had clearly defined, short-term goals, and understood specifically how to get there, they got there. I was the CEO and did little more than direct. By the end of the period, they were tired—not me.

"When you're finished, we'll laminate them and hang them in the hallway," I said.

I wandered into the hallway, ostensibly to check on something, but I wanted to see if my presence in the classroom was necessary. They continued working. I thought back to Pete's teacher-success story about leaving his students alone in the classroom during a science experiment. This day would be my success story.

Later in the day, a teacher came by to drop off some paperwork. He stopped dead as soon as he saw Wilson and Francisco. "What are they doing here? You cannot sit those two boys together. They're special ed, and they don't know how to behave."

Everyone craned their necks to glare at Wilson and Francisco, who lowered their heads and peeked up at me. Just when they were starting to fit in, they were forced outside again. All the kids made fun of the special education students. Now a teacher added to the denigration in front of the entire class.

The next morning they returned. "Please, Miss," Wilson said, giving me a charming but desperate toothy grin. "Please let us stay in your class." It happened day after day. All he wanted was to belong to a real classroom. I sat him in the second row, next to Big Bird. Francisco sat in back. Francisco was well behaved but less motivated to work. Wilson took off like a bottle rocket. He was like Pedro—clever, cheeky, and best guided with interesting activities, not pink slips.

I had made a mental note to go and talk to the special education teacher, Mrs. Q., but every free period was taken up with preparations for our field trip to the aquarium. I finally did call. She wasn't in her office. Then I forgot. A week after they both joined us, the phone rang in my classroom. Wilson was hard at work practicing past tense. Francisco was absent.

"Ms. Asquith? You got Wilson?"

"Yes," I said. "I was planning on coming and talking to you about him today."

"Well, he's been marked as absent. He needs to come upstairs."

"Oh, okay. I'll send him up. But he's expressed an interest in staying here, and since he doesn't have a teacher and it would be all right with me, we should talk about it."

"Wilson is special ed. He needs special ed services," she said.

"Well, I've already got special education students in here, and they don't receive any special services." Without thinking I added, "And it's not like he's receiving anything at the moment."

I didn't mean that as a slight—it was an honest assessment. Why should she mind? Clearly she was overburdened and understaffed.

"Well, if he were going to be in a regular ed class, he would have to have written documentation from his parents and IEP adjustments and XYPs. . . ." She went on and on, detailing all the red tape. The phone dangled at my ear, as I watched Wilson scrawling answers in a notebook. I understood her point: the school ought to keep track of its students. Yet it hadn't done so all year. Why the insistence on starting now, when it could only harm the student? Why not err on the side of the student? She was fighting to put him back where he was supposed to fit. If she failed, she would have to deal with paperwork. Wilson had been deprived of an education for months. He had gone all year without a teacher, a classroom, or a lesson. That was permissible, but incorrect paper-work could never be forgiven.

Wilson noticed my unhappy stare and sensed he was the cause of it. He shrank behind his notepad.

"I'll come up and talk to you about it," I said to her.

A moment later I told Wilson: "Hon, you've got to go upstairs."

His face fell. The other children watched as he grudgingly picked up his notebook and trudged out. He paused outside, then shut the door softly so as not to disrupt the others. I turned back to my class, minus one.

***

Wilson's special education class was on the third floor, but his wasn't known as the most notorious—that title went to Rogia's P68 classroom. This group would have scared Jovani. P68 was the level-three student headquarters. If we teachers could have only excised this class altogether, the hallways during class time would have been practically empty. For these kids, setting curtains ablaze and pulling the fire alarm were too basic. They had pushed down the principal, knocked over the music teacher, assaulted Ms. Fernanda with scissors, screamed obscenities at Mr. Whitehorne, and openly committed sex-related acts so vile for twelve- and thirteen-year-olds, it was too upsetting to contemplate. They might not have acted this way had the school administration not locked them upstairs, given them nothing to do, and cycled so many inexperienced and mean-spirited babysitters through there that they had become the animals that we treated them as. This was why I couldn't believe it when I heard that the principal had found a substitute teacher willing to stick it out in there. Mr. M. had been with P68 for a full month.

I had seen him in the teacher's lounge. He was a grandfatherly looking white man who wore a bomber jacket with military pins on each side. When not in class, he sat in the teacher's lounge, listening to Rush Limbaugh on his mini radio. Mr. M. was paid $70 or so a day to substitute. That money wouldn't have been enough for anyone to endure an hour alone with P68. My students told me that his class watched TV all day.

These were the toughest kids to teach, the 2 percent factor, and I wanted to see how he handled them. So I asked him one morning if I could sit in on his classroom and observe, which was not unusual among teachers. All morning as I passed his room I could see him reading magazines at his desk, which was dragged in front of the door. The students sat in circles on top of their desks. I knocked around 11:30 AM. He put down his magazine, jumped up, and announced, "Okay, everyone, get into a circle." Six kids, five boys and one girl, moved around. Their average age was about fourteen.

"Hello, Ms. Asquith," Mr. M. said. "We were getting started as you knocked."

Mr. M. dragged some desks forward. "Hey, you—zip it," he said to a boy wearing a baseball cap who was talking.

"Hey Mister, when we going on our field trip?" the boy replied.

"We're not going the way you act," Mr. M. said.

The student shoved the desk he was pulling and shot back "I don't care!"

"Exactly, you don't care," Mr. M. replied. "That's the problem. You don't care. I mean all of you, second-person plural."

I sat in the back. I didn't know what Mr. M. was hired to teach, what the official responsibilities of a long-term substitute were, or even what the curriculum for a special education class was. I did know that these six students had been with Mr. M. for 80 percent of the day, and they would be for several more months, and there was not a single textbook in the classroom. There were no notebooks, no schedule posted, no student mailboxes or personal spaces, no decorated bulletin boards, no class rules, no smiley signs or encouraging posters, no student work hanging, and certainly no teaching or learning happening. The only thing scrawled on the chalkboard was "The 3 branches of government, Legislative, Executive, and Judicial."

"Now," he began, propped up on a desk in the middle of the students, "How many branches of government are there and what are they?"

Several students glanced at the board where Mr. M. had written, "Executive."

"Yes," Mr. M. exclaimed, "That's right, and legislative," he answered himself. "Okay, and how many senators do we have in that?"

The students shouted out guesses: "Five." "Fifteen." "Oh, oh, oh, one thousand?"

Mr. M. waved them all away. "No, no, no!" Finally, someone guessed one hundred.

"Who said that?" Mr. M. asked. "Joe! That's right. Acknowledge yourself."

Joe just sat there. "Now, what's the third branch?" Mr. M. asked. A couple kids continued guessing. Two students tapped each other on the shoulder. Mr. M., who was leaning back on a desk in the middle of them, stopped and pointed at them.

"Now, would you do me a favor?" he asked, his voice raising. "Would ya listen? It's judicial. Now, this is for a pretzel and a soda: I'm president. If I want a judge there, do I just pick him?"

Two kids yelled out "Yes!"

Mr. M. shook his head. So they shouted out "No!" And Mr. M. said, "Good job! That's right. The answer is no."

The lesson continued like this, with Mr. M. drilling students who couldn't read, write, or do basic math, on obscure questions on U.S. government. Yet despite the fact that the students clearly had no idea what the answers were or what their teacher was talking about, they earnestly struggled to answer correctly, beaming when they guessed right. For a moment, they looked like a dysfunctional family that couldn't relate, but knew each other and had fallen into a comfortable pattern of mistreating each other. Oddly, the students had affection for him. Mr. M. stopped at one point and said gruffly, "Hey, by the way, I'm very proud of you guys."

Soon, the students grew bored. One of them snuck behind Mr. M., dancing around and making faces. The kids ignored him, but Mr. M. whipped around. "Your mother will get a call from me. SIT DOWN."

The kid shrugged. "SIT DOWN!" Mr. M. screamed. He was so loud I winced.

"No!" the student shouted, then slunk to the back of the room and kicked a chair. He sat in the corner, facing the wall.

Mr. M. announced it was time for math.

"Okay, let's try some division," he said. "How many state senators do we have in Harrisburg?"

The girl shouted, "Twenty-five!"

"Close," Mr. M. said.

"Fifty!"

"Double that," Mr. M. said. "Now, let's see, if there's two hundred members in the House, and each represent about 55,000 constituents, that's about the size of Veterans' Stadium. Now, let's do division. How many is that?"

No one even had a pencil or paper out. The students had stopped listening and were randomly calling out numbers. Mr. M. quizzically stared at the desk in front of him. "Now, um . . . so . . . how many state senators do we have?"

"Hey, you farted," Douglas yelled out, and everyone laughed.

"Okay, Douglas, I'm going to write you up." Suddenly, there was a knock on the door, and Douglas jumped up to open it. A boy of about thirteen sauntered in wearing jeans, a black T-shirt, and a gold earring shining near his closely cropped buzz cut. He surveyed the room and cocked his head back, staring at me.

Mr. M. glanced over and then very purposefully ignored him. The boy leaned to his friend. "Who she?"

"She here to watch Mr. M.," he said.

The kid looked at me and then at his friends in a circle. He said loudly, "Oh, what? Is he teaching us something today? Hey, Mister, today we doing work?" he said.

I bit my lip to keep from smiling. And Mr. M. thought his kids were dumb.

Mr. M. yelled, "Get out!" Then again: "GET OUT!" The boy backed up toward the door but looked directly at me and spoke very clearly.

"He never teach us work," he said, and Mr. M. got up and walked toward him. I thought he might push him out, but the boy stumbled backward. "This is the first time he teaches us anything," he said, and the door swung shut. Mr. M. returned to his routine. A girl asked, "Mr. M., a woman ever been president?" He distractedly turned to her.

"I think you will see a woman as president in your lifetime," Mr. M. said. "I think Elizabeth Dole would have made a fantastic president."

It was time for me to leave. As I walked toward the door, Wilfredo wondered aloud, "I never seen a black president," and Mr. M. stared at him. For once he had nothing to say about politics.

As I turned to shut the door, I glanced up and saw all of them looking at me. The whole class stopped talking. I thought about how they circled Mr. M. and tried so hard to answer his questions. That wasn't affection—that was desperation. Only about half of these students showed up for the class yearbook photo, in which just one kid smiled, and they were combined with the other teacherless classes, H81 and P78. The rest had empty expressions. Unlike all the other classes, there was no teacher in their class photo.

The principal would then order Mr. Whitehorne to fill out their report cards, so they could receive made-up grades for math, history, English—all the subjects they'd never even received a quiz in. Their eyes clung to me as I was left. There she goes—"nice" Ms. Asquith, with the pretty classroom and classroom projects outside her door and her class rules and holiday parties and field trips; a teacher who loved her students; one of those "real" teachers, who, for some reason, they would never get.

***

The following morning, someone sprayed a fire extinguisher all over my door. The enlarged photos I hung outside with "Team T61 & T62" got wet and wrinkled. I wondered who it was and if it had anything to do with Mr. M.'s class, but I didn't say anything.

At 8:25 AM, an unfamiliar, older boy walked in and sat down in the back row of T61 class. He stretched out his legs and glared at me.

"Who are you?" I asked. He ignored me.

"He in our class now," Josh said. I took in the tight black stocking cap on his head.

"Who are you?" I had to ask again.

"Javier," he answered.

Something about him put me on guard. He had an arrogant swagger. He was older than my other students. He had my ignorance to his advantage. No one told me a thing about him. Not having any information about a student, even his name, forces the teacher to have conversations like the one I had:

"How old are you?" I asked, squatting next to his desk.

"I don't know," he answered glibly. Josh snickered.

"Well, when were you born?" I asked, and he repeated, "I don't know."

"You don't know, or you don't want to tell me?"

He just stared at his desk.

"Well, I respect that," I said. "You don't have to tell me. That's your personal information."

I got up and walked away.

Of course, I didn't really feel that way. I felt like demanding he tell me or get the hell out of my classroom. He was baiting me into a power struggle. I would be smart to avoid one so early on. This bought a little time to think about how to handle him.

I tracked down Mrs. G.; she didn't know anything about him, either.

"We are not a dumping ground for the rest of the school's problems," she said, as if I had invited him in. She made some phone calls and found out he came from Ms. Soleimanzadeh's sixth-grade class on the third floor.

"Why was he transferred to me?" I asked.

He was her terror student, disrupting class, threatening her, beating up students, she said. She couldn't handle him anymore.

"So he's in my class?!" I yelled.

"Now you see what we have to deal with here on the bilingual floor?" Mrs. G. asked.

I dashed over to Ms. Soleimanzadeh's room. She was standing behind her cluttered desk looking exhausted, not acting the least bit guilty.

"He's extremely bright, but totally lacking in social skills. My advice is whatever you do, don't get into a confrontation with him," she said.

She already had five more students than I did, and her room was a disaster. I heard that she had taken her class on a field trip downtown to the Liberty Bell, and even called the TV stations to get some publicity, and when she arrived bedlam broke out. Her students ran all over the place and trashed the trip. Afterward, she took three days off school to recover. She needed help, and we should stick together as teachers. Also, I wanted to feel confident that T61 was tight enough and running smoothly enough that we could absorb one more. There was something fearsome about Javier, but I knew that, if not my class, he would end up with Mr. M., and that could be dangerous.

"Okay," I told her. I'd take him. . . .

***

That night I felt queasy—a mixture of fear, anger, resentment, and guilt was building up inside me. So I decided to release these emotions the only way I could: with an article in the *Public School Notebook*, a free quarterly newspaper devoted to the school district.

During my next coverage, I interviewed all the special ed kids, then I called home and interviewed their mothers. After school, I interviewed the head of recruitment downtown. The article was a critical but straightforward look at the effect of the vacancies:

> On a recent Thursday afternoon, while most students at Julia de Burgos Bilingual Middle School worked on their subjects, José G. and Donnielle M. aimlessly circled the school halls, stopping in the gymnasium, then at the lockers and finally ducking inside an administrator's office to hide from the school security.
>
> "We run around the hallways because we don't got a teacher," said José, 14. "We don't learn nothing—just a wasted day."
>
> Seven months into the school year and the problem of teacher vacancies in Philadelphia schools is as grave as ever, some say with slim signs of improving. Across the district, thousands of students such as José and Donnielle arrive at school each day to face a revolving door of untrained substitutes, disorganization, busy work, and trouble because their classroom has no assigned teacher.
>
> Yet many worry that unless the Office of Human Resources devises some new and drastic sales pitches as the recruiting season begins, they'll face the same problems or worse next year. The school district's Office of Human

Resources pegs the number of vacancies district wide at 200, down from 250 in September, out of a total of 12,000 teachers district wide. The School district defines vacancies as any position not filled by an appointed teacher.

But that number does not capture the extent of the problem. Many vacancies have been covered by rotating long-term substitutes, or schools have cut out positions for mentally gifted, Spanish computer, English as a Second Language, and other teachers. Nor does the district count the hundreds of untrained apprentice teachers as vacancies, although they can receive no training before they step into the classroom, are not certified, and have a high rate of turnover.

Most schools just deal with the shortage day to day, with teachers forsaking their prep time and students subjected to new fill-ins every 45 minutes. In some schools, the library has shut down because the librarian covers classes.

"We've never had it so bad," said Harriet Liss, the roster chairperson at Julia de Burgos. "It's devastating for staff because they're bombarded with coverages and of course it hurts the kids and disrupts the whole learning process."

I ended my article with:

Until a teacher arrives, students like José and Donnielle are resigned to cut class or face another substitute. Although another long-term substitute has been appointed to his class, he was absent on this day.

"All they do is give us crossword puzzles all day long, and if you don't want to do it the teacher gets mad," says Donnielle. "But everyone is sick and tired of doing crossword puzzles."

Donnielle's mother, Debra H., says she has complained but is slowly giving up hope that her son will gain much from this year.

"He hasn't had no education—he hasn't had any work," she said. "He just goes from one teacher to another. Sometime I don't even send him."

When the article came out, Ms. Vinitzsky photocopied it and placed it in each teacher's mailbox. She loved it and called me a hero. I heard the principal was furious. She never spoke to me about it, though after the article, all my field trip requests were denied, and our class never received the Ice-Cream Scoop books that she'd said she ordered for us. She brushed me off each time I'd ask her, and eventually my students forgot about them.

***

Javier was exceeding my worst expectations. He was very bright and had been well behaved for a short time, but then grew wild and violent. Sometimes he would listen and pay attention in the morning with me. Sometimes he laughed like a madman, got up, and walked out of class. Other times he'd threaten the students and would get into fistfights with Pedro. If I sent him to Mrs. G., she sent him back immediately. Sometimes Ms. Vinitzsky took him, but other times her office was full.

One day I intentionally went to Mrs. G.'s office to phone his mother. I told her everything that had been happening in class. I didn't even bother with trying to find three positive things to say; I just cut to the chase. Her voice was tired and impatient.

"Javier needs medicine for problems he's got," she told me. "He's finished it and I haven't picked up the refill yet."

I knew Javier was on some kind of medication to calm him down. He talked about how he hated it because it made him drowsy and dulled.

"When he misses it, it's worse because it's addictive," she added.

"Okay," I said, because I couldn't think of anything else to say. I hung up and turned to Mrs. G. "Do you think the mom can be useful in helping us with him?"

"No," she said. She could see me slumped in my chair, and her voice was soft and sympathetic. "After a certain amount of time they give up. She has three children. The oldest girl is eight months pregnant. Who knows who the father is? The middle one is the best one, and Javier is special education."

"I didn't know that," I said.

"The parents get so beaten down they don't care anymore, and the kids know it. Do your parents love you?" she asked. The question caught me totally by surprise.

"Do your parents love you?" she asked again.

"Yes," I said. "Of course."

"Well, ask these kids," she said. "Some say yes, but most will just look at you. Or say 'I dunno' or 'no.' And when you have problems, where do you go?" she asked. "Home? Well, these kids don't have a home. Or the problem is home."

I thought about Josh, who'd complained about his alcoholic father or a shooting he heard outside his window. I thought about Vanessa and Frances, whose dads were in jail, and about Pedro, who wanted to live with his mom instead of his grandma. I tried to imagine my own life without the unspoken love and stability of my parents and home.

"Try to imagine how they feel," Mrs. G. said. I nodded and left her office.

When I got in my car, I thought about what she'd said. Was it true that some of these parents didn't love their children? I couldn't think of a single parent who didn't come to meetings, return my calls, or try hard for their child. Even Jovani's mom clearly loved her boy. The parents I met worked hard and had aspirations for their children, and they were just as overwhelmed as the teachers were. What I did see in a lot of them was frustration and a feeling of powerlessness. Looking at the education their children received, how could they feel otherwise? Was it their own fault, or was it the school's?

***

The only people more terrifying to the principal than downtown administrators were special education parents. We were so "out of compliance," as Mrs. G. called it, that one phone call to a lawyer could put the district in the center of a million-dollar civil rights lawsuit, as it had in the past—and that meant someone would get dismissed. So when I secretly notified Wilson's grandma of the battle between me and the special education woman for her grandson, she called the school. They were now suddenly "happy to discuss this." Wilson was moving in with me.

Wilson's grandma's thick, broken English was a little difficult to understand, but I guessed that Wilson had said nice things about me because she got right to the point. "I want Wilson with you," she said.

Wilson grinned. He'd returned to my class whenever he could escape, and in only weeks he had risen to become one of my favorites. Wilson had an abundance of energy, creativity, and spark, like the new kid at the school who had finally made friends. When I directed his energy to schoolwork, he flourished. When he got an answer right, we shared a little smile. He was ambitious, too, always asking to stay after school. He did not seem to have a learning impediment like Jovani, who was not even listed as special education. I began to wonder why Wilson was even labeled as such.

"Wilson has been wonderful in class," I told her. "He participates, he reads, he works well with others and is making friends. And I'm so proud of the way he pushed to get into our class. To be honest, I don't understand why he's listed special education."

His grandma explained that while she was working as a teacher's aide at Wilson's elementary school she had noticed him memorizing words rather than learning them. She thought special ed would help.

"I don't know if I did the right thing," she said. "He never liked it."

I asked Wilson: "Why didn't you like it?"

He shook his head. "It makes me feel bad."

We talked awhile about Julia de Burgos school, and I was stunned at how Wilson's grandma had been kept in the dark. His grandma had no idea that Wilson's special education teacher had left early in October, supposedly for health reasons, and that he had had only rotating substitutes since then. She thought we had a real special education program and had been blaming Wilson for his pink slips.

I told her that most of the special ed classes didn't have teachers and the classes were out of control. I said Wilson had begged me to be his teacher. She listened with a mix of anger, pity, and pride. We chatted for nearly half an hour. We'd become a united front by the time the special ed teacher, Mrs. Q., barged in.

"Oh, hello. Good to see you. Hiiiiii, Wilson," she smiled, carrying stacks of paperwork." She beamed at Wilson as if he were her class pet.

The grandma straightened up and stared at her. "I don't know you," she said coldly. "I want my grandson taken out of special education. The teacher say he is doing really well with her, and he's been here only three weeks. Well, he didn't do well in special education classes," she said.

The special education teacher's smile disappeared. She took out some paperwork and began to flip through it.

"I evaluated him," she said in a grave tone. "He reads at a second-grade level. His math is at a third-grade level." She rambled on about his decoding skills, using a host of special education jargon. Wilson's grandma looked confused.

"Now, I still need to get an IEP on him," Mrs. Q. said.

"What that mean?" Wilson's grandma asked. She looked uncertain. "I don't want him in special ed no more."

Mrs. Q. slowly repeated "I-E-P," and then continued her esoteric analysis of Wilson's "decoding skills." She was hanging on tight to him. Moving Wilson into my class would involve doing seven pages of IEP paperwork. The paperwork had to be done—even if there was no teacher to look at it.

Wilson's grandma still wanted Wilson to stay in my classroom.

"Well, we could put him in the learning disabled category, and have him included in Ms. Asquith's classroom," Mrs. Q. said. "This way he can still receive special services. Ms. Asquith can come to me and say, 'I need this and this for Wilson,' and it will be the principal's responsibility to provide those resources."

Legally, she was right, but in reality, there were no "special services" available. Where had she been all year? I routinely asked for help for my special education students and was ignored. Jovani had plummeted into desperate territory without a word from Mrs. Q.

"Why not just move him into regular education status?" I asked. Wilson nodded.

She ignored me and spoke directly to the grandmother. "There's no guarantee that next year he'll be with Ms. Asquith. He won't get this special arrangement or such a small class size. If things change at all for him, the door will be open for him to get more services."

In special ed he hadn't even had a teacher. Was that an extra "special service"? My frustration rose, and I sensed a fight brewing. It felt as though we were both tugging at the grandmother's sleeves. Wilson sat between us, gazing from left to right as if he were watching a tennis match. Looking at him, I knew there was no point in going into all our school's problems. So I asked directly, "Does his grandmother have the legal authority to change him to regular education?"

The grandma jumped in: "Oh, yes," she boomed. "I know my rights. I moved him in, and I can move him out."

Mrs. Q. said, "I don't recommend that." In the end Wilson's grandma relented, leaving us with a compromise of sorts. Wilson would retain the special education label, but he would stay in my class.

The following day, Mrs. G. found out. She was furious. She banged on my door in the middle of class.

"I can't believe you did this," she said. "He's a terror."

She was clutching a thick sheath of pink slips she had dug up on him. "These say he steals. He punched a hole in the wall. He's out of control. Do you know what you've gotten yourself into?"

I glanced over my shoulder at Wilson, who was chewing on his pencil eraser. I said, "Well, he hasn't had a teacher. He's been fine with me."

"I don't want one pink slip on him," she warned, walking around the corner. "He's yours. Not one."

After school one day, while driving a student home, I spotted Wilson alone in an abandoned lot overrun by weeds, staring at a wall. Block-long pockets of North Philadelphia were vacant. Some were so large you could stand in them and almost forget you were in the city. I pulled the car over. Wilson was wearing a ratty blue shirt and his book bag lay on a dirt pile a few feet from him. Smack. He slammed his hand against the deteriorating brick wall. He inspected the mark. I rolled down my window.

"Wilson?" What was he doing? As much as I liked him, I had bouts of self-doubt, that I was missing something—that he had some crazy Dr. Jekyll/Mr. Hyde complex and was going to turn on me any day.

"Hi, Miss," he said, waving.

"Hon, what on earth are you doing out here?"

"I'm smacking bugs for my chameleon to eat," he said, scraping a carcass off the wall. "Miss, you said you'd call my grandma if I did good all this week. You forget?"

He was right. I had forgotten. I pulled out my cell phone. I hit the speed-dial button marked "Wilson."

His grandma answered.

"What he do now?" she yelled.

"No, I'm calling to say he's had a great week, and did a super job on his report, and I'm really proud of him."

His grandmother said, "Ohhh? That good. That goooood!"

I passed the phone to Wilson, who was gesturing wildly and beaming from ear to ear. "See, Grandma?"

***

Auditors from the federal government arrived at our school to investigate our special education program. A student's right to special education is protected by federal law, established under the 1975 Individuals with Disabilities Education Act. This act states that a child has a right to any service necessary that ensures they have equal access to public school. For some students, this meant a tutor or a seat closer to the board or extended time on tests. I wasn't certain what the one hundred or so special education students at Julia de Burgos needed, but considering that they didn't even have a teacher, I could only imagine the trouble we were in for.

Mr. Whitehorne told me they chose at random two students to interview. "They picked Rogia. Can you believe it?" Mr. Whitehorne exclaimed. I wanted to high-five him.

I hadn't seen much of Rogia since I'd tried to help her back to her attic classroom last fall. Sometimes she stopped in my classroom, and we did art projects together. She tried to hang around with the cleaning ladies after school, but she stole things off their cart, so they shooed her away. Mostly, she continued to wander the halls, getting screamed at and pushed from room to room.

I prayed that Rogia would describe in full detail her experiences at Julia de Burgos. This was her chance to be heard. We would finally be caught, and things would change around here.

The morning after the special ed auditors announced their visit, a memo from the principal arrived in our mailboxes.

"From now on," the memo read, "H87 special education class will only be covered in their room, and you are to teach them math or reading. There will be a curriculum and lesson plan on the desk."

By the time the special education investigators showed up, the principal had combined Mr. M.'s class with another special education class that hadn't had a teacher. Mr. M. was moved to a bigger room on the third floor, and three teaching aides were pulled from classrooms and given to him. The principal also moved many special education students into other teachers' classes, like mine, Ms. Rohan's, and Mr. Rougeux's. One boy was Josef, from Mr. M.'s room, a tiny, shy boy who rarely spoke and had been sent to me the day the fight broke out in Mr. M.'s room. He had simply showed up at my door one morning clutching a note. I had no paperwork on him; there was no explanation. "I'm in your class now, Miss," he said meekly. I thought I remembered him from H87. From the first day of class, he was a wonderful student: overly timid, but sweet, obedient, and eager to please.

If I ever wondered what a school year without a teacher did to a student, this change made it abundantly clear. When he arrived at my door, he was practically mute. He never raised his hand. He rarely even reacted. He was so unresponsive that at first I wasn't sure he spoke English at all.

One day, after a week or so in my class, I put an assignment on his desk, and he pushed it away. "I hate tests. I'm gonna fail," he whispered. Another time, I gave him a worksheet along with the rest of the class, and his face froze in such trauma and pain he began to fidget and squirm. "I can't," he said, and simply, "No." So Josef spent most days just sitting and staring at the backs of students and not talking to anyone.

I didn't know how to diagnose him, except by acknowledging that he'd spent the past eight months in an unsupervised and out-of-control room with five or six, and often a dozen, bigger boys. The littlest boys were always terrorized, and in that classroom no one would have stopped them. Josef was yet another one of those students who retreated the only way he could, by closing himself off to the rest of the world.

***

At the Friday-night meeting of the Pedagogical Society at J Street café, we all agreed that Mr. Whitehorne had had the toughest week. He was in the middle of a conference with a parent when a student burst in and told him to "Fuck off." When Mr. Whitehorne ordered him out, he refused.

"What could I say?" asked Mr. Whitehorne. "This is a teacher threat at Julia de Burgos: 'If I get one more problem from you, I'm going to start a disciplinary transfer. That means you'll be moved to a different school, because we can't handle you. I don't know when it will go through, if it goes through at all. It will take hours of my time, and your teacher's time, in paperwork. Nine times out of ten, your mom will be able to successfully protest it and have it thrown out. But listen up! You could be transferred, within a year or two. Maybe.'"

We all laughed. It was true. We had nothing left to throw at our students. They ruled the school.

"What happened with those special education auditors?" I asked.

"We passed the inspection," Mr. Whitehorne answered nonchalantly. "We sailed through."

"You're kidding," I said. I was astonished. "How could we possibly have passed?"

"It was a lot of smoke and mirrors," Mr. Whitehorne said. "They chose two students to interview. Rogia was absent that day, and they prepped the other student. They told kids not to come into school, and they hid the other bodies in the basement. Then they threw a lot of kids into different classrooms. They put all the teachers on their best behavior, and moved the after-school tutors from upstairs into the classrooms as aides," he said.

Mr. Whitehorne told me that the investigators looked at the paperwork, and if it was in order, the school passed.

"Don't forget," he added, "even if we're found out of compliance, what does that mean? It's not like the state or federal government will force us to hire more teachers, because then they have to give us the money. We've been fighting all year for more money. If they accuse us of something, they have to give us the money to make improvements," he said. "They pass all these laws that make them look good, but they don't give us the funds to implement them."

Driving home from the bar, I passed our school at Eighth and Lehigh. Behind it, in the neighborhood, people gathered outside on their stone perches. I once thought they were junkies. More likely they were my students' brothers or mothers. Tomorrow morning, bottles, needles, condoms, and cigarette butts would greet Juan C and Big Bird in their pilgrimage to school. No workbook could help that. No federal audit would change that. No amount of money could combat that influence. I no longer knew who to blame or what to do with that blame. So I went home, made dinner, and invented something new to teach for the next day.

15
Rally

All those who have meditated on the art of governing mankind have been convinced that the fate of empires depends on the education of the youth.

—Aristotle 384–322 B.C., Philosopher

T61 was going to meet the new mayor. If we couldn't improve our school from the inside, a trip to see a higher authority might help. Philadelphians had elected John Street on the strength of his promise to turn schools around. He was visiting Edison High School in North Philly. All the education big shots would be there, and our principal offered to pay overtime to teachers who showed up and waved Julia de Burgos signs. We were encouraged to bring students. In English class, we did a writing exercise in which they described the school:

— This school is awright but things happen in this school like a fire and a boy who had a knife and the third floor is like crazy kids. But in the second floor bad thing start. The first floor is awright. Daniel O.

— I think Julia de Burgos need a lot of thing. They need teachers to teach the children to write and read because is the most impotents thing. They need a new Julia de Burgos because this is mess up and ceiling broken down. If you touch it, it broke down. But the good part is that I'm glad to have a teacher who teach us things. We go on field trips. Noemi.

Ms. Rohan and I brought ten kids. I offered to bring Josh, Miguel, Big Bird, and as a special reward for an afternoon of good behavior, Jovani.

I had ulterior motives for inviting Jovani. He was still terrorizing T62's classroom, and I'd continued to handle him as well as I could, but I had done a terrible thing to him. A few days earlier we'd been finishing vocabulary exercises in our workbooks. As always, my control of the classroom was precarious. I had walked past desks, pasting insect stickers on their books that said "GREAT!" and "SUPER!"

Jovani had stuck his fist in the air and called my name. I had raced over and saw he had completed an entire page. "Wow, good job, Jovani," I had said. Then I checked his answers. They were wrong. Not only one—all ten of them were wrong. These weren't minor mistakes. He had simply plugged words in at random.

"Is this right, Miss?" he had asked, his eyes pleading.

I'd stared at the workbook. If I'd told him they were wrong, he'd have slammed down his workbook and torn across the room, distracting everyone. If I'd explained it to him, I'd have to review every question with him and ignore the rest of the class. It would have taken twenty minutes. Jovani had been in the suspension room when I'd explained the material, so his poor attempt had hardly been surprising. Other hands had waved in the air.

I'd murmured to Jovani: "Yes, hon, that's great." I'd pressed a sticker of a bear holding a pot of honey against his page. He was beaming.

I brought him on a teacher trip as though I could somehow compensate. I drove back to Third and Indiana to pick him up. My students knew where to go, and we found his row house, next to several crumbling buildings.

Josh and Big Bird were already squished into the backseat of my car. As I jumped out, my plan was to get out and get back as quickly as possible. I banged hard on the blue-painted door. His mom opened it a few inches. When she saw me, she pulled the door wide open and smiled.

Jovani came stumbling out with an oversized puffy black jacket hanging off his tiny frame, like a cloak on a wire hanger. A little brother trailed after him, then clung to his mother's legs and wailed as Jovani sprung down the stoop. Jovani ignored him.

"Where we goin'?" he demanded.

"We're going to meet the mayor and hear him talk about our school," I said, glancing around as we walked to the car. A group of men watched us from the corner.

"That's all they gonna do is talk?" he said, kicking stones on the ground. "I don't wanna go."

I was jingling my pockets nervously for the car keys. When I reached the car, the other boys had locked the doors from the inside. Sunk into their seats, they peered out at us, saucer-eyed.

"This is a bad neighborhood, Miss," said Josh as I got in.

Josh lived three minutes away. I looked back at the decaying buildings and purplish sidewalks. Dirty diapers were slung atop a pile of cinderblocks. A man slumped against a wall nearby. This wasn't the family neighborhood the other boys lived in.

We got onto a main street and relaxed. Edison High School was five minutes north. When we arrived the students spilled out of my car and scampered up to the front doors. They seemed much more excited about seeing Edison High School than listening to the mayor.

Edison had about 2,400 students and was the high school for the Puerto Rican community in North Philadelphia. More than half of Julia de Burgos's graduates went on to Edison. Edison was not the worst high school in the city, but it was close. The dropout rate was more than 66 percent.

The community had fought from the early 1960s until 1988 for a new Edison school building, and when the city finally agreed they spent $50 million building the most expensive school in the city. Yet, for all the money poured into Edison—for all the years of community protests that their children were held back by an old building and unequal school funding—the new building hadn't helped much. In fact, many say the school grew more violent. Among the 685 students that became Edison's first freshman class in 1988, 85 percent dropped out by 1992. Since then, the school had been plagued by teacher turnover, violent lunchroom brawls, knife fights, shootings, and gang warfare. Between 1988 and 1995, nine Edison students were killed in crime-related incidents in the community. They were all buried in the New Cathedral Cemetery across the street from Edison.

Yet Edison High School was the neighborhood school, and Vanessa was enamored of it. She said that cute boy, Bebe, was a student here. She couldn't believe how big the lockers were. "Miss, I wanna go here," Vanessa said.

"You said you're going to CAPA," I reminded her, referring to the prestigious performing arts school she'd spoken of months ago. She didn't answer.

When we entered the auditorium, I was amazed to see the stage decorated with signs from each school. Teachers were cheering and singing school songs. A handful of teachers from De Burgos waved glittering signs that the kids had painted. They read "We Want a New School!" Jovani tried to sneak upstairs to sit in the bleachers, so I kept him firmly planted by my side. Vanessa attached herself to my other side.

When the mayor arrived an hour late, the auditorium took on the mood of a pep rally. One by one, the mayor called out schools. Representatives cheered when their school was named. Those teachers who were there only for the overtime pay lingered near the door. They cheered obediently for Julia de Burgos. The principal was trying to curry favor with the administration. "Listen for when they call our school," I whispered to my kids.

Jovani turned to me. "Who are we?"

I looked at his face to check what he meant. "Julia de Burgos, hon." And he nodded. Vanessa and Ms. Rohan laughed.

The new mayor promised to be the city's "education mayor," and repeated, "I am for public education!" The crowd roared. He made three main points: schools were underfunded, teachers needed a fair contract, and school employees should be held accountable. To each point, the crowd cheered and waved signs. At the end he gave us an opportunity to approach the microphone and ask questions. Several teachers repeated his demands, and a few from Julia de Burgos made their case for a new building. One of my top students, Luis, leaned over to me. He wanted to ask when we were going to get a new school. Jovani said he wanted to say something, too. I agreed.

Luis looked straight at the mayor as he spoke into the microphone.

"Um, I want to talk about my school, Julia de Burgos." The soft child's voice against the sudden silence made everyone lay down their signs and listen. He cleared his throat.

"I really like it there, but like the school's not so nice. The bathrooms are really dirty and the pipes are broke. And there's always fights in the hall, and the other day part of the ceiling fell in and almost hit a teacher. Some days, it's like I don't want to come to school no more. That's it. Thank you."

A woman had tears in her eyes, and I felt like crying, too. The mayor nodded, "Thank you, son."

Jovani danced behind him, so I nudged him forward to the microphone. He had volunteered, so I assumed he had something he wanted to say. He stood there for a second. Then, he raised himself up on his tiptoes, causing his lips to bump the microphone, and echoed his steady breathing throughout the room. Everyone turned to see who was at the microphone. "Jovani?" I whispered. "Go ahead."

He twisted his neck and stared up at me, frozen. His eyes were wide and lit up. The mayor raised his eyebrows. After ten awkward seconds of silence, I tugged at Jovani's sleeve, and we returned to our seats. I never found out what it was that Jovani had to say.

***

I took the kids home, dropping Vanessa off last. Lately, she'd even been sleeping through the separate, more challenging assignments I'd given her. "Have you given any more thought to changing middle schools next year to Conwell?" I asked her. Conwell was a considerably better middle school in the neighborhood that was application-only.

"Yeah, Miss," she said.

"Well, I want you to reapply for Conwell Middle School next year and go if you get in."

She shifted uncomfortably as we bumped down the potholed streets of Erie Avenue, past the row houses and the abandoned buildings. Streetlights flickered across her face.

"It's nice, Miss, but I'm used to my own friends. I don't like to go into things and meet new people. I'm not into trying new things."

"You'll make friends there, too," I said. We crossed a bridge over railroad tracks. The giant building looming in the distance was an abandoned factory. I thought about Vanessa's mom, who was in her early thirties and had grown up in the neighborhood. She answered all my calls, visited the school on parents' night, and said she didn't want her daughter to have the life both she and her mother had had: working in a low-wage factory, being financially dependent on a boyfriend, having few choices.

"C'mon, Vanessa. You said you wanted to go to CAPA, the honors high school. Julia de Burgos won't get you there."

She stared out the window. I tried to tell her that her time was running out. What would she learn with someone like Mr. Jackson as her future English teacher? Despite all her aspirations and abilities, if she let Julia de Burgos waste away all her opportunities now, she would end up at the blunt end of other people's bad choices. She didn't want that, did she?

She shrugged and tucked her chin into her jacket lining.

We pulled up to her house. The one next to hers was abandoned. On one side, the windows were dark cavities. On the other, the house had crumbled into a pile littered with street trash.

"Listen, Vanessa, our class is pretty good this year. I mean, we get work done. But look around the school. Not all the classrooms are like that. If you get placed with a bad teacher, you could waste the whole year not learning anything, and my worry is that you'll fall so far behind you'll never get into a good high school."

"All right, Miss," she said, giving me her sweet smile. She hopped out of the car and ran up the stairs.

16
The Toughest Students

One morning, Jovani came into class massaging his neck. He ignored the other students and moved right to my desk, burying himself in my hip.

"I got into a fight, Miss," he said. "I can't do my work because I hurt my neck. I can't turn it," he said, rubbing his neck.

Jovani had gotten into plenty of fights before, but he'd never mentioned them to me. In class, he did what he'd mostly been doing for the past couple of weeks, which was wander without purpose. He drew circles on the board aimlessly or went to the back of the room to glue Popsicle sticks together. At times I convinced him he was my little helper, and he policed the aisles, awarding stickers or tickets to the students who completed the simple grammar work that stumped him. He relished that job, pleading for it each day. He felt useful, for once, maybe even powerful. The kids didn't smirk at him, like they did when he picked out coloring books at the library. They clamored for his attention. He took his job seriously. He didn't hand out the stickers to the popular kids, or the girls. His motive was to please me and to do his job well. Once, he even carried a girl's workbook over to me to settle some confusion as to whether she had really finished the entire assignment. She had, and this earned her a sticker.

On this day, he lingered in my room while everyone else went to lunch. He climbed up onto the chair next to my desk, folded his knees underneath him, and leaned his elbows up on my desk.

"I'm leaving, Miss," he blurted out. "We going to New York."

My first instinct was to assume this wasn't true, but as he gave me more details, I realized he really was leaving.

178

"How did you hurt your neck in a fight?" I asked.

"My neighbor did it," he said. He said his neighbor was eighteen and had been bothering his mom the night before. "I went out to get him, and he yanked me by the head."

Jovani shifted to show me how the neighbor had reached across him from the right and grabbed the left side of his head by the ear. His feet slipped off the chair.

"He hit my mom, you know, so I hit him back. They my family. I do what I gotta do," he stated, with a hard emphasis on the Is and an arm-jabbing, neck-rocking cadence that reminded me that despite his small frame Jovani could instantly turn into the toughest student in my class. He shifted around some more. His worn boots weren't even totally touching the ground, and on his bony frame was an oversized, stained gray turtleneck that he wore several times a week, if he came to school that frequently at all.

"We leaving," he said softly. "My stepdad hit my mom, and she don't want that no more."

His toughness fell away, and he looked like a lost little boy. "I'm gonna say good-bye," he said.

Then he laid his head in the crook of his arm and cried. He buried his eyes away so I couldn't see them, or maybe so he couldn't see me. His angular shoulders shook and he breathed heavily. I stroked his head. He sat like that for a few minutes, sobbing to himself. "I don't wanna go," he cried. "I'm gonna miss my dad."

Jovani had never mentioned his dad before. I didn't even know he knew him. He had never mentioned any male figure in his life, unless it was some older boy trying to beat him up.

He stopped crying after a while and said, "You drive me home, Miss?"

We walked out of the classroom and down the hallway to the parking lot. He had wiped away his tears and clambered into the front seat, excited to sit beside the teacher. For a moment, I wondered whether he really was leaving or whether this was a ploy to get attention. As sorry as I felt for Jovani, I wasn't going to put anything past him.

"I'd like to come in and talk to your mom, Okay?" I said.

"Miss, don't tell my uncle we leaving. He don't know. Miss, what you gonna say? You gonna talk to him?"

"I won't say anything, Jovani," I answered.

"Miss, you gonna see my house. In my house we got two couches now," he said.

We turned onto Third and Indiana. Jovani bounded up the three steps of his stoop and pushed open the cracked door of his row house. There wasn't even a mailbox outside. I heard a man's voice. I stepped inside the dark hallway reeking of pot. To my right, above the living room, a hole gaped from the ceiling, spewing plaster and wires. The two couches that made Jovani so proud were pushed against the wall. They didn't face each other and were faded and torn.

A man lifted himself off the couch. He was in his twenties, dark-skinned, and had a goatee to match his cropped buzz cut. His eyes were sunken into his head and smoke trailed from a roach in his hand. For a split second, I imagined Jovani looking like that in ten years, but pushed the impression out of my mind. He approached me. Back in the fall, during the Puerto Rican Day Parade, I would have been scared, but I felt I had earned a place in this neighborhood since then, and at the very least I could distinguish between dangerous situations and the rest.

He looked embarrassed.

"Oh, hi. You're Jovani's teacher? His mom's not here."

"Who are you?" I asked.

"I'm his cousin," he said. I turned to follow Jovani back to the car. "Hey, um, I'm really sorry about this," he added.

"It's not me you should apologize to," I said, and closed the door.

In the car I asked, "Does he do that all the time?"

Jovani peered up out the window and watched the row houses pass by.

"He smoke cigarettes and he smoke that drug. He don't do nothing else. They smoke it all the time. I'm not allowed to be in the room, or it gets in me and they'll see it when I go to the health clinic. I have to go upstairs or outside."

I thought about Jovani being constantly kicked around so they could get high. I began to see how he must have looked at me and my classroom and my Rules and Consequences and pink slips.

I had always known it wasn't Jovani's fault, which was why I had grappled with how to discipline him. Jovani's family had a responsibility to deliver him to us each day washed, fed, with a notebook and pencils, and ready to learn.

After school, his parents had to make him do his homework—not make the teachers run around, phoning and visiting the houses, to get him to do it. Sending Jovani into our classroom each and every day was unfair to the rest of the class and to the school system. I didn't know much about the mother's situation (it certainly must have been desperate). But I did know that there were a lot of families in this neighborhood who struggled and yet still provided for their children and held up their end of the invisible partnership with the school. Jovani had ruined so many other students' opportunities to learn. What would happen when he finished school and was let loose on society?

We reached his aunt's house, but Jovani's mom wasn't there, either.

"She at the welfare," his aunt said.

He loped up the stairs, his jacket dragging behind him. Suddenly, I had a flashback of the humiliating experience months earlier in which I had driven around in circles trying to find Jovani's house. My relationship with Jovani had deepened so much since then. It felt odd to think that I was ever so angry with him. Just reflecting on that day made me blush. Mr. Rougeux had said Jovani had probably just been trying to spend more time with me. Since we had become so friendly, and I was doing so much to help him, I decided to bring it up.

"Do you remember that day I tried to drive you home, but you wouldn't tell me where you lived?"

Like that, his expression brightened and that old mischievous, catlike grin reappeared. "Yeah."

"Why did you do that? You know, I was trying to help you."

I should have let it go. Why did I have to dig up that afternoon? Deep down, I suppose I was still humiliated. I didn't really want an explanation. I wanted an apology or a slightly guilty look, at least an acknowledgement.

He leaned his head back and peeked up at me. "Miss, I told you where to go. You dropped me off at the school and wouldn't let me back in your car."

He was smiling to himself again. That wasn't the answer I wanted. Clearly, I wasn't going to get it.

We said our good-byes. Three days later Jovani stopped coming to class. I never saw him again.

***

While Jovani was endlessly frustrating, I never disliked him. I somehow always managed to separate my personal feelings from my role as the teacher. With Javier, I wasn't sure I could still do that.

I had now turned into one of Javier's many targets, and his sole purpose in class had become to lash out at me. Javier made me feel helpless, and I resented him for it. I knew he needed medicine, but I had struggled for two months to appease him, taking him on field trips and persuading Mr. Rougeux to allow him to work alone in his computer room. I had even arranged for a Puerto Rican lawyer to visit my class as a guest speaker, in part because Javier always said he aspired to be a lawyer.

Unfortunately, the lawyer took a longwinded route to explain the origins of the legal system, and everyone had tuned out. Most students had suffered silently, but Javier had been impatient. He had thrown pieces of paper into the air and poked the girls around him. Finally, he had stood up and bounced a rubber ball. I had to interrupt the speaker and confront the problem.

"Give me the ball," I said, as everyone looked on. I confiscated it, but then he blew papers off Odalis's desk, so I told him to leave. I didn't see him for the rest of the day, until he appeared outside my door last period waving through the window. I went out to get him, and he ran down the hallway. Then he reappeared, knocking on the door and yelling at students so it was impossible for anyone to concentrate. What could I do? Ms. Vinitzsky's room was full, and Mrs. G. refused to take him. A good teacher prevented this from happening by being organized, showing compassion, and being consistent with discipline. How did I build a relationship with a student dropped into the class with just three months of school left?

I ignored the banging, but then he came inside and picked up my phone and dialed random numbers. "Hello?!" He shouted into the phone. I walked over to him, and he dropped it. Then, he grabbed José R.'s book off his desk and dodged between desks to the back of the room, waving it in the air.

"Heyyyy," slurred José R., lugging himself out of his chair. Oddly, ever since Javier had joined the class José R. had been calm and obedient. Thankfully, most of the class didn't like Javier and wasn't paying attention to him. I didn't want to be dragged into a fight, so I tried my old trick of pretending a reporter was in the room, observing everything. How would I want myself portrayed in an article? This worked for a minute, but my temper fought back such maturity. José R. was traipsing down the aisle in pursuit. I cut him off and confronted Javier.

"Javier, please sit down. Javier, give me the paper. Javier, no one in the class is interested in your showing off. You're embarrassing yourself."

He yelled, "So what! I don't CARE! You're embarrassing yourself." He dodged between desks, and I felt stupid chasing him around. "Gimme my ball back!" he shouted. "I want my ball back."

He was so wild-faced and angry, I wondered if he was having a reaction to his medicine. He slipped past me, marched to my desk, and picked up a packet of stickers. He waved them so close to my face they brushed my nose. I swatted to grab them, but he yanked them back at the last second.

"I'm going to take these, then!" he yelled. He kept waving the stickers in my face before the whole class.

"I see them, Javier," I said, gritting my teeth. "They're stickers."

I turned away from him, livid, and busied myself with a student's question. Soon, it was 2:50 PM, and I prepared to dismiss the class. I wrote on the chalkboard, "Quiet down. The longer we talk, the longer we stay after school."

I turned around and tapped on the board to draw their attention. The students were laughing. I looked back to see Javier standing behind me erasing the board. I picked up the chalk and rewrote it, and he stood there waiting and then erased it again. I was so outraged and exhausted, I simply could have lost my composure right then and there and shoved him down. I'd pinned my hopes to the notion that no student was beyond reach of a good teacher. Either I wasn't that great of a teacher, or Javier was beyond reach, because nothing was working. It crossed my mind that Javier might hit me. He was only thirteen, but already my height, and I presumed much stronger than I. If he attacked me or punched me, I was alone here. I clenched my teeth and said the only thing that came to mind.

"Javier, you are out of control. Do you realize that? You are out of control."

It was my last card, and thankfully it worked. The intensity in my voice must have scared him. His face went blank, and he ran out the door and down the hallway. I turned on my class.

"What is wrong with you guys?!" I cried. "I asked you to be quiet."

I felt bad that I had taken my frustration out on them, but I needed to be back in control for a minute. I'd never had a student belittle me like that and in front of the class whose respect I'd worked long and hard to earn. I was a teacher, but as I stood there seething with rage, I realized I was also human.

***

As May stumbled into June, the school veered into madness. All day long screams echoed in the hallways. "Fuck this school! I hate this fucking place! You motherfucker! What the fuck!" I could hear them in the teachers' lounge, the bathroom, and my class. They rang in my ears driving home. The police were called four separate times in one day. There was a fight in the cafeteria. A seventh-grader was picking on some kid, and when Gigi, the hallway monitor, stepped in he screamed in her face, "*vete al mierda*," which is Puerto Rican slang for "eat shit." When Hector, the school police officer, stepped in and tried to take the boy out of the cafeteria, the kid punched him in the face. So Hector pushed him against the wall and roughed him up, then handcuffed him.

All my kids came running up from lunch bouncing off the wall and shouting about police brutality and saying the boy had a knife. When they came to class like that, it made it twice as hard—and usually impossible—to settle them. Rumors that several students had knives made me nervous to walk around the hallways. My kids didn't dare ask to go to the bathroom anymore.

When I'd hear a swarm of kids coming, I'd duck into my classroom and hide, for fear of having to confront them. I didn't know what was worse, confronting the students and risking their wrath or ignoring them and feeling impotent. I hated to admit it, but I was scared. Pack mentality reigned, and teachers caught in the wrong place at the wrong time could be in real trouble. Several had already been punched and pushed down. One afternoon, I saw Mrs. Jimenez fumbling desperately to lock her door and then, literally, running out of the building for her car. Ms. Vinitzsky's room was so overcrowded, she stopped accepting any more students. Mrs. G. was absent, and so was Ms. Rohan.

Mr. Rougeux's room, in which students calmly prepared for final exams, was the eye of the storm. Mr. Rougeux had created from scratch final exams in all his subjects. He'd also created review sheets and mock exams for his pupils to study. This kind of schedule was probably standard at schools across the country. At our school, only a handful of teachers were organized enough to give real final exams that mattered. I had put together a final exam in reading class only.

While teachers had the relative safety of their classrooms, the students had to actually go out into the hallways. If a student wasn't an instigator, he was a target, like Big Bird, who was picked on for his huge size and gentle nature. For a few weeks I couldn't understand why he arrived late and hung around after 3:00 PM, waiting for the buses to leave and the crowd to clear. His struggle broke my heart. He didn't want to break the rules and anger the teachers, but when he got jumped, not one teacher would be there to help him. In my classroom, Javier disappeared for a week, but then suddenly reemerged. The morning he returned to class, I settled everyone.

"I have to talk to you all about something serious," I said. I pulled out my stool and sat in front of T61. "I'm proud of our class. We are well behaved; we do a lot of fun stuff, learn a lot, and we take the most field trips. Because of that, we've gotten seven new students in the last two months, and I'm happy they're here. Everyone in here follows the rules, and I've been proud and happy with all of you. The reason why we're doing so well is that everyone in here follows the rules."

I turned to Angela, a student who had been moved into T61 by her mother a month earlier. She had been in another sixth-grade classroom that was notoriously out of control.

"Angela, you told me in your last class that no one followed the rules. Can you tell me what that was like?"

"It was terrible," she said. "We never learned nothing. Everyone just ran around all day. They hit the teacher, and he cried three times. We didn't go on not one field trip."

She said exactly what I'd hoped. I took a deep breath and prayed this was working.

"Well, it's come to my attention that we have a problem. We have one student who is not following the rules, and that upsets me. We have a student who erased the board while I wrote on it. We have a student who walks in and out of here and bothers other students and disrespects me."

I didn't look at Javier, but I didn't have to. Everyone else did. Josh gave him a sneer.

"What happens in society when people don't follow the rules?"

"They go to jail?" Vanessa said.

"That's right. Society decides they can't live in it anymore, and they are removed. Well, I don't want any of my students removed from this class. But we can't have one student just ignoring the rules, because it brings everyone down."

My brutally honest approach was risky. It was a direct plea for help with a student that I couldn't handle on my own. I felt like my class's solidarity was being put to the test. Kids could be so fickle with their loyalty. Had I built up enough trust that they would support me? Javier sat stone-faced, and no one else spoke.

"Do I have your support with the rules, and are we agreed that we want everyone to follow them?"

Ten students said yes, and Javier shouted, "No!"

I repeated it again, more forcefully, and this time everyone said, "Yes!"

Did they truly support me? In the hallway after class, Javier pushed through the crowd and hissed, "You did that on purpose."

I looked him in the eye and said, "I didn't say your name."

"Everyone knew it was me. You just tried to embarrass me," he said.

"Look, Javier," I said locking the door as we walked out. "Everything I said was true. And you brought it on yourself. Start behaving."

Javier disappeared for the rest of the day, and I sent in a pink slip on him for cutting, just to cover myself. I saw it later, on the floor under Mrs. G.'s desk.

***

I saw Javier only once or twice more during the school year. He showed up a week after our blowout and got into a fight with Pedro. I pulled him by the arm and he screamed, "Don't touch me!" Then he ran into the halls and sprayed a parent with a water bottle in front of the vice principal. Javier was suspended for days. By the time he returned, with his father in tow, his prescription had been filled. The father promised this would calm him down. The next time I saw him I had to call on him twice.

"Javier? Javier?" He looked sedated, his lids half closed. His lips parted, and he said "Huh?"

17

Good-bye

Most people are mirrors, reflecting the moods and emotions of their times; few are windows bringing light to bear on the dark corners where troubles fester. The whole purpose of education is to turn mirrors into windows.

—Sydney J. Harris, 1917–1986, Chicago journalist and teacher

For most of the school year I had fretted over the future. On some days, teaching clearly seemed to be my calling. Working with the students left me feeling invigorated and inspired, and the emotional attachment to the students was so strong that the prospect of leaving my new home in Julia de Burgos felt gut-wrenching. Another year offered the opportunity to rectify my mistakes and put to use all I'd learned. I wanted another shot to do it right. And I didn't want to leave my kids. I dreaded saying good-bye.

But then there were the tough days. The fights, the arsons, the petty battles with the principal and the administration, and the sense that a handful of students were running the school. By May, this all pushed me over the edge, and I wasn't sure I could keep my sanity or my dignity for another year. This job was too physically punishing, too mentally exhausting, and I was afraid of becoming so accustomed to all of it that I would stop wanting to make a difference. I went to Mrs. G.'s office to tell her.

"I've decided not to come back next year," I said softly.

"What are you going to do?" she asked.

"Probably go back to journalism," I said. "I don't have a job yet, but my family and friends are in New York, so I'll go there."

"I understand why you're leaving, you know," she said. "We're raising everyone else's children. I stay in it because I like it. I wouldn't do anything else. But I realize I'll never be rich. I'll never make more than $70,000. I have a master's, and anywhere else I could make a lot more. But I like what I do. They sure don't make it easy on you!"

Her phone rang. No doubt Mrs. G. had a million things to do.

I had thought she was cynical, but maybe she was just realistic. She had immediately sized up Jovani and tried to get him "out of our hair," while I had insisted on "reaching him" and just spread myself out too thin. I invested so much time and energy in him, and to what end? In doing so, he ruined class and contributed to destroying many children's only chance at learning. Perhaps my time would have been better spent focusing on the kids who weren't as lost as he was. So whose strategy was right—Mrs. G.'s or my own?

I wondered how the other teachers at the school had changed and adapted over the years. Had they all started out like me? Our school was so dysfunctional that at some point, it was only natural to start adapting. I felt myself adapting. I remembered how outraged I'd felt walking into Rogia's special education classroom and the anger with which I had earlier dismissed my team teachers. These reactions were so naive in hindsight. Every teacher reacted to these tiny affronts differently. The Venezuelan teacher turned a blind eye; Mr. M. the substitute blamed the students; the principal hid the problems for her own ambition; Mr. Rougeux's talent lifted him above it all; Mr. Whitehorne's strength enabled him to bend when he had to and fight when he thought he could win; and Ms. Fernanda, the new English teacher, quit in protest. How was I reacting? I had stayed the year, longer than most. But I could not come back. Sitting with Mrs. G., I realized she would probably have loved to have had things improve. She was stuck here, though, dealing with the situation the best way she could. She had two little children, a husband, bills to pay, and given all her responsibilities she couldn't afford to be fired or to dedicate her life to overturning the monstrous school system. In a way, that was hero's work.

I wanted to be a success story and to have a message that new, idealistic teachers could succeed in this environment. I could see now that it was much more complicated than I had ever imagined as a twenty-five-year-old.

I took a deep breath and said sincerely, "You know, I've never thanked you for all your support."

She smiled. "Good luck. Send us a postcard."

***

Passing the row of sixth-grade lockers—skinny rectangles bunched together on top of each other—made my heart hurt a little. I boxed up the last of my things, straightened the desks, and swept the floor. I had a pile of my decorations and workbooks to give to Ms. Rohan for next year. I packed up all the books we'd read: *Bridge to Terabithia, Iggie's House, Chicken Soup for the Kid's Soul, Where the Red Fern Grows, Pedro's Journal, Harry Potter and the Sorceror's Stone, Tuck Everlasting,* and *Scorpions.*

The principal announced another faculty meeting in the library, this one about grades. Mr. Whitehorne told me the Puerto Rican–dominated cluster was looking to replace her with a Spanish-speaking principal, and two major fires in one school year would be sufficient justification.

I'd been worried about grades, which were due shortly. My big question was whether I should hold any child back. I didn't think it would help them much, but I wanted to be tough and have standards and live up to my word that if you don't try, there would be consequences. I felt that was only fair to the students who did listen and make an effort.

What would the principal suggest? She talked about holding a hard line with the kids. She'd pushed us to do "everything that we can to help each student" because "failure is not an option." She'd set up a ton of roadblocks for any teacher who tried to fail a child.

"As you fill in the mark-sen sheets with each student's final grade, search your soul," she said, a slight smile playing on her lips. "See if you really want them back here next year. Ask yourself if there is nothing you can see in reviewing their grades that can help them move on," she said. "Because if you retain them, we will have to deal with them again next year!"

The teachers burst into laughter. From all sides of the room came shouts of "Have mercy!"

I glanced at Mr. Whitehorne, who sarcastically called out, "Well, our promotion rate just took a hike." Laughter spilled from all sides of the room. Teachers were high-fiving and chuckling—nudge-nudge, wink-wink—with the principal.

"Okay, okay," the principal said, catching her breath. "Now, now, it is a professional that realizes that at a certain point we've done all we can. And it is a professional that realizes when you can give all you can, and when you say, 'I have nothing left for them,'" she said. "Studies show that coverage students have poor attendance rates and poor academic performance. . . ."

A teacher stood up and cut her off.

"Yeah, so leave your ego behind!"

A hearty applause broke out. "No pressure," the principal said gleefully. "I'll support you either way. However, if you retain them, they're yours next year!"

The meeting was over. After the faculty meeting, I caught up with Ms. Ortiz.

"What happens if I tally up my kids' scores and see that I have some who have failed?" I asked. "Do I fail them?"

"Every teacher uses their discretion," she answered. "To me, if a kid makes an effort, any effort at all, I'll pass them," she said. "I'm failing two kids, and these are kids that just never showed up and never did any of the work."

"But what about the kids that, say, can't read?" I asked.

"I'll pass them, anyway. Otherwise, they end up like some of these kids you see running around here that are way too old for this place," she said. "It doesn't matter, anyway. They'll push them through."

"What do you mean?"

"They'll promote them, anyway. They always do, especially if a parent comes down and complains. That's why I always keep very good records. But, in the end, the administration passes them. It's like the principal said, do you really want them back next year?"

***

I gave two students Fs: José R. and a girl named Jen. When we received our report cards, though, they all said the same thing at the bottom: "PROMOTED." Someone had changed my grades from 55s to 65s.

I confronted the principal, who said, "Cross it out and write 'RETAINED.'" When I pointed out to her that crossing it out on the hard copy didn't change anything on the school computers, she told me to "make a copy and leave it on my desk." I knew she had changed the grades, and she wouldn't change them back. What did it matter?

I returned to my classroom. Oddly enough, José R. was back early from lunch and waiting for me. "Hiiiiiiii, Meeeesssss," he slurred.

He was grinning and held a gigantic binder in his arms. I felt that familiar mix of pity and resentment toward him that had made him such a troubling student to deal with all year. He saw the report card in my hand.

"That mine, Miss?" he asked slowly.

I looked down at it, mostly Cs and Ds on the page. I thought about all the times I had threatened José R. to work or he would fail and be held back. He had ignored me. I felt like if I handed him the report card, he would laugh at me. *I told you so, Miss. I know this system better than you do!*

I sat down next to him. "José, I have your report card here. It doesn't say it yet, but you've failed two subjects, and you may have to repeat sixth grade."

At first he looked shocked, and I thought my bluffing had worked. All year, I'd warned José R., and I couldn't help feeling that, finally, the teacher had some power in her classroom.

"José, I've been trying to help you all year, but you see, there are consequences for your actions."

"Noo, Meeesss," he sang. "Because I'm moving schools."

And then he began to laugh and laugh and laugh. "I'm moving schools."

Even though I had his grades in my grade book and pink slips to show he had fooled around and bothered other students all year, test scores to show that he couldn't read or write well, and a diary full of my failed efforts to intervene and help him, none of it mattered. He was right.

He would move on. He would be falsely promoted, probably up to twelfth grade, if he wanted.

Together we sat alone in his sixth-grade classroom. I surveyed our room, taking in the cracked fluorescent lighting overhead, the used workbooks stacked up on the shelves, the trash and graffiti outside the window, and back at José R., who had stopped laughing. He was sitting still, looking at his teacher.

***

— Dear Ms. A I am happy to sign your yearbook. Have a nice, and safe summer don't forget to call me, you are a good teacher and very nice teacher to. I love you don't forget me. Vanessa.

— From Miguel Ramos you're the best teacher.

— I won't forget you, by José R.

— I love you by Josh

— From Miguel C Con mucho carino de tu estudiante

— Dear Ms. A, Thank you for being a teacher this year. I don't know who we would have as a teacher if you would not come to this school I would have never meet a young beautiful intelligent and kind teacher like you. I hope you have a great summer and can be happy where ever you are. Thank you alot. Missed, but not forgotten, love ya, Jennifer C.

— Ms. Asquith even though I was absent 40 days I still enjoyed being in this class. I'm going to miss you a lot. "I give Ms. Asquith an A+ beause she teached us well & she always told us we can when we thought we couldn't. Iris.

— Ms. Asquish is a very nice teacher, she teach very well. I love you beacauses you give good work. My teacher always match on her cloths. I tell her she dress very nice and good, I love you. Jose M.

— I would give you an A because you taught us a lot of things like how to read longer words. And, because she tried very hard to teach us how to read better and teach us how to write cursive.

— Ms. Asquith you teaches good and if you don't understand something she will always keep explaining it until you get it.

— Ms. Asuqith comes every day with a smile even though I don't. She is a good and fun teacher and I really adore her. Juanita

— We got a good teacher that help us so we can learn. I got the best teacher in the school because we won the ice cream scoop reading contest for the most reports we beat everyone and we can do anything because we are the best. Daniel O

— Dear Ms. Asquith have a safe summer call me I won't forget you. you gave fun work sometime and you had taught us well and had a good time going over work even if we wasn't supposed to. B)

because you gave us way to much work no offense. C) I wish you could stay here for next year. Loves Rodolfo

— A- she a good teacher but not enough break. you give too much work. You always be teaching us something. Even when we not learning, we learning. Pedro

Epilogue

Eighth-Grade Graduation Day

Afew years later I returned to the neighborhood for my students' eighth-grade graduation. Of course, they were another teacher's students by then, but I still felt close to them. I missed them, a lot. We had stayed in touch for a while, but over the months, as testament to their transient lives, they moved houses, moved in with grandmas or cousins, or had their phone service disconnected, so we lost touch as their phone numbers changed.

Eighth-grade graduation at Julia de Burgos Bilingual Middle Magnet School was always a lavish affair, primarily because the majority of students never went on to high school. This year it was also historical. My former sixth-graders were now the class of 2002, the final graduating class of the school at Eighth and Lehigh. After nearly one hundred years in operation, the school district had finally voted to shut the school down. Down the street, at Fourth and Lehigh, the site of the former Quaker Lace Company, a brand-new $26 million Julia de Burgos Bilingual Middle Magnet School was about to have its grand opening. The cafeteria had floor-to-ceiling windows. The lunch ladies had working ovens and prepared fresh salads and fruit. The special education classroom had a door leading to a small outdoor courtyard with flowers. The hallways felt airy, sunny, and clean. There was even an elevator. The school had been expanded to include kindergarten through eighth grade. Unfortunately, my students would never experience the new building, but those a year below them would start the following year.

Downstairs in the windowless cafeteria of the old building at Eighth and Lehigh, students made last-minute preparations for the graduation ceremony. Their gowns swooshed just past their knees and closed with one button in the front. Many had attached American-flag pins over their hearts—a gesture of solidarity after 9/11. The girls were in heels, some a little too high to walk casually. They usually slicked their hair into tight buns that sat atop their heads, but today their hair was down and ironed straight so as to fit under their caps. They ran their long nails through the front strands of their hair.

"I'm nervous, Miss," said Iris, one of my former sixth-graders. "I stayed up last night to do my hair and nails. Then I got up at 5:30 this morning. I got my mom, my aunt, my mom's boyfriend, and my cousin out there."

Big Bird was standing in the back. He had shelled out $45 for his cap and gown and a final yearbook. Big Bird wore a gold chain across the front of his gown and posed for a photo with his best friend, Juan C. "It's cool," said Big Bird. "I'm happy." Big Bird said he wasn't going to Edison. He'd been accepted into Swenson High School, which was out of his neighborhood. His sister, Jocelyn, had gotten pregnant and decided not to go to Temple University.

They told me Pedro had transferred to a suburban school closer to his mom. Some of my students were awkward around me—they were different people now at thirteen and fourteen than they were at eleven and twelve. They now had squeaky voices and were tall.

Students lined up against the wall. "Tassels to the right!" shouted Ms. Rohan. One girl spat out her gum. They began their march.

Upstairs the auditorium was slowly filling. A student was setting up the electric piano for the music teacher. Blue balloons were taped to the stage and a glittering sign was pinned to the curtains. Falling plaster and rainwater had ruined the first twelve rows of seats, which were roped off. The morning air was just beginning to warm the room and the bunches of helium balloons hung motionless in the stagnant air. The morning promised to be a broiler, and several parents had begun to fan themselves. Parents settled into the wooden, fold-down seats, wearing tank tops, Hawaiian shirts, and lots of gold jewelry.

Ms. Rohan fought back tears. She had carried these students from sixth grade to graduation day, and it was as much her celebration as theirs. Unlike most new teachers, she had stuck it out the entire year, and had even stayed two more. This year would be her last. She was leaving for a school in Florida. Behind her was Mr. Whitehorne, who had just turned sixty. He was one of the few teachers who'd been here since the school's opening fourteen years earlier, and who was moving to the new school, where he would stay for two more years and then retire for health reasons. He wore a red bow tie to graduation, and his massive wave of white hair blew back. Mr. Rougeux was still teaching and in the crowd also; but for him as well, this year would be his last. He was leaving for Harvard University graduate school, after which he would get a job in technology in the Pennsylvania State Department of Education. Ms. Ortiz was still here, strutting around in her high-heeled black boots. Ms. Fernanda had left the year I resigned, as did Mrs. G., although she would later return to the new Julia de Burgos as an assistant principal.

I stood in the back with the seventh-grade math teacher. "I think about half of them will graduate high school," she said. "This year's group has been really good. They had dreams. They didn't just come in with nothing. But still, I would say about only half."

For ten minutes, the students slowly streamed in. Honor-roll kids wore yellow sashes, so they walked in first. I spotted Wilson, who, unbelievably, was wearing a yellow sash. Later I chatted with his grandma. "Can you believe?" she kept saying. "He doing so good. I just can't believe."

"Pomp and Circumstance" played on the piano. Relatives jumped up to snap photos. The American and Puerto Rican flags were carried to the front of the room. Students said the Pledge of Allegiance in English and Spanish.

Two honor students read a poem by Langston Hughes, a radical black poet who spoke out against injustice. The students recited the refrain, "America never was America to me."

> *O, let my land be a land where liberty*
> *Is crowned with no false patriotic wreath,*
> *But opportunity is real, and life is free,*
> *Equality is in the air we breathe*
> *(There's never been equality for me,*
> *Nor freedom in the "homeland of the free")*

Unlike most of the graduation ceremony, the students sang this poem with passion, barely needing the script in their hands. This was the poet that, forty years earlier, new teacher Jonathan Kozol was fired for teaching in a Boston elementary school, the experience upon which he based his classic book, *Death at an Early Age*. That book spoke out about the terrible conditions, the falling ceilings, and broken windows of poor inner-city public schools. Looking around the auditorium, I realized how little of what Kozol fought for had changed.

Many teachers had called this year a special year, for reasons unknown even to themselves. It was perhaps just a class that had had an unusually good mix. Or, maybe there had been a few popular kids who'd also happened to be respectful and polite, and they had set the tone. Whatever it was, there were thirty-seven honor students this year, fourteen more than last year.

The children sang "The Star-Spangled Banner," "La Borrinqueña," "Lift Every Voice and Sing." These were the kids who had made it through eighth grade, no small feat in this neighborhood. Of the forty-five students in both my and Ms. Rohan's classes, ten had already dropped out of school.

***

After graduation, I found Vanessa on her stoop with a four-month-old baby boy. I had expected to find her weary, repentant, even embarrassed. Instead, she was in great spirits and gave me a hug.

"Oh, Miss, you back at the school?"

"No, I'm visiting for graduation."

She told me that after sixth grade, she had been skipped to eighth because she was already fourteen. She began cutting class with her friends and disappearing for the afternoons. When she was elected prom queen, she was already pregnant. She decided to keep the baby, and his father—Bebe- –went with her to the hospital for the birth.

During our conversation, her mother and grandma held the baby. The mother looked tired and annoyed.

"I kept telling her, don't get pregnant," she said, rolling her eyes. "Now the Baby Daddy in prison."

I asked Vanessa when her own father was getting out of jail.

"I dunno," Vanessa said. "It don't really really matter because I never see him, anyway."

The mother looked on, disappointed.

"She was doing good, but then she fell in love with Bebe and she stopped doing all that."

"No, Mami, I met Bebe earlier, and I was still getting good grades," she insisted.

Vanessa turned to me. "Class with you and Ms. Rohan was fun. It was never a problem to get up in the morning and go to school. But the other teachers don't care."

"What about college?" I asked. What about the special arts school, I thought, and Villanova?

She told me about a friend who had attended a job training course. This friend had told her that college wasn't as useful as job training. So she was going to start going to job training school, maybe next year, maybe in hairdressing.

I asked Vanessa about the baby's father, and this was the only time her cheerful facade cracked a bit. "We broke up last month," she said quietly.

I had a few more students I wanted to see. I gave her my phone number and told her to call me if she needed anything. We hugged goodbye.

A few months later, Vanessa got pregnant again. At sixteen, she was already a mother of two.

***

I visited Rodolfo next. I tracked down his uncle's phone number, and they invited me to the uncle's house that afternoon, not far from Julia de Burgos. Rodolfo threw open the door. "Hey, Miss!" he shouted, and hugged me. The house had a pool table, a gumball machine, and a TV propped up on a chair in front of a couch. It must have been a fourteen-year-old's dream—living with his much looser uncle. Each day, his uncle took him to work and trained him.

Rodolfo told me he had been kicked out of Julia de Burgos in seventh grade, and was now at CEP, a disciplinary school. He said he was about to drop out.

"Miss, school's not for me. I don't like all that reading." He leaned over the pool table, cue in hand, and sunk a shot.

His uncle stood nearby. "We gotta plan for him," he said. His uncle was an entrepreneur and was starting electrical businesses and other technical work. He had a habit of taking under his wing the young guys in the family and turning them around. "I'm gonna do the same for him," he said about Rodolfo. "I just want to give him a skill. He's already doing cable. His brother know how to do wiring. I just say, if you got a skill, you'll be all right."

Sometimes they'd go to the big houses in Lower Merion, near Villanova University. The uncle liked to show them how other people lived.

"I say, you can have that if you want."

Rodolfo grinned and showed off another pool shot. "I'm doing good, Miss. I'm happy."

***

The principal was not invited back to Julia de Burgos.

In 2002, I called on her for an interview, offering her a chance to tell her side of the story. Calling the principal was one of the most frightening things I did. Even though I was long gone from Julia de Burgos, she still intimidated me. I was pleasantly surprised she agreed to meet.

After Julia de Burgos, the principal had been offered a job as principal of Showalter School in Chester Upland School District, about thirty minutes south of Philadelphia. Showalter was one of a handful of schools taken over by "Edison Schools Inc.," a for-profit company that was permitted to test the feasibility of privately managed public schools. The principal ran that school for several years. While there, test scores in the PSSA (Pennsylvania System of School Assessment) and the SAT-9 skyrocketed, according to the *Philadelphia Inquirer*. In fact, the year the principal was at Showalter, the school's PSSA scores jumped 62 percentage points in math and 39 percent in reading; from fewer than 20 percent of the students being proficient in math, to more than 70 percent. It was almost unbelievable.

On the day of our meeting, we spoke for more than an hour in her office. I had hoped to crack the ice—to finally receive some insight into the school year from her perspective.

"I did the best I could with the limited resources I had," she said. She pointed out that the school had had nine vacancies and eleven new teachers, no official program, a tiny budget, and she'd had only two weeks to prepare for the position. She said she was never received well because she was white and didn't speak Spanish and was appointed by the school superintendent instead of selected through a committee of teachers. Yet she maintained that the year was a "success."

"I raised student grades by having each parent of a failing child meet with me and go to Saturday School, keeping students there till 9:00 PM to get homework done. And I made teachers describe why students were failing and how to improve those grades. It was not just on paper that they improved."

"So you think it was actually their performance that was being raised as well as grades?" I asked.

"Absolutely, because their grades reflect their performance," she said. "Prior to my arrival, failure was accepted at Julia de Burgos. When you change that, and you're there until 9:00 PM and on Saturdays, you prove you can make a difference. It takes a terrible toll on you personally, and I was exhausted at the end of the year."

We talked about the bilingual program. I explained that I had no program at all—no books or curriculum, nothing to teach.

"It was intended to be a bilingual program, but as it was written, with the staff we had—it was not implementable," she replied. "The goal was to have the whole school be bilingual at the end of a certain period, but to do that you'd need staff trained, and with such constant turnover it was difficult to do. Our plan in the beginning was to keep it, but as I realized we didn't have a Spanish special ed teacher or enough teachers generally, I had to revisit."

I asked her about the special education students. "Why did we have to cover up the problem?"

She said the problem was never hidden. "We tried to get more teachers, and when we couldn't we tried to provide some continuity through myself or the vice principal. Special education kids never fail. A teacher must revise their individual education plans if a student is not passing. Many students did do work through after-school programs or the Saturday school."

"But they didn't have a teacher all year," I said.

"There was always a teacher in there. They didn't get what they should have gotten, but they did get instruction. It wasn't one hundred percent, but under the circumstance we did the best we could," she said.

"What happened when the special education auditors arrived to investigate our school's special education program?"

"We did very well," she said.

"How is that possible? We had no program, no teachers," I asked.

"There are two kinds of audits. This is the paper one. The other one looks at services," she said.

I always felt she put her career ahead of the students. In the end, the students finally caught up with her.

In 2005, a group of students accused her of cheating on the standardized tests. The *Inquirer* article about the incident reported: "Students told teachers that she had given them test answers or that they found some bubbles already filled in on their answer sheets during the administration of the PSSAs."

She was fired from the Chester Upland School District.

***

Through the dirty windows at Eighth and Lehigh, desks can be seen piled up in the dusty hallways. There are broken ceiling lights and newspaper strewn everywhere. The school doors are locked, and officially no one is allowed inside for safety reasons. After the teachers moved many of their things over to the new building, the looters arrived. They pushed crates against the sides, cut through the wire bars and glass, and climbed into the school to take what they could.

Ten miles away, Northeast High School is still open. Its neighborhood is no longer considered a part of the Philadelphia suburbs. The city has a new ring of suburbs even farther out toward the rolling countryside, and good schools out there have attracted many families out of Northeast's neighborhood. I drove up to Northeast and met with the principal who showed me some of the school's early history—the old clock, the plaque, the trophies. Looking around the halls, I noticed that the school was racially diverse. The principal told me that in the past ten years the neighborhood had undergone a lot of changes. It was changing "racially, socially, and economically." In 2003, Northeast's student body was 50 percent white and 50 percent black and Hispanic—the same as it had been in 1957, the year the school moved.

***

A few miles north, Ronny was flipping hamburgers in a convenience store that his dad owned. He glided between the grill and the condiments counter, long fingers wrapping sandwiches into white paper like he could have done it with his eyes closed.

"How do you like it here?" I asked.

He shrugged. "I been doing this for, like, seven years now," he replied.

Ronny told me he had stuck it out through seventh grade, and then dropped out. Looking back, I realized he never stood a chance: He had moved from the Dominican Republic when he was eight, too early to have properly learned Spanish in his country and too late to easily learn English in this country, at least, not in the Philadelphia school system. If he had been placed in an English-only program, he might have been able to learn English. But instead, Julia de Burgos bounced him around bilingual programs, which of course were essentially Spanish-only classes. He picked up a little English, a little Spanish, and was left language-less. He was still unable to read English.

The awning on Ronny's neighborhood corner store said, "Open 7 days a week. For all your shopping needs." In front, three guys in oversized white T-shirts ate their sandwiches and drank ice tea in a circle. Inside, two aisles separated three shelves of Butterfingers, bread, sodas, and Goya products. In the back, Ronny ran the deli, while his cousin manned the cash register behind a Plexiglas window, with an ice-cream counter below.

Ronny had matured into a gentle-natured, kind, and graceful young man. He wore a large, red plaid shirt and baggy, low-riding jeans. During our school year together, he had openly told me that if he didn't pass, his father would make him leave to work at the store, which is exactly what happened. I knew Ronny had tried hard to practice his reading and sought help—I remembered that day he shouted at José R. to "shut up, man!" No help was offered. I caught him too late, and with too little time remaining.

He thanked me for promoting him, but said that his father thought schooling was a waste of time. Ronny's dad also owned a restaurant up the street from the corner store. I visited with him.

"I wanted him to learn and to be successful, but it just didn't work out for him," Ronny's dad said, leaning on the counter of Tierra Dominicana. "He couldn't learn how to read. I don't know why. Then he got old, and it was embarrassing for him to be in the class with all the younger kids. He felt like he was less than the other boys."

So in a school that was doing nothing for him, Ronny, along with his father, had decided on another course. He and his cousin would take over the father's convenience store. Each year he would make payments to his dad for it, and eventually it would be his. He wouldn't make anything the first year and probably would never make more than $18,000 annually. Meanwhile, his sister was heading for college.

"My sister say she going to make in one year what I make in two. I know she right."

Ronny told me he liked working, and that he was happy here because it was something that he owned and it was work that he was good at. He had bigger dreams at one point, and he'd given them up, at least for now. He said he regretted leaving school, he wished he could have stayed, and he would wish it for the rest of his life. The first September morning after he dropped out was the toughest. The neighborhood was buzzing with excitement about returning to school—all the kids had new clothes and notebooks, and the buses were arriving. Ronny lay in bed, listening to the first-day energy as his sister's alarm rang and the shower turned on. Then, the porch door swung open, clicked shut, and the house was quiet again.

"That first day of school I felt bad. You know—everyone was getting ready, buying new clothes, and everyone was so happy to be back in school. Suddenly, all the kids were off the street. The morning of the first day back, my sister woke up, but I stayed in bed."

He rested his thumb and index finger on his eyelids and stayed silent for what seemed like minutes. I realized he was crying. I waited, and finally he looked up at me again.

"I saw everyone go off to school all happy. Everyone ask where I was—why wasn't I in school. I told my pops to tell them I was in the Dominican. But I wasn't."

He looked around the deli.

"I was here."

Afterword

In spring 2007, I made my final visit to see my former students before the publishing of this book. Most would be nearly twenty years old and, had they followed the path their young, naive sixth-grade teacher had envisioned, they would be finishing their freshman year in college.

Finding them was a challenge. Out of a class of about thirty-three, I was only able to catch up with about six students. I had stayed in touch with a few of them, trading e-mails or phone calls, but their lives had always been transient. Some moved with their families back to Puerto Rico; most shuttled around their extended circle of grandmas, cousins, ex-husbands, and mom's new boyfriends. Parents were in and out of jail, and phones got disconnected.

The only student I spoke to regularly, about once every other year, was Vanessa. This was in part because she liked to stay in touch, and partly because she'd lived in the same house from sixth-grade until now. Her neighborhood had gotten much worse since I was her teacher (in 2006, Philadelphia saw nearly four hundred murders—the highest in ten years). I was eager to catch up as we'd fallen out of touch when I went to Iraq in 2003. From Baghdad, I filed stories for two years mostly on the school system and the U.S. efforts to rebuild it after Saddam. It was always interesting to compare the two school systems. In the poorer, rural areas, the Iraqi schools had much less infrastructure; often sixty students were crammed onto benches, sharing books in classrooms with no windows, much less air conditioning. The teachers ran their classes with iron fists—no open discussion, nothing but rote memorization. Classroom control wasn't a problem the way it was at Julia de Burgos.

When I called Vanessa, she sounded delighted to hear from me. "Miss," she said, "I'm trying to get into this school downtown. But it's $30,000 for three years, so I don't know."

When we met, I could see Vanessa had blossomed into a beautiful young woman, with manicured hair and matching purse, belt, and shoes, a vibrant giggle and a polite, thoughtful nature. At seventeen she now had two children from two different fathers, neither of whom were around. She was now

205

working at Taco Bell full-time as a cashier, having dropped out of high school in tenth grade.

Vanessa gets up at 7:00 A.M., dressing and feeding her kids and getting them to a Head Start program where they were already learning to read. She arrives at work early each day, and her shift runs from noon until 7:30 p.m. Then she comes home, spends time with her kids, and goes to bed. This is her schedule six days a week. She doesn't drink or go out and despite her long workdays and two children, Vanessa didn't seem physically haggard or tired at all.

"I want to give my kids a better life," she said.

We chatted about the other students. Rosalia had a child and was working as a supermarket checkout girl. Big Bird was joining the Navy. Two other students were dealing drugs. I had gone by Ronny's dad's store, but there was a new owner.

"Was anyone in college?" I asked.

She gave me an exasperated look. "I doubt anyone even graduated high school."

"How about you, Vanessa?" I asked her. "What happened?"

Her mood changed, and her eyes filled up with tears.

"I hated high school. There was no point in being there. The teachers don't care. They weren't like you and Ms. Rohan. You made class interesting and you took us places on Saturdays. The teachers at Edison didn't care."

"But, Vanessa, why do the teachers have to care?" I asked. "Why didn't you care enough to keep going?"

"Well, I had my kids to raise. My grandma passed away in July 2002, and she was watching the kids. After she passed, I had no one to watch them."

She said the first pregnancy was a mistake. "I don't know what happened. I was stupid," she said. While she was pregnant, her boyfriend started cheating on her. After she gave birth, a neighbor in his late twenties regularly came by and flirted with her. They started dating and she got pregnant again. They stayed together for two years, but she eventually decided he was a bad influence.

"He wanted to go out into the streets and sell drugs, and he had gotten locked up. I didn't want my kids around that."

Vanessa described these years almost as if they were a blur—as though she wasn't really sure why she did what she did. Her sense of isolation did little to help. She has no Internet access, no connections from school, and almost no role models to speak of. Had she wanted to make more of her life, there was no one to guide her toward doing so. She seemed to have no idea of the first steps needed to get herself out of her situation. "My life is passing me by," she said.

In 2006, she tried to move her life in a different direction. She went online and found a high school in Florida that offered diplomas via the Internet. She took a test and received her degree. "It's not a GED," she said. "It's better. It's a real diploma."

Watching TV late at night, Vanessa saw an advertisement for a culinary school in Philadelphia. This was the school she had mentioned on the phone. She convinced her cousin to drive her to the open house on weekday evening, but she learned the tuition was much more than she could afford. She didn't really want to be a chef, but she didn't know what other options she had.

"Do you have anyone to ask questions to about how to get a job?" I asked. "Or how to write a resume?'

"No. My mom always discourages me," Vanessa said.

Indeed, Vanessa's mom seemed to have a philosophy to life that planted a small voice in Vanessa's head saying: "don't try." And that was the only voice Vanessa heard. In the five hours we spent together having lunch and hanging out, her mom (who was watching Vanessa's children) called her cell phone six times.

After lunch, I drove Vanessa to the bookstore where I had taken her as a sixth grader. We pulled a number of employment reference books off the shelf, and looked at some areas she might be interested in. After reading all the different career options for young women without college backgrounds, she got excited about being an executive assistant. We wrote down some Web sites of training programs and night schools. In the next few weeks, I watched Vanessa struggle to follow up on this information. Given the costs, she had no Internet connection in her home. Then she had to start working the graveyard shift at Taco Bell because another cousin changed jobs and couldn't pick up her kids anymore. Getting Vanessa to reach her potential clearly was a path ridden with the small annoying obstacles of just getting by that people with money don't ever have to think about.

It's now been eight years since I first met Vanessa as a twelve-year-old girl with long black hair and a dimpled smile. I could tell by the way that she had grown up and matured that this time, we would stay in touch. I know I'm not ready to give up on her yet. More important, she isn't ready to give up on herself.

Acknowledgments

Of all those involved in this book, my deepest gratitude goes to Mark Bowden, whose encouragement, inspiration, and wisdom made this book happen. From the first lunch in which we discussed the journal over taquitos in North Philadelphia, through several versions of the manuscript, he has remained my deepest inspiration and the best friend a writer could hope to have in her life.

Almost everyone involved in *The Emergency Teacher* participated out of compassion and support for the subject. Ken Nolan spent hours at Starbucks in London reading early drafts, and bringing humor and creativity to the task. I thank him. Jonathan Dahl brought his sharp mind to the early drafts. My sister Nikki taught me how teaching is supposed to work, and helped me in the classroom. Sebastian Junger gave me perspective and patience in the writing process, and is a good friend for it. My best friends Jen Hughes and Claire Edmondson have always been there, in the background, singing my praises.

Harry and Rosemary Wong pushed me to research the best practices in teaching and showed me that through optimism, determination, and hard work, it is possible to make a difference in the schools. The late activist Marla Ruzicka was the motivation to finally finish this project. She knew how to make things happen, and taught me to follow my dream.

At Julia de Burgos, I have the deepest appreciation of Ron Whitehorne and Lance Rougeux—not only for befriending and supporting me during my first-year struggles, but for staying in my life beyond and believing in this book. They are heroes to the Philadelphia public schools. I would also like to thank Ms. Rohan, Mr. Marr, Ms. Vinitzsky, Mrs. G. and Ms. Ortiz for their friendship and kindness.

Several of my students helped me in long interviews afterward, especially Big Bird, Ronny, Wilson, Rodolfo, and Vanessa. They have many talents to share with the world.

Thank you to the Temple University archives department and the staff at Northeast High School, board members, and alumni. I also drew my research from the good work of education reporter Dale Mezzacapa.

Finally, thank you to my mom, who taught me to love literature, and my dad, who taught me the value of education.